Martin

All the best with lectures!

Karl.

L E X U S

LEXUS
THE RELENTLESS PURSUIT

How Toyota Motor went from "0-60"
in the Global Luxury Car Market

CHESTER C DAWSON III

John Wiley & Sons (Asia) Pte Ltd

Copyright © 2004 John Wiley & Sons (Asia) Pte Ltd
Published by John Wiley & Sons (Asia) Pte Ltd
2 Clementi Loop, #02-01, Singapore 129809

This publication is designed to provide accurate and authoritative information with regard to the
subject matter covered. It is sold with the understanding that the Publisher is not engaged in
rendering professional services. If professional advice or other expert assistance is required, the
services of a competent professional person should be sought.

The views in this book represent those of Chester C. Dawson III in a private capacity, and should
not be taken to be representative of *BusinessWeek* or its parent company, the McGraw-Hill Companies,
or of Chester C. Dawson III as a representative, officer or employee of *BusinessWeek*, or its parent
company, the McGraw-Hill Companies.

Other Wiley Editorial Offices
John Wiley & Sons, Inc., 111 River Street, Hoboken, NJ 07030, USA
John Wiley & Sons Ltd, The Atrium, Southern Gate, Chichester PO19 BSQ, England
John Wiley & Sons (Canada) Ltd, 22 Worcester Road, Rexdale, Ontario M9W ILI, Canada
John Wiley & Sons Australia Ltd, 33 Park Road (PO Box 1226), Milton, Queensland 4046, Australia
Wiley-VCH, Pappelallee 3, 69469 Weinheim, Germany

Library of Congress Cataloging-in-Publication Data:

0470-821108

Typeset in 11/15 point, Palatino by Red Planet
Printed in Singapore by Saik Wah Press Pte Ltd
10 9 8 7 6 5 4 3 2

CONTENTS

For
Alyssa and Sean

"Our vision for the future is very clear and it doesn't include being in anyone's rearview mirror. In the 10 years since Lexus was launched, it often has been referred to as a "textbook example". I don't know who's going to be standing in front of you at the Detroit Auto Show 10 years from now, but I do have a feeling they'll be talking about another successful chapter straight from that standard-setting business publication, 'The Relentless Pursuit of Perfection'. "

—former Toyota Motor Sales U.S.A. Inc. Lexus division head Bryan Bergsteinsson, speaking to the press at the North American International Auto Show in Detroit on January 5, 1999

INTRODUCTION AND ACKNOWLEDGMENTS

My journey toward writing this book had many starting points, but the primary impetus arrived in the form of a mysterious brown envelope one day in late May of 2002. As a correspondent in the Tokyo bureau of *BusinessWeek* magazine, I was accustomed to receiving unsolicited mailings from discontents, kooks and—occasionally—admirers. But this one stood out because it was marked with the logo of a major corporate icon. Inside was a neatly stapled set of internal case studies—mostly written in Japanese—by the Toyota Motor Corporation along with an assortment of newspaper clippings on the auto industry. It turned out to have been sent by a Japanese acquaintance whom I had met with once for dinner—and then never again. How this person obtained the "eyes only" documents from Toyota Motor or why they were passed on to me remains a mystery. But one thing was clear: I had been handed the keys to unlocking the secrets of Toyota Motor's first "world-class" luxury car, the Lexus LS 400. At the time I already was in discussions with John Wiley & Sons (Asia) Pte. Ltd. about a possible book project, but I had hesitated to sign on due to the demands of my work schedule and, frankly, lack of any particular insight. In fact, I only had begun to cover the Japanese auto industry with any depth after joining *BusinessWeek* in 2000. Prior to that, my reporting on cars was mainly limited to noting how a handful of automakers, including Toyota Motor, seemed impervious to the slow meltdown of Japan Inc. in the 1990s. But once bitten by the car bug, I began to grasp the importance of the industry to the world's leading economies and to average consumers around the globe. More so than even sports, talking about cars is truly one of the few surefire conversation starters. Everybody's got a favorite car story—even those of us who live in cities such as New York and Tokyo where ownership is often the exception rather than the rule. The arrival of the mysterious manila envelope was the nudge I needed to start connecting the dots from what I had learned in the course of my reporting on Toyota Motor, the world's luxury-car market and the auto-industry in general. Since formally embarking on this book project a year ago, I have pored over all manner of material in Japanese and English and culled notes from interviews with dozens of auto-industry hands, on and off the record. Even so, I am the first to admit my lack of expertise under the hood and in the showroom. Any flawed descriptions, interpretations or analysis are therefore solely due to my own inexperience and shortcomings as a writer.

With that caveat, in this book I hope to shed some light on the manufacturing and marketing of one of the automotive world's most impressive success stories to date—the Lexus brand. In the space of 10 years, Toyota Motor's luxury division evolved from the butt of jokes to become the preeminent benchmark for quality among the world's top vehicles. Not only have Lexus cars won more J.D. Power & Associates awards than any other brand of automobile, but Lexus also has been the best-selling luxury car in the U.S.—import and domestic—for the past four years in a row. Having spent more than a decade based in Tokyo, I never failed to be struck on trips back to the U.S. by the ubiquity of a luxury icon that doesn't even exist in brand-obsessed Japan (but not, as it turns out, for much longer—Toyota Motor plans to introduce Lexus into its home market in 2005.)

With this year marking the 15th anniversary of the brand since its debut in amid a snowstorm at the Detroit auto show in 1989, it's an appropriate time to look back and attempt to divine the secrets of Lexus's success. From its hallmark quality and top-notch customer service to the dedication of Toyota Motor's employees and the brand's distinctive advertising, Lexus has been nothing if not...relentless. The final chapters of the book look at some of the challenges faced by the brand and give a peek at what's in store for the Lexus line-up.

I would like to thank the many, many people who have provided material, editorial and emotional support for the writing of this book. First and foremost, to Wiley (Asia) and its indefatigable publisher Nick Wallwork, who chased me for many months to sign on with him and exhibited remarkable patience and persistence in the process. Recognition is also due to my eminently capable editors at Wiley in Asia: the dogged and relentlessly upbeat Selvamalar Manoharan, who shepherded the project on a day-to-day basis, and skilled wordsmith John Owen, who smoothed over the many rough spots in my raw copy. Although this work has no official sanction by Toyota Motor (for that, I recommend the company's own upcoming work, *The Lexus Story*), I am indebted to the many current and former executives, engineers and sales associates of Toyota Motor Corp. (TMC) in Japan, Toyota Motor Sales U.S.A. Inc. (TMS) in the U.S. and the Lexus Division of TMS who offered their stories to me. I would like to extend particular thanks to TMS senior vice-president J. Davis Illingworth Jr., who oversaw the first years of the Lexus brand's sales in the U.S., and former TMC executive advisory engineer Ichiro Suzuki, the godfather of the LS series. Both men put up with incessant questioning in the course of several interviews with me. Special thanks also go out to TMS group vice-president and general manager of the Lexus Division Dennis E. Clements; former TMS executive vice-president Robert "Buck" McCurry; TMS vice-chairman Yale Gieszl; former TMS vice-chairman Jim Perkins; Toyota financial services president and CEO George Borst; TMS executive vice-president and chief operating officer James E. Press; Toyota Motor Manufacturing Canada Inc. president Real "Ray" Tanguay; Toyota Motor Marketing Europe president and CEO, Tadashi Arashima;

former Toyota Motor Asia Pacific senior vice-president, Richard "Dick" L. Chitty and former TMS project manager John French. I am also grateful for the unending assistance of Toyota Motor's global media relations staff. In North America, that includes TMS corporate communications division external communications manager Mike Michels; Lexus division national public relations manager William "Bill" L. Ussery; Charlotte Lassos of Lexus public relations; TMS processing archivist Amy Lucadamo; TMS national strategic news manager Nancy Hubbell; Toyota Motor North America vice-president for external affairs Veronica Pollard; Toyota Motor Manufacturing North America media relations manager Daniel Sieger; and TMS northeast public affairs manager Wade Hoyt. In Japan, I would like to thank the members of TMC's public affairs division international communications department in Tokyo, including general manager Shigeru Hayakawa, group managers Tetsuo Kitagawa and Shinya Matsumoto and assistants Monika Fujita, Liu Hong, Paul Nolasco, Hisayo Ogawa and Shino Yamada. Among the many TMC engineers I spoke to in the course of my reporting for *BusinessWeek*, I am especially grateful to RX 330 chief engineer Yukihiro Okane and ES 330 chief engineer Kosaku Yamada. Lexus division vice-president Takashi Sakai, Lexus development center product development group managing officer Takeishi Yoshida, Lexus planning division general manager Shinzo Kobuki and Lexus brand planning group manager Yukihiko Yaguchi also provided invaluable assistance. Specific thanks are also due to the helpful staff at TMC's Global Design Center in Toyota City, including senior general manager Hideichi Misono, Lexus design division general manager Kengo Matsumoto, group manager Simon Humphries and Masako Nagai of the resources administration department. I must not fail to mention my debt to the current and former employees of TMC and TMS who spoke only on the condition of not being identified in order to protect their long-term ties to the company. These brave souls provided documentary evidence and oral insight which helped fill in the many blanks in Toyota Motor's official history of Lexus. Among the many auto-industry outsiders who contributed in some way, shape or form, I would like to offer special thanks to current and former members of ad agency Saatchi & Saatchi's Team One unit based in El Segundo, California who helped me piece together the advertising side of Lexus, including current Saatchi & Saatchi New York office CEO Scott Gilbert and J. Walter Thompson Detroit office co-president Tom Cordner. A tip of the hat is due as well to photographer Makoto Ishida, who snapped a few memorable pictures of me monkeying around on the LS/GS assembly line in Tahara, Japan, including the one used on the inside back flap. I also would like to express my gratitude to *BusinessWeek* magazine, which took a chance on an untested local hire with a news wire background when it brought me on board. In particular, I am indebted to editor-in-chief Steve Shepherd, managing editor Bob Dowling, and Tokyo bureau chief Brian Bremner. Each contributed in his own way to honing my skills as a reporter, researcher and writer. As far as inspiration is concerned, I point to two seminal works with which I dare not compare this work but which provided me with basic reference points for a my narrative framework. These are David Halberstam's breathtaking 1986 book *The Reckoning* on the rise of Japan as an automotive power and the relative decline of Detroit, and *Rich Nation, Strong Army: National Security and the Technological Transformation of Japan*, a fascinating 1994 study of Japan's pervasive "techno-national ideology" by Richard J. Samuels, Ford International professor and head of the department of political science at Massachusetts Institute of Technology. Finally, a word of thanks to the friends and family members who provided critical support while I undertook this project and unfailingly encouraged me even when the task seemed too daunting, especially my parents, Chester Jr. and Ruth, and my partner, Miyuki.

Chester C. Dawson III
June 2004

A note on Japanese names:
Although Japanese convention is to use the surname before the given name, for purposes of standardization, all names in this book are written with the given names first.

It is 3:00 am, February 12, 1987. I'm at the Tokyu Hotel in Nagoya. A combination of jetlag and excitement makes it impossible to sleep. Today, I'm going to see the super-secret F1 for the first time, in my new role as Corporate Manager of Special Projects at Toyota Motor Sales, U.S.A. (TMS). My title is a little misleading. There is only one special project, and it doesn't even have a name. As I stare at the ceiling of my hotel room, my mind takes me back to the previous December when TMS president Yuki Togo first told me about the F1.

As I walked into his office that morning, Yuki bounded from behind his desk to greet me, his round face wreathed in a charismatic smile. We sat down — he right next to me — and he told me of the F1 car and its importance to Toyota. The F1 was the brainchild of Toyota Motor Corporation (TMC) chairman, Eiji Toyoda, and it must not fail, he said.

It was Yuki's opinion that the F1 could not be sold as a Toyota in the U.S. but must be sold as a new brand through a new channel.

"Many directors do not agree with me about this second channel," he said. "They say, 'Yuki, you are crazy'. Many directors believe the finest car ever built by Toyota should have the Toyota name. I believe we must have a new second channel." After a brief pause, he went on, patting his breast pocket: "I have a resignation letter. I told Dr Toyoda [TMC President, Shoichiro Toyoda], 'Trust me'. We can make it happen," he continued, passionately. "If it fails, I will resign immediately!"

Yuki studied me closely, raised his two hands in the air and waved them excitedly at me. "This is a big job, Dave," he said. "I'm counting on you to make it happen!"

In the sleepless hours, I look again at what we're up against. If the F1 is to be sold from a separate luxury franchise, the dealers will have to build costly new facilities in prime locations and will have no service, parts, or used-car business to help cover their expenses. They will need to sell 40,000 of the new vehicles in the first year just to break even.

An uneasiness settles in my stomach. I am 44 years old with four sons and a fifth child on the way. Life is good. Why is this happening to me? Why can't I just stay in the Toyota Division? But "why?" doesn't matter much at this point. One thing is for sure; Yuki is right, there is no choice but to make it happen.

At 8:00 o'clock, I meet my colleagues in the hotel lobby: John Koenig (Toyota Product Planning Department), Yuki Azuma (Japan Staff Coordinator, Product Planning Department), Tetsuro (Ted) Toyoda (Japan Staff Coordinator for Special Projects), and John French (Staff Member for Special Projects), who have also made the trip. This is the first time that American managers of this low rank are being permitted into the design center's styling review facility, known as the design dome. The F1 has already been through seven unsuccessful design reviews. Since the F1 is to be sold only in the U.S., the decision was made to allow the younger managers to see the car.

We pile into the car for the hour-long drive to Toyota City, home of Toyota Motor Corporation's world headquarters. It is a typical winter day in Japan; cold and crisp and not a cloud in the sky. Everyone is tense and quiet. We all know how important this day is going to be.

On the road to Toyota City, I review our present situation in my mind. Four years earlier, chairman Eiji Toyoda had made the courageous decision to have Toyota build the best car in the world and during those years the full force of the company's resources had been thrown at this secret project. The F1 was not to be benchmarked against the "best car" in the world but, rather, against every individual best *part* in the world: the best transmission; the best suspension; the best audio system... The emotional decision not to sell the F1 as a Toyota has been made.

The situation in the U.S. market is difficult. Trade friction and anti-Japanese sentiment are running high. This has resulted in the Voluntary Restraint Agreement between Japan and the U.S. governments. It means that for every F1 to be brought into the U.S., there will be one fewer Toyota brought in, and this is sure to upset the established Toyota dealers, who are already low on inventory.

Honda has launched a luxury-car division, Acura. It has the four-door Acura Legend, priced at US$19,298, but it is not doing well. In a September 1986 headline, *The Wall Street Journal* had asked the question, "Has Honda stumbled?" and went on to say, "Honda's decision to pursue the affluent buyer has brought it face to face with its well entrenched European competitors who dominate the luxury market worldwide."

Kevin Wilson of *Autoweek* had issued an ominous warning: "That even Honda doesn't get a free pass into the prestige performance should be a lesson to other aspirants (i.e. Toyota)."

The president and CEO of Volvo North America, Bjorn Ahlstrom, said of the Japanese attempt to enter the luxury market that it would be a "marketing flop".

In 1986 there were 15 million cars sold in the U.S. Of those, 925,000 were luxury cars. Cadillac was the number-one luxury car, with over 300,000 sales. Cadillac and Lincoln accounted for 55% of the luxury market but all of their cars sold for less than US$30,000.

Mercedes-Benz, considered to be the number-one luxury prestige nameplate, sold 93,000 and BMW, which was considered the number-one luxury performance nameplate, sold 92,000. The rest of the market was made up of Jaguar, Audi, Volvo, Saab, Bentley, Rolls Royce, and exotic sports cars. However, of the 185,000 Mercedes-Benz and BMW sold in 1986, only 85,000 were four-door sedans selling for over US$30,000.

For the F1 to sell 40,000 units in its first year, it will have to significantly expand the over-US$30,000 luxury four-door sedan market or win over 50% of the buyers of the established nameplates, Mercedes-Benz and BMW.

Just as troublesome, the F1 is a four-door sedan that is to be priced at around US$28,000. The exchange rate in 1986 was 200 yen to the dollar. But now, in 1987, it has appreciated 22%. It is becoming clear that this F1 car will be priced well over US$30,000 by the time it comes to market in two years. The highest-priced car Toyota sold in the U.S. is the Cressida, at US$16,680. Who is going to pay US$30,000 for a Toyota-made luxury car with no history, prestige or image? Toyota has a reputation as a very conservative, risk-averse company. It's clear that the F1 project is going to be a huge gamble.

We arrive at the design dome and have to check in at the security gate. After showing our IDs and being thoroughly checked over by the guards, Ted Toyoda leads us into an unimpressive, dingy, gray lobby with a heavy odor of stale cigarettes. The design dome is behind closed doors and we are asked to wait outside. I am pacing back and forth impatiently when a whirling dynamo of a man bursts through the door. He has bright eyes and a huge grin. He eagerly shakes everyone's hand. I like him right away. He is Ichiro Suzuki, chief engineer of the F1, and a 28-year company veteran. Most of his career had been spent in the chassis engineering department until he joined the chief engineer ranks in 1984.

Mr Suzuki invites us into the design dome. Here, the huge round ceiling makes it impossible to see any horizon, and gives an immediate sense of an expansiveness reinforced by the seamless high-intensity lighting.

The dome makes voices echo and even the quietest conversation can be heard from across the room. We look around for the F1 and are dismayed because there is no car. Instead, there are five chairs in front of a podium and a screen. Before we are to see the car, Mr Suzuki wants us to understand the engineering effort that is going into F1.

First the engine. It will be a completely new motor, sharing no parts with any other built by Toyota. It will be the company's first 4-liter V8, 4-cam 32-valve fuel-injected motor. It is to achieve 250hp, go from zero to 60 in 7.9 seconds and have a top speed of 150 miles per hour. It is to be powerful and whisper-quiet. Most importantly, it is to achieve something no other luxury car can do; get 23.5 miles per gallon, thereby avoiding the gas-guzzler tax — a seemingly impossible goal.

Next, Kunihiro Uchida the chief designer makes the styling presentation. Mr Uchida has been with the company since 1966. He graduated from the Tokyo National University of Fine Arts and Music and also studied at the Art Center College of Design in Pasadena, California. The F1 has already failed seven design reviews and rumor has it that Mr Uchida has lost 20 pounds from the stress. His problem is that most luxury cars of the day have a coefficient of drag between .38 to .40. The most aerodynamic sports cars of the day have a coefficient of drag of .32. For Suzuki to achieve his design goals for an engine capable of a top speed of 150 miles per hour while achieving 23.5 miles per gallon, the coefficient of drag will have to be .29 — another seemingly impossible goal.

Knowing that the buildings, the other cars, even the vegetation, will all affect how the F1 will look on the road, Mr Uchida and seven other designers had lived in Newport Beach, California, for three months to get a feel for the American market.

Finally, the moment of truth. Because it's a sunny day, we are invited to see the car outside. As we walk out into the cold morning air, my cheeks tingle. I am aware of the beating of my heart. I expect the F1 to be covered, allowing Mr Uchida a dramatic unveiling. But, as we walk around the corner of the building, there it is, standing, uncovered in the bright sunlight.

The silver F1 is shimmering on the turntable at a rear three-quarter view. It has sleek, smooth, elegant lines. The dual exhaust immediately catches my eye. The car begins to rotate on the table; the side view looks solid, substantial and steady. A wave of warm relief sweeps through me. As the F1 comes around to the front, it looks youthful and aggressive. We glance at each other, trying to read each other's thoughts. We can tell by the smiles that we all know this car has potential. I feel a surge of optimism.

We spend the next 20 minutes carefully going over the car. There are a number of concerns. While the front is youthful and aggressive, the grille looks unfinished, busy, and needs some chrome to make it a little less menacing. The 15-inch wheels are too small and the wheel design is uninteresting.

On a scale of 10, we grade the rear view 9.5; the side at 9.0; and the front at 8.0. Overall, we are thrilled that something can look this good this early in the development process. We go back inside to look at an interior mock-up.

The interior design engineer, Tomohide Yamada, explains that while the domestic luxury cars in America are super plush, the European cars have a Teutonic harshness. The F1 is to have the best of both worlds, creating a luxury atmosphere to accommodate the tastes of virtually every human being who might get into the car. The interior will be all high-tech elegance, with the world's first electro-luminescent panel. The seats are to be a special leather, neither too soft nor too hard. The cabin is to be surrounded by special sandwiched-steel panels that will make this the quietest car in the world to accommodate the world's finest audio system.

After a full day of briefings, we gather in a conference room with Mr Suzuki and all the engineers. It's now 5:00 pm. We have all gotten about four hours of sleep in the last 48 hours. It has been an exhilarating day but my mind is groggy and I'm getting a slight headache from the jetlag. As we sit around the conference table, a light, positive mood fills the room. Mr Suzuki asks me if I have any questions. I'm not sure if a young, low-level manager such as myself should dare ask the senior chief engineer any questions about something to which he has devoted so many painstaking hours and so much energy. I whisper to Ted Toyoda on my right and he nods to me to go ahead. I explain to Mr Suzuki how impressed we are with the car and thank him and the engineers for their great effort...but I am curious about one issue. Both of our main competitors, Mercedes-Benz and BMW, have tool kits and first-aid kits in their cars. I see no plans for such items in the F1.

There is a moment's silence. Even though Mr Suzuki speaks English my question is translated into Japanese to make sure everything is communicated properly. Before the translator finishes, Mr Suzuki glares at me. The mood changes from one of celebration to one of unease as Mr Suzuki erupts into an angry diatribe in Japanese that goes on for five minutes. When he is done, Ted sheepishly explains that Mr Suzuki is frustrated. After spending all this time in trying to develop the best possible car in the world from an engineering standpoint, he is upset that we would waste his time on minor issues like first-aid kits and tool kits. These will only add weight to the car and make it even more difficult to avoid the gas-guzzler tax. I retreat quickly, saying I did not mean to be offensive and certainly appreciate the tremendous work that he and the engineers have done.

Riding back to Nagoya I have a growing feeling deep inside that I am blessed to be a part of something very special.

On September 1, 1989 the Lexus LS 400 (F1) went on sale in the U.S. Automotive journalists hailed the styling of the LS 400 as elegant and refined. It had a 250hp motor that went from zero to 60 in 7.9 seconds and had a top speed of 150 miles per hour. It had a coefficient of drag of .29 and did not attract the gas-guzzler tax.

The interior was judged the quietest cabin in the market, with the world's finest audio system. It still had 15-inch wheels as a concession to avoid the gas-guzzler tax, but Mr Suzuki had listened and it did have a tool kit and first-aid kit.

Today, Lexus is sold around the world. It has received some 86 J.D. Power awards in excellence for quality and customer handling and the LS 430 has been rated the most trouble-free car in America by J.D. Power for the last seven consecutive years. Lexus has sold over two million units and has been the number-one luxury brand in America for the past four years.

That feeling I had 17 years ago after I had seen the Lexus LS 400 for the first time; that feeling that Lexus was going to be something very special, turned out to be true. It was and still is.

J. Davis Illingworth, Jr.,
Senior Vice-President, Toyota Motor Sales, U.S.A. Inc.,
and former General Manager, Toyota Motor's Lexus Division

■ ■ ■

CHAPTER ONE

THE TOYODA WAY

T he day was like any other in the waning, achingly humid spasm of late summer on the plains outside the city of Nagoya, in the dead center of Japan. The heavy air barely circulated under a relentless late-summer sun. Wizened farmers with leathery skin worked lush rice fields cut into squares like so many patches on a vast verdant quilt. Surveying their lot in ankle-deep, primordial mud, they prayed autumn typhoons would spare their top-heavy crops before the harvest. For more than a millennium, the farm hands who populate the fertile lowlands in the Mikawa region believed themselves to be at the mercy of mercurial deities. The demon-like *Fujin*, the wind god with green-tinged skin, and the horn-headed god *Raijin*, bearer of the thunderclap whip, ruled with an arbitrary hand.[1] They were said to control the fortunes of Japan's rice-dominated commerce up and down the coasts of her four main islands. Today, the archipelago is swayed not by the whims of weather gods, but by the tides of a global economy. Yet the agrarian values of those living in the Mikawa region are much the same as ever. They prize insularity, loyalty and, above all, shrewdness. For nearly 300 years, the area was a conservative stronghold of the Tokugawa dynasty, or shogunate, which ruled Japan until the country was thrust into the modern era in the late 1800s.

It was on this historic firmament that a mighty fortress rose: the headquarters for the 20th-century equivalent of Mikawa's warlords. These are the modern rainmakers who run the world's second-largest auto-maker. Just upland from thousand-year-old rice paddies, amid the remnants of an ancient red pine forest, lies the Spartan headquarters of Toyota Motor Corporation. And it was here, on a simmering August day in 1983, that the senior-most officers deliberated a calculated gamble to tinker with a successful strategy of producing budget vehicles for a mass market, and spending billions of dollars launching a single luxury car.

It was not a decision taken lightly. The populace of Nagoya — and, to a more limited extent, the whole of Japan — looks to Toyota Motor as a powerhouse, one which anchors the economy of the industrial heartland between Osaka and Tokyo. The modern-day samurai who run this corporate giant are credited with keeping the sons and daughters of Mikawa off the farm and in high-wage jobs with good benefits. This, in turn, fills local tax coffers and has spawned an industrial complex of thousands of affiliated businesses — from brake makers to taxicab companies. "Companies in this city have long been protected by their parent company, Toyota," said Nobuhiko Narita, director of Toyota City's industrial and labor policy division. Altogether, this "parent company" alone directly employs some 65,500 workers in Japan.[2] But these days it sells more cars in North America than it does in its home market. Indeed, in the past 20 years, Toyota Motor has grown from a niche player in the market for cheap compact cars into the world's second-largest automaker after General Motors. It boasts a healthy 10% share of the global market (and 11% in the U.S. alone). By the end of the decade, the company aims to capture 15%, which would put it on par with General Motors. Increasingly, the Toyota group has a car for every segment, be it 660cc-engine Daihatsu minicars such as the Naked model, designed for the narrow streets of Tokyo, to the hulking and Hummer-like Mega Cruiser, with its 37-inch tires for use by Japanese military forces, or the 20-ton Hino Profia Teravie heavy-duty truck for long-haul cargo. That's to say nothing of the Camry, America's most popular car for five of the past six years. Today, Toyota Motor is one of the top 10 most profitable companies on the planet and enjoys a market capitalization of US$130 billion — greater than that of Ford Motor, General Motors and DaimlerChrysler combined. And, unlike GM and Ford, which in recent years have earned more from sideline businesses such as their financing units than through car-making, Toyota Motor has remained faithful to its core automotive business, which accounts for 92% of its profit and revenue. Compare that with the largest vehicle manufacturer in the world, GM. It earns only 83% of its revenue and 7.6% of net income from its car operations. Most of GM's profit comes, instead, from its high-flying financing unit, GMAC. Toyota Motor, on the other hand, remains committed to what it calls *mono-zukuri*, or "making things". It's almost a quaint conceit in comparison with GM's finance-driven business acumen. And it's one of the most basic elements of Toyota Motor's famous but little-understood production system, which got it where it is today — closing fast on GM for top honors. How it got there owes a lot to its success in carving out a large chunk of the global market for luxury cars.

And that goes back to *mono-zukuri*. Teruyuki Minoura, a senior managing director and former head of Toyota Motor Manufacturing North America, has said that, "When we talk about mono-zukuri at Toyota, it is more than just manufacturing. It involves the idea of creating a product. It implies a love of creation. It also encompasses the sense of craftsmanship: making and crafting a product with expertise and with high quality. At Toyota, we believe what makes human beings different from other animals is our desire and ability to 'manufacture', in this larger sense." Expanding on these almost theological underpinnings, he went on: "Without manufacturing, we believe, there is no civilization. From the simple tools of the stone age to today's high-tech space shuttle, it's all part of the same continuum. In order for human societies to continue to prosper, we must continue to have manufacturing."[3]

In other words, what Toyota Motor does best is the antithesis of outsourcing, with which much of Corporate America seems so enamored. Most of what Toyota Motor makes is manufactured in-house — or in cooperation with its close-knit *keiretsu* family of suppliers in which it owns large ownership stakes. This includes not only longtime satellite companies, such as instrument-panel manufacturer Toyoda Gosei Co. and brake-maker Aisin Seiki Co., but also foreign companies which have developed strong working relationships with the group. Ohio-based ball-bearing maker Timken Co., which supplies Toyota Motor's North American factories, is among them. All believe strongly in the importance of actually making the things they sell, and each works hard to forge long-term relationships which extend beyond any one car project. This means jointly designing parts for new models under development, and collaborating — not cracking heads — to reduce costs through innovation and greater efficiencies. That's a far cry from Detroit's top-down approach, which demands across-the-board cuts from its harried suppliers. "We are dedicated to the entire relationship; from product innovation to service and support," said John Dix, Timken's vice president of automotive business development.[4]

Origins of Lexus

While Toyota Motor has maintained a fairly traditional approach towards business fundamentals, the company has undergone a tremendous transformation. From a market-share and revenue-driven manufacturing monster, it has become a lean profit-making machine with a US$30 billion war chest. Toyota Motor has jettisoned its growth-at-any-cost philosophy in the passionate pursuit of profits. To understand why, consider that its operating profit margin of more than 8% in 2003 was up from a mere 2% in 1993. And much of those profits come from Lexus.

The tectonic shift at Toyota Motor dates back, in large part, to a hush-hush board meeting at the company's headquarters in August 1983. At that top-secret session, Toyota Motor's top brass debated a car project so sensitive it was codenamed with an encircled letter F, or *maru-efu* (and later known internally as the F1 program), a nod to its make-or-break status as the company's (F for) flagship, No.1 vehicle.[5] Chairman Eiji Toyoda posed a question to the company's senior executives, designers, engineers and strategic thinkers — the Toyota Motor joint chiefs of staff. "Can we create a luxury car to challenge the very best?" he asked. To a man, the assembled generals of Toyota Motor's far-flung empire answered in unison: Yes — "A 'yes' full of conviction. And more: Toyota *must* take on this challenge", as the official Toyota history tells it.[6] In fact, however, not everyone was sold on it from the start. Shoichiro Toyoda, the son of the company's founder and successor to Eiji as president and chairman, had some initial misgivings. He wanted to stick with what Toyota Motor did best — build cheap cars for everyman.[7] But Shoichiro, like most others who may have had initial misgivings, later changed his tune. "The question has been put to me, that with all of Toyota's success in the United States over the past 30 years, why did we spend billions of dollars, and invest thousands of man-hours in research and creative designs to launch a new line of elegant vehicles? Perhaps you have heard that I am not fond of riding in limos built by someone else," he jokingly told a gathering of American dealers shortly after the debut of the first Lexus. "From here on, I no longer will have to ride in vehicles made by Cadillac or Lincoln or Mercedes-Benz."[8] Eiji Toyoda's decision to move upscale hit the jackpot. Not only is Lexus the most profitable division of Toyota Motor, one that auto industry analysts estimate accounts for up to one quarter of the entire company's annual earnings, it is one of Japan's most profitable export goods. As *Fortune* wrote with great foresight 15 years ago: "The inside tale of how Lexus came into being is rich in lessons for anyone who yearns to develop up-market products."[9]

A cousin and protégé of the company's founder, Eiji Toyoda became transfixed by the idea of a luxury car in the summer of 1983, as he sifted through his thoughts while organizing a book to commemorate the company's 50th anniversary. To him, it seemed a natural progression, especially since at that time Toyota Motor had taken an 8.1% share of the global market — more than any other Japanese car-maker at that time. "Toyota," as the company notes somewhat modestly in a confidential internal analysis, "was on the rise in both size and standing."[10] But the chairman didn't embark on the odyssey to create a luxury car from scratch on a whim. He knew all too well that any upscale car Toyota Motor produced would have to be every bit the equal of the Mercedes top-end S-Class or BMW's vaunted 7-Series sedans. The downside risks were substantial. It would be fantastically expensive to engineer a luxury car with a new, high-powered engine with little to go on but hunches and a vague sense of marketplace demand. Even if Toyota Motor got everything right under the hood, the car would need to excel in areas such as creature comforts and opulent styling inside and out — which were not exactly the company's strongest points.

An even greater challenge had to do with reputation. Toyota Motor had no track record. It would be asking a lot of buyers to lay down tens of thousands of dollars on something that might appear to be little more than a fancy Corolla. This was a risky proposition considering that the dominant players traded off their established brand names to sell cars. Would anybody pay top price for a Toyota, even one sold under another name? It was an open question. "Getting the Lexus out of Toyota, whose forte is rolling out wheels for the world's millions, is like producing Beef Wellington at McDonald's," sniped *Fortune* in a less clairvoyant remark.[11]

It was more than a philosophical matter for Toyota Motor because of the money involved. The company, while comfortably in the black, could ill afford to pursue a misguided vanity project. But some argued it stood to lose more from staying out of the luxury market than by jumping in when its most loyal customers — baby boomers — were moving into their peak earning years and would soon be looking to buy more expensive cars. Toyota Motor wanted a high-end product line to prevent these loyal customers from defecting to other brands. The idea was to build a gilded bridge between the compact-car buyers of today and the luxury-car buyers of tomorrow. What's more, it also needed to safeguard its revenue in an era of increased U.S. import barriers, to stay neck-and-neck with Japanese rivals who were planning their own luxury lines, and to keep its engineers motivated with new challenges. At home, it sold the stately Century, a boat of a car with a 5.0-liter V-12 engine, used to chauffeur Japanese CEOs and cabinet ministers around the streets of Tokyo. The often empty front passenger seat on this and other Japanese luxury cars were built with a removable cushion so that the back-seat passenger could stretch his legs through to the front seat. But at US$125,000, the car was deemed too expensive to compete in the mass luxury market. Besides, Toyota Motor needed to update its export line-up with a car-lover's car designed primarily to be driven, not a limousine to be driven around in.

Most importantly, Toyota Motor smelled opportunity. Existing producers of luxury cars had grown fat, happy and increasingly out of touch with the demands of a new generation of car buyers. So, in a move that spared no expense and cemented his legacy as one of the automotive world's greats, Eiji Toyoda gave the orders to move into the luxury market.[12] Six years and a billion dollars later, the very first Lexus was born. To Toyoda, it was not a matter of cost, only a matter of time. In his words: "For us, this was not only a tremendous challenge and a dream to fulfill but also an inevitable decision."[13] Yet even the most zealous proponents of a Japanese luxury-car program in the early 1980s could scarcely imagine what Toyota Motor would unleash upon unsuspecting rivals a decade later. The company's luxury division, the Lexus brand, has grown from a car enthusiast's afterthought into the leading luxury brand in the U.S. It usurped Cadillac for that title in 2000 and has kept it ever since. In its debut year in 1989, sales of the untested brand's two models — the flagship LS and entry-level ES sedans — totaled just 16,302 cars. Two years later it became the best-selling luxury import and added a third model, the SC coupe. In 2003, Lexus sold more than 259,000 cars and boasted a fleet of eight different vehicles, including three sport utilities — the most of any luxury brand. An estimated 1.3 million vehicles sporting the Lexus L are still being driven on the roads of America, a testimony not only to the brand's popularity but also the durability of its cars.[14]

CATERING TO THE MASSES

Not so long ago the word "premium" was never used in the same sentence as a Japanese brand name. That was true for any number of household products in the 1960s and 1970s. Many of the trinkets stamped "Made in China" today carried a "Made in Japan" stamp back then. But the stigma of being perceived as a cheap and bland product was especially true for the country's small and underpowered automobiles. The key to Toyota Motor's success historically had always been selling large numbers of mid-range cars with mass appeal. While Toyota Motor sought to expand its horizons beyond that with Lexus, it used some of the same basic strategies in the luxury segment as it did in the low end of the market. Rather than seeking to outmaneuver Detroit with larger engines and gimmicks, for example, Toyota Motor did it one better by selling best-of-class quality cars that — while not cheap — still undercut the prices of the competition. This was a strategy it later used to sell the Lexus line-up. Only by offering greater value, Toyota Motor reasoned, could it hope to compete with the likes of Ford, GM, Chrysler and Nissan Motor, a favored son in its home market. Hammering away at costs and operating on razor-thin margins became institutionalized at Toyota Motor decades ago, something insiders wryly refer to as "wringing the water from a bone-dry washcloth". While other auto-makers allowed costs to creep up by virtue of their preoccupation with bigger engines, flashier designs and so on, Toyota Motor worked hard to keep costs to the customer in check. It kept up with the latest technology to remain competitive, but mostly concentrated on leveraging economies of scale. High production volumes of nearly identical models allowed it to spread out fixed costs for development and manufacturing. Revenue from each additional model made on an existing production line fell straight through to the bottom line. But much of this "profit" was immediately recycled into R&D or passed on to the consumer in the form of lower prices. For Lexus, the company combined that cost consciousness with an unending dedication to flawless manufacture. Cutting corners to cut costs has never been part of the Toyota Motor game plan.

In Toyota Motor factories, engineers routinely probe for potential glitches and, once these are uncovered, work closely with assembly-line workers to eradicate them. Procedures such as multiple inspection stations and the modern manifestation of the company's *poka-yoke* system — color-coded robotic lights that flash when a worker errs — reduce the number of careless mistakes and prevent small problems from cascading down the production lines. Using these techniques, Toyota Motor honed its skills at home, while planning a move into the U.S. mainstream. In the three years between 1969 and 1973, Toyota Motor moved up from being the world's fifth-biggest auto-maker to establish itself at No. 3, after GM and Ford. The Corolla compact, first introduced to the U.S. in 1968, the Corona sedan of 1969, and the sportier Celica coupe, which made its debut a few years later, won over a new generation of American drivers more concerned with fuel mileage and tailpipe emissions than raw horsepower and wheelbase length.[15] They were not only the first export-grade Toyota Motor models to match the quality of rival European cars, they were also much cheaper. This was a key competitive advantage in the volatile 1970s. Amid the twin shocks of the oil crises and stagflation, the American passenger-car market shrank, after hitting a peak of 10.95 million vehicles in 1978, down to a low of fewer than eight million cars by 1982. As a result, the Big Three all reported losses in 1980. In a last-ditch effort to counter this, Detroit rolled out smaller cars designed to compete with the Japanese, among them the ill-fated Chrysler K-cars and GM X-car. But Toyota Motor solidified its position as front-runner in the compact-sedan market.

It wasn't just early adaptation to tighter U.S. government-mandated fuel-emission restrictions (which Toyota Motor initially fought) and higher fuel prices that gave Toyota Motor a leg up on the Big Three. Trademark attributes such as providing more value for money and a laser-like focus on quality is what really propelled the Japanese from the sidelines into the mainstream. Toyota Motor's exports — most of which were earmarked for the U.S. market — skyrocketed from 4,000 cars in 1957, to 158,000 by 1967 and 1.41 million by 1977.[16] By the 1980s, Japan had the segment locked up and its car-makers rapidly moved up into bigger sedans. Again, the same traits that served Toyota Motor so well in budget and mid-sized cars would also work to its advantage when it moved into the luxury segment. "Over the years we have concentrated our efforts and abilities on quality, reliability and value for the broad automotive market," said Eiji Toyoda. "But our tradition and capabilities had reached the point where building an automobile in the grand style (sic) was a natural challenge to accept."[17]

It's impossible to understand why Toyota became America's best-loved manufacturer of luxury cars without delving into the company's history — if only to find out what makes it tick. Many drivers might be surprised to learn that despite the company's well-documented commercial success, Toyota Motor's early development as an auto-maker owes more to supplying armies than catering to suburbia's Soccer Moms.

EMPIRE OF THE SUN

In fact, the company started out as the pet project of a family black sheep of sorts. Its founder, Kiichiro Toyoda, the scion of a well-to-do clan of automated-loom makers and a man with a certain wanderlust, took up his father's passion for automobiles after losing out to his more business-minded brother-in-law for control of the family company. His interest in cars was kindled by a tour of American and British auto and machine-tool factories in 1929.[18] On his return to Japan the following year, this mechanical engineering graduate of the prestigious Tokyo Imperial University set about building an automobile prototype. Kiichiro's team spent most days — and many nights — dissecting import brand models assembled from ready-to-assemble kits at Ford and GM factories in Japan.[19] Close at hand was a dog-eared copy of Henry Ford's book *My Life and Work*. Although Mitsubishi produced the first passenger car in Japan in 1917, Detroit quickly gained control over the bulk of the Japanese auto market. This was thanks largely to local assembly of auto kits shipped from the U.S. At a time when their country was just beginning to industrialize, ordinary Japanese were greatly impressed by American car-assembly factories. In 1930, one Japanese newspaper reported without a trace of irony that Ford's plant in Koyasu "has joined the Imperial Theater House and Mitsukoshi [department store] as one of the famous places to see between Tokyo and Yokohama". GM, meanwhile, boasted that its 40,000- unit annual capacity plant in Osaka put it in "the position of being the largest automobile manufacturer and seller in the Orient".[20] That grand title would not last long.

But Toyota brand cars remained a dream deferred for Kiichiro. He entertained fanciful notions of building Asia's largest auto factory using what he'd discerned from the entrails of import models, but in reality it was handouts from the family business that enabled his dingy Nagoya workshop to continue operating. Yet by the early 1930s, what was once more of a hobby than a business venture had grown into a 1,000-man R&D operation skilled enough to produce decent motorcycle engines. Encouraged by senior officials in the Imperial Japanese Army — which had begun to run amok in Northeast China and grow increasingly influential over all aspects of policy — Toyoda managed by 1935 to produce a prototype car called the A1. Notable only for being developed domestically, it was little more than a pale imitation of a 1933 Chevrolet DeSoto Airflow.[21]

Despite being blessed by a Shinto priest, the A1 was succeeded by only two other prototypes before being dropped altogether. Yet it was an educational milestone. Sensing a shift in political tides, Kiichiro hitched his fortunes to the Japanese war machine. Instead of producing civilian cars, he hoped to win a license for making trucks needed by the army. On August 25, 1935, just 24 days after the passage of a protectionist law that would effectively shut down Ford and GM's burgeoning businesses in Japan, Toyoda introduced the G-1, a field-truck prototype with a heavy-duty suspension and a radiator grille inspired by a traditional Noh dancing mask.[22] Commercial truck sales began three months later at a price of 2,900 yen, well below cost but — crucially — 200 yen cheaper than its American competitors.[23] Such aggressive pricing became a tactic that was to serve Toyota Motor well for decades to come. With the writing on the wall for U.S. car-makers in Japan, Kiichiro was able to hire GM's top Japanese sales executive many other experienced administrative employees and even a few of GM's local auto dealers. Production rose to 50 trucks a month, but the vehicles were plagued with problems, including cracked rear axles. It was enough of a going concern, however, to enable Kiichiro to set up a research lab in Tokyo and start developmental work on two new prototypes. Dubbed the AA and BB, these were big, bulbous-nosed vehicles with waist-high front grilles, prominent fenders, protruding headlamps and Jeep-like flat windshields. In 1936, Kiichiro's connections and ambition were amply awarded. His venture received one of just two permits allotted under a new law regulating the manufacture of all vehicles.[24] With this government imprimatur guaranteeing a measure of success, Toyoda Automatic Loom gave its auto division a proper name: Toyota Motor. In written Japanese, the newly coined word "Toyota" required two fewer strokes to write than the 10-stroke family name, Toyoda. This was deemed fortuitous because eight is considered a lucky number in Japan. It was also a lot easier to pronounce and more modern sounding to the Japanese ear than the surname Toyoda, which literally meant "fertile rice paddies".[25]

By 1937, now employing 3,000 workers, Toyota Motor Co. became a fully fledged company in its own right. Most of the founding capital was put up by the Toyoda family and the powerful Mitsui *zaibatsu* industrial combine of cross-owned companies,[26] which was increasingly under the influence of Japan's militarist government. The investment was hardly altruistic. Japan was on a war footing, as full-scale battles raged against Chinese armies following the so-called Marco Polo Bridge Incident north of Beijing in 1937. Toyota Motor's first big order — for 6,000 trucks — came from the army that same year.[27] Two years later, Toyota Motor and Nissan Motor Co., which received the only other license to produce vehicles, were churning out 10,000 trucks each to meet military procurement orders.[28] To keep up with the steady demand from the Japanese army, Kiichiro built a new factory 20 miles (32 km) east of Nagoya, in the rural municipality of Koromo, later to be re-christened "Toyota City". There, Kiichiro appointed his young cousin and protégé, Eiji, to oversee the construction of the plant, which began operations in record time in 1938. This became known as the Honsha plant, which is still operating today and which served as a crucial laboratory for many of the production techniques at the heart of the Toyota Way, including "just-in-time" parts delivery, *kanban* inventory control and *kaizen* continuous improvement. Military orders boomed and the Koromo factory quickly expanded its production to full capacity. Just a year after its formal establishment, Toyota Motor recorded a profit of 800,000 yen — a handsome sum for the time. In fairness, Kiichiro was probably no more nationalistic than other well-connected businessmen of his day. Flamed by sensationalist media coverage of Chinese boycotts and sabotage aimed at Japan's factories in China, few Japanese felt much empathy for their Asian brethren. The Toyoda family, which had set up spinning-and-weaving operations in Shanghai as far back as 1921 and had become the leading equipment supplier to Japanese textile mills in China, had a huge stake in the re-imposition of "order" in the war-torn neighboring country — by force if necessary.[29] What's more, Toyota Motor was a prime beneficiary of the flagrant protectionism of the day. In 1939, GM and Ford had been forced to pull out of Japan, forfeiting the market to Toyota Motor and its sole domestic rival, Nissan. Meanwhile, Kiichiro Toyoda forged ever-closer ties with suppliers, creating an embryonic *keiretsu* network for sharing technology and information. Where Toyota Motor couldn't source the parts from outside manufacturers, it continued to build them internally. And those parts-making units eventually grew into companies in their own right, including Denso Corp., the former Nippondenso Co., which was spun off from Toyota Motor in 1949. Buffeted by the war effort, Toyota Motor began to rationalize its business to conserve ever-scarcer resources. It was in this environment that the company adopted such core practices as just-in-time production, which was designed to maximize efficiency and minimize inventory. In what would later become a staple of Toyota Motor factories, Kiichiro is said to have written out the motivational slogan "Just-In-Time" in oversized characters on a banner and had it hung on the factory wall.[30] Even as demand for Toyota Motor's trucks peaked, it was clear by 1944 that the tide had turned against the Japanese war effort. Toyota Motor continued to churn out its heavy-duty trucks, amphibious vehicles and aircraft engines as a veritable ward of the Ministry of Munitions. To cope with the wartime shortage of able-bodied adult male workers, it hired a motley assortment of substitutes to keep production lines running. These included children, common criminals and even patron-less geisha. The army was so desperate for trucks — and parts were in such short supply — that Toyota Motor made some "one-eyed" trucks with no front brakes and with just a single headlight installed.[31] A day before Japan's surrender on August 15, 1945, and the end of World War II, American B-29 bombers struck Toyota Motor's main truck plant in Koromo, destroying half the factory in a fiery blast. But in a sign of the company's resiliency, just one month later it won approval from the U.S. to start limited production of trucks for the occupying forces. It thereby escaped the fate of many other companies which were dissolved as a result of their ties to Mitsui and other *zaibatsu*. Post-war chaos notwithstanding, Toyota Motor staggered on.

WORKING OUT THE KINKS

Ironically, after surviving the war and the subsequent American-orchestrated economic purge, Kiichiro Toyoda lost his job in 1950 and died two years later. His death came after the commercial launch of the company's first car, the ill-fated SA model, but far too early for him to witness the company's eventual success in passenger cars. Kiichiro was forced to resign as part of a deal to settle a strike prompted by a bank bailout of Toyota Motor which led to layoffs of 1,600 workers on his watch. Within months, under the leadership of its new president, Shotaro Kamiya, the company bounced back as production skyrocketed. Once again, military trucks saved the day, this time commissioned by the U.S. for use by American troops fighting the Korean War. In the summer of 1950, Eiji Toyoda, by then a Toyota Motor managing director and soon to be named executive vice-president in charge of technology, spent weeks on a Ford Motor-sponsored tour of American auto-assembly plants and tool-makers in New York, Ohio and Rhode Island. Excited by the possibilities he had seen, he returned to Japan in October. Impressed by the scale of the American plants but scornful of the inefficiency he witnessed, he sensed an opening and immediately took up his mentor's zeal for mass-producing a commercially viable passenger car.[32] One of his first steps was to transfer Taiichi Ohno, who had accompanied him to the U.S., from Toyoda's post-war loom operations to the automotive business. Ohno, a high school graduate and textile machine-shop hand who was also a relentless tinkerer, became the godfather of that gospel of manufacturing efficiency, the Toyota Production System. Ohno went on to train average line-workers in Japan to handle the quality checking and repair work carried out solely by specialists in Detroit. He also pioneered breakthrough procedures to improve efficiency, such as the *kanban* index cards still used today in Toyota Motor plants to track inventory in real time, an analog precursor to modern bar code systems.[33] As Ohno worked his magic on the factory floor, Eiji busied himself with the roll-out the SF model. Based somewhat awkwardly on a truck platform, this car was truly Toyota Motor's first sports utility vehicle. But it was a commercial flop, selling only about 200 a month by mid 1952. A successor, the Toyopet

Super, fared somewhat better. It was dogged by defects, however. Even as Ohno worked to fix the faults, it wasn't until 1961 that Toyota Motor adopted a system of Total Quality Control to halve the number of glitches on the production line. Eiji Toyoda was nominated in 1964 to head an all-out campaign for Toyota Motor to win a coveted prize in Japanese industrial circles named after quality-control guru W. Edwards Deming, whose ideas had become a huge intellectual force in the Japan of the 1950s. In 1965, Toyota won the award. Two years later Eiji became the fifth president of Toyota Motor.[34]

Well into the 1950s, Toyota Motor remained largely a supplier of trucks to the U.S. military. Its output of cars, for example, made up only about a third of the 15,994 vehicles it sold as late as 1953.[35] It wasn't until 1966 that Toyota Motor sold more cars than trucks. Yet trucks are what allowed the company to survive those early post-war years. "These orders were Toyota's salvation," One Toyota Motor president later recalled. "I felt a mingling of joy for my company and a sense of guilt that I was rejoicing over another country's war."[36]

Of course, Toyota Motor was hardly alone in its dependence on military orders. Companies such as Nissan, tire-maker Bridgestone, and engine-manufacturer Kawasaki also relied heavily on U.S. military contracts, as MIT professor Richard Samuels writes, "to train their first post-war generation of engineers in the most advanced manufacturing technologies".[37] The steady demand kept Toyota Motor's factory humming and earned the company enough money to invest in its first hit: the 1955 Crown sedan. This car instantly became Japan's best-selling taxi-cab model at a time when few Japanese could afford their own family car — a position the Crown continues to hold onto to this day. Of course, it helped that American and European car-makers were effectively locked out of the market by a 34% protective tariff that applied to all but the smallest imports for most of the 1950s and 1960s. Though the duty was reduced to 17% in 1969, it wasn't phased out entirely until 1978. By then, vehicle imports had been largely priced out of the market. As a result, Detroit's share of the world's second-largest car market shrank from as high as 60% in 1953 to an insignificant 1% by 1960.[38] Without the protective wall of tariffs, however, the car fared less well overseas. A 1.5-liter

Crown was exported to the U.S. in August 1957 (escorted by Miss Japan), but was quickly — and quietly — withdrawn when the expected sales didn't materialize. It was simply too underpowered for American highways. A Ford executive called the Crown "a heap of junk".[39] The failure to break into the world's biggest auto market would haunt the company for years to come. It also reinforced a conservative bent that led Toyota Motor to shy away from taking other big risks in the years ahead. The company developed a reputation for being less of a great innovator than a great imitator — a producer of models which improved on existing designs. Even today in Japan, Toyota Motor is mostly known for allowing other auto-makers to test the waters before wading into a new segment and then liberally borrowing design cues. Some say that this explains its dominant 40% market share in Japan. Toyota Motor's biggest fans readily concede that the company rarely wins points for style with car-buyers and motoring magazines. Instead, the company targets as many buyers as possible with inoffensive, if bland, offerings. Critics say Toyota Motor has followed that same road in luxury cars, and it's hard to deny the obvious styling similarities that some Lexus models share with Mercedes, BMW and even Britain's Jaguar (now a unit of Ford Motor Co.). Toyota Motor freely admits to having used these cars as benchmarks. "Eiji Toyoda suggested we create a vehicle that would join the ranks of BMW's 7-Series, Jaguar and the Mercedes S-Class," said Kazuo Okamoto, who served as deputy and then chief engineer of the original LS sedan.[40] Imitation truly is the sincerest form of flattery.

"THEY WANT TO DESTROY US"

Once Toyota Motor committed to jump into the luxury market, for reasons outlined later, it leveraged top-flight quality and service as a way to break into the market dominated by well-established players. "Inside Benz and BMW the thinking was: 'We own this market'," said Richard "Dick" Chitty, who oversaw the brand's service operations in the earliest days. "Lexus took them totally by surprise."[41] Exhaustive market surveys showed that, ironically, luxury cars had some of the lowest levels of customer dissatisfaction. This was despite — or perhaps because of — the fact that they were also the vehicles with the highest profit margin for manufacturers, who seemed to expect their very best customers to complain. Toyota Motor would do no such thing. Its luxury division stole the march on its rivals immediately upon its release in 1989, impressing both American car-buyers and a cynical auto press. "The upper management of BMW and Mercedes-Benz were pooh-poohing the idea of a Japanese luxury brand," said former Lexus division chief Jim Perkins. The first LS sedan came across as a state-of-the-art product at a rock-bottom price. "The troops are mobilized, the dogs of war unleashed. Toyota Motor seems ready to let the Germans feel its sting," wrote *Car and Driver* magazine. "For the European luxury-car makers, the days of sitting contentedly on their status symbols are over."[42] Former BMW chairman Eberhard von Kuenheim went so far as to accuse Lexus of "dumping", by selling cars for less than it cost to make them; a charge Toyota Motor strongly denied.[43] Clearly, European luxury marques felt threatened. "I don't think the Japanese intention is to live together with us. I feel they want to destroy us," said BMW's Wolfgang Reitzle. "They can roll over costs in this segment to their mass-produced models. They can lose money for the next three to five years only to make market share. We have to live out of the income of the luxury-car segment."[44] But BMW and Mercedes were quick to catch on to Toyota Motor's efficiency gains and had made up much lost ground by mid decade. Mercedes passed Lexus, which was dogged by a lull in new products, to re-take the crown as the best-selling luxury import in 1995. "In the mid 1990s, we hit another wall," said current Lexus division head Denny Clements. "Our competitors responded with improved products."[45] But Toyota Motor's luxury brand quickly regained its footing with new cars such as the sleek GS luxury sports sedan and smooth RX crossover sport utility vehicle (SUV). By 1998, it was not only back on top of imports but also, for the first time ever, outsold the domestic luxury brands. Demand for luxury cars climbed to unprecedented levels, from 1.11 million units in 1989 to 1.9 million by 2003, pushing up luxury's share of the overall U.S. market from 8% in the mid 1990s to 11% today. Tellingly, the Lexus share of this grew from just 1.5% in 1989 to 14% in 2003.[46] "We have spent all this money," company president Shoichiro Toyoda said during a visit to the U.S. in 1989, "because there is a strong market for a luxury car such as the Lexus."[47] But even he didn't know then just how right he was about that.

As the market expanded in lock-step with the accelerating U.S. economy in the mid-to-late 1990s, there seemed to be enough growth in the high-end auto business to fuel expansion for everybody; or almost everybody. In earning its pole position in the U.S. market, Lexus arguably did the most damage to iconic American brands such as Cadillac and Lincoln. Both of these U.S. marques suffered greatly from mass defections to Lexus and, by the late 1990s, the hyper-competitive Germans. Sales of traditional domestic luxury cars plummeted from 465,844 in 1989 to just 289,422 in 2001.[48] While Cadillac has enjoyed something of a resurgence since then, there's little mystery why so many buyers of American luxury cars switched to Lexus. After all, what really makes the Japanese brand appealing to its biggest fans is the smooth ride and easy handling which the American brands are best known for. Those characteristics are typically shunned by the autobahn-loving Germans, who view driving as a two-hands-on-the-wheel pursuit and stress performance and prestige. German cars tend to have stiffer suspensions, tight handling and multiple engine variations; traits shared with high-performance racing vehicles. Many Americans, on the other hand, tend to see driving as a matter of getting from Point A to Point B with as little discomfort as possible — preferably with a hot cup of coffee or take-out Krispy Crème donut in hand. So Lexus took on the American brands that catered to the weekday commuter and Sunday driver. It won these people over handily with superior cabin appointments, fewer breakdowns and good old-fashioned dealer service. "We wanted to build a Benz with a Cadillac interior," recalled Dick Chitty, one of the brand's founding fathers in the U.S.[49] Detroit will always maintain a core base of drivers who "Buy American", but Lexus has undeniably eroded Cadillac's once-unassailable position by coupling comfort with quality. No surprise then that the average age and income level of a Lexus car-buyer overlaps Cadillac's core constituency of 60-year-olds. These days, you're just as likely to spot senior drivers behind the wheel of an ES 330 as a Cadillac DeVille, to the point where *BusinessWeek* raised the question: "Doesn't Grandpa Drive a Lexus?" The median age of Lexus buyers is 52, four years older than that of Mercedes drivers and nine years older than BMW drivers.[50]

BOOT CAMPS AND BANK ACCOUNTS

Lexus has become so successful that it's no longer the bargain it used to be. When the brand made its debut, the LS carried a base price of US$35,000, or about US$10,000 less than the BMW 535i and the Mercedes 300E. Nowadays, the price difference has narrowed. The LS starts at US$55,000 today, about the same as an E-Class Benz. It's not only because BMW and Benz charge less for their cars; Toyota Motor can now charge more. And it would argue — not entirely without merit — that on the basis of performance the LS is the equal of the S430 Benz and 745Li BMW (both of which have a base price of US$72,500). *Consumer Reports*, for example, compared those two cars with the LS 430, the Cadillac DeVille, the Audi A8 L and the Jaguar XJ8. Its conclusion? "The Lexus LS 430 was not only the least expensive of the group, but also scored the highest and is the only car we can recommend."[51] By those standards, of course, the flagship Lexus is still a tremendous bargain. The higher price tag that Lexus can now command is of immense importance to Toyota Motor because profit margins are so high on luxury cars — at least double those of ordinary compact sedans. Lexus accounted for just 259,755 of the two million cars Toyota Motor sold in the U.S. in 2003. Yet those relatively small volumes are high value-added and make up a large proportion of the company's profits. While Toyota Motor won't disclose the brand's profitability for competitive reasons, it's safe to assume Lexus has played a major role in lifting Toyota Motor to its estimated 2003 earnings of US$7.2 billion. That's twice the level it reported in 1999. Industry analysts note that 70% of the company's profits come from the U.S. market, and that up to a quarter of that is derived from 14 years of steady growth at Lexus. It has become by far the most valuable division of Toyota Motor.

The brand's list of achievements is long — and growing longer all the time. Lexus has consistently taken top honors in the J.D. Power and Associates quality ratings, the gold standard for the auto industry. In the 2003 Vehicle Dependability Study, which tracks the number and type of problems owners have with three-year-old vehicles, Lexus took top spot for a ninth straight year — or every year since it has been eligible. Also in 2003, for the seventh consecutive year, the LS was named as the premium luxury sedan with the fewest problems of any vehicle (76 per 100 vehicles) charted by J.D. Power. It was a new industry record. As a key component of its marketing strategy, Lexus takes out full-page advertisements in major newspapers to promote its achievements. And it strives to back these claims up with service par excellence. Beyond common courtesy and efficiency, Lexus has gone the extra mile. This extends from providing loan cars at most repair shops, to on-site putting greens at some dealerships and free fresh-cut roses at others. To ensure that its "sales associates" were up to the company's standard, Toyota Motor sent 560 newly recruited sales and service people to two-day "boot camps" before the brand was introduced in 1989 to grill them on Lexus minutiae and groom them to cater to (almost) every whim of customers. Assigned to study-teams with names like "Blue Thunder", the recruits endured training sessions that finished as late as 10 pm. They were instructed to eschew the cold, distant approach of Acura as well as the over-friendly pitch of Cadillac dealers. Instead, they aimed to be honest brokers, who are genuinely well informed about their cars but not pushy. Of those early recruits, about 22% came from jobs selling or serving European luxury marques, while some 15% had worked for American luxury brands such as Cadillac and Lincoln. Fully 83% boasted at least some college experience, and two-thirds were under 40. Most expressed relief at not having to rely on the hard sell. One reporter who attended a session attested to the caliber of the sales force by remarking: "There's not a plaid sportscoat in sight."[52]

Toyota Motor also deserves credit for setting the standard for the now widespread practice of certifying pre-owned vehicles. It started the program for its luxury division in 1993 at a time when used-car programs put in place by Jaguar and Mercedes-Benz were faltering. "Certified" is marketing jargon for trade-ins sold at authorized showrooms. By standardizing used-car sales with check-ups and extended service warranties, these programs prop up resale values, which buoy new-car sales and bolster a brand's image. It's a virtuous circle that has helped Lexus retain an air of exclusivity despite record sales. "In terms of value creation, through their used-vehicle certification programs, Lexus and Toyota rank among the highest of all vehicle manufacturers," said *Brandweek* magazine.[53] J.D. Power & Associates found that buyers of certified used luxury cars pay an average of US$3,000 more per vehicle than those who bought non-certified versions of the same models. "We like to say they're like new," said Marv Ingram, chief sales manager for the Lexus certified pre-owned program.[54]

As much as resale values are factored into a car-buyer's decision, few on Madison Avenue would contest that unique advertising is what put Lexus on the map. A series of innovative campaigns brought Lexus into the living rooms — and onto the shopping lists — of millions of Americans who'd never heard of the brand. "We're trying to make the car look like art," said David W. Wager, former president of New York-based advertising agency Saatchi & Saatchi's special unit dedicated to Lexus.[55] Who can forget the sight of the shiny LS with a pyramid of champagne flutes delicately stacked on its hood as an engine purred at full strength underneath? That's what the ad-company insiders credit with starting the Lexus legend. But that was just the beginning of a series of innovative campaigns. There can be few who haven't heard the tagline "The Relentless Pursuit of Perfection", which *Brandweek* magazine called "arguably one of the most effective of the [20th] century".[56] Crafting the brand's image is so important that Saatchi & Saatchi, Toyota Motor's chief global advertising agency set up its special unit — Team One — at El Segundo, California, to deal exclusively with the brand. Some 240 staff are assigned to convince the rest of us that the Lexus magic is real. How real? One study commissioned by Lexus in the mid 1990s found that most Americans thought of it as an independent company, not as a sales division of Toyota Motor. Many guessed that Lexus is based in Europe. The very word, a neologism based on the name "Alexis" and the word "luxury", has taken on a life of its own, being used occasionally as a term to describe the quality of other products, as in the "Lexus of sake" or as in "Lexus-ized" — a term comedian Jay Leno has used in his automotive musings for *Popular Mechanics*. All of this is fine with Toyota Motor, as long as it adds to the prestige of the brand. "We think of our brand equity like it was a bank account," said James E. Press, the former head of the Lexus division and current executive vice president of Toyota Motor Sales U.S.A. "You are either making deposits or withdrawals."[57]

SUV SUPERPOWER

But as nice a wrapper as the ads and marketing provide, the product is what makes Lexus cars stand out. From the outset, Toyota Motor has endeavored to give its luxury line the edge. With the first LS sedan, for example, car enthusiasts took note of the graceful acceleration and the seven-speaker stereo option — and all for thousands of dollars less than the competition. What Lexus lacked in heritage, it made up for in sheer "value for the money", according to Shinzo Kobuki, general manager of the Lexus Planning Division in Toyota City. "The product was strong enough to knock out the competition."[58] No styling element was overlooked. Debates over the shape and coefficiency drag — the flow of air around the car — went on for months until a suitable silhouette was selected from hundreds of prospective designs. As Toyota Motor recounts: "Lexus designers concerned themselves with expressing the LS400's superlative aerodynamics and elegant style. They attended to details as minute as the radius of a headlight lens, how the gap between the hood and fender looks from the human vantage point, surface quality and lack of seams in a window molding. To refine and complement the LS400's shape, they sought out new materials, created special finishes, [and] researched the flow of air around an automobile body." The interior detailing underwent similar scrutiny. "Imagine a high-speed cloud with a leather interior," gushed *Car and Driver*.[59] "These guys thought of everything," cooed *Road & Track*.[60] *M Magazine*, too, extolled the virtues of the brand: "The only way Toyota can improve its new Lexus LS 400 is by figuring out how the car can make wake-up calls and brew fresh coffee."[61] Where parts that would meet the high standards set out for the LS didn't exist, Toyota Motor created them from scratch. "A luxury automobile is enjoyed first and foremost from the inside. Here Lexus designers and engineers sought to create a warm, serene, comfortable environment — one that respects the human being in both [the] functional and esthetic senses."[62] The follow-up entry-level ES and sporty GS met — and exceeded — crucial industry benchmarks for comfort, handling and speed. And the SC coupe gave the staid brand a pinch of sexiness. State-of-the art technology became a hallmark of the brand; something which dovetailed nicely with its Japanese roots. Indeed, car-buyers who know Lexus only as an extension of Toyota Motor have come to expect the latest in high-tech from it. The auto-maker has worked hard to live up to that image, with features such as Mark Levinson audio systems and the Lexus Link emergency-help system. What really put Lexus into a class by itself, however, was the RX sports utility, the very first luxury "crossover" vehicle. To date, in the U.S. alone it has achieved sales of more than 472,000 vehicles. The popularity of the RX stems largely from its unique blending of the tall ride of an SUV with the soft ride of a sedan. In fact, it shares the same basic body framework as the Camry and ES sedans. The car's ungainly, humpbacked silhouette is more homely than menacing, despite valiant efforts by Team One to portray it otherwise in ads. But the high seating and roomy hatchback give it all the SUV pedigree needed. The RX is especially popular among women. Indeed, for the latest model, the RX 330, Lexus appeals to a demographic of mostly married females in their mid-40s with household income over US$125,000.[63] In other words, Lexus has become the preferred brand of the well-heeled Soccer Mom.

The competition took notice only after initially dismissing the RX as a freak accident of engineering. The BMW X3, the Mercedes M-Class, the Cadillac SRX and the Acura MDX all compete for a slice of the growing market for luxury crossover SUVs. But none have succeeded like the Lexus RX line. Toyota Motor has built its status as a purveyor of SUVs to the rich and famous with two other, higher-grade vehicles: the LX and the GX, making Lexus the only luxury brand with a stable of three different SUVs. This proved to be a smart move. Sales of luxury crossovers went from zero in 1996 to 14,569 the following year. Annual demand zoomed to 238,543 units by 2002.[64] The RX has been so good to Lexus that when the time came to upgrade the 2003 model, Toyota Motor made only the most minor alterations — a more powerful engine, a longer wheelbase, slightly better fuel economy and optional xenon headlights that rotate as much as 15 degrees in the direction the vehicle turns. "The original RX 300 became the template for a new kind of luxury vehicle, one that many competitors are now following," Denny Clements, Lexus general manager, said in a nod to the ancestry of the 2004 model RX 330.

THE LAST LEXUS SALE

For all that, in many ways the deck was stacked against Toyota Motor when it waded into the luxury market in 1989. To make it work, the company committed everything it had to the project. The first model evolved out of some 450 prototypes that represented the work of 60 designers, 24 engineering teams, 1,400 engineers, 2,300 technicians and 220 other support workers. Development costs alone — not to mention the expense of setting up a dealership network — reached at least US$1 billion[65] (some estimates put it closer to US$3 billion[66]).

To put this into perspective, for a typical new product launch Toyota Motor generally crafts, at most, two or three full-scale prototypes, which generally involves a maximum of 200 engineers and rarely costs more than US$500 million. Eiji Toyoda essentially gave a blank check to the team assembled to make the first Lexus. But the team entrusted with this task set exceedingly stringent parameters for themselves. Half-way measures would not be tolerated. The car must be faster, more fuel efficient, quieter and also less expensive than the top-grade cars of all rival brands. The engineering dilemma was enormous: how to fit a 4.0-liter engine in a car which needed to be light enough to skirt the gas-guzzler tax yet also sufficiently insulated to muffle noise and vibration? Yet Toyota Motor managed to do just that. As a measure of how much effort went into its development, one former president of the company joked that so much money had been spent on making the car flawless that Lexus shouldn't need a servicing network in the U.S. since it should never break down.[67] In fact, the very first Lexus did suffer a minor, but embarrassing, glitch just three months after being introduced. But as we'll see later, fast footwork and full disclosure would turn a potential fiasco into a big PR win.

Another hurdle the brand faced was heavy competition from Japanese rivals. Toyota Motor was not the first of Japan's auto-makers to wade into the luxury market. Honda had set up its Acura division in the U.S. three years earlier. Nor was Toyota Motor the sole star of the 1989 North American International Auto Show. Nissan also launched its luxury marque and was seen by some as having an edge over Toyota Motor since it had a reputation for more attractive, better-engineered cars. Later, of course, Nissan's Infiniti brand stalled and Acura failed to fulfill its potential, allowing Lexus to establish itself as the dominant Japanese luxury player. Among the many reasons for this were the strict rules against overlap in the pricing of Toyota brand and Lexus models. Jim Press, who ran the Lexus division in the mid 1990s and who now serves as COO of Toyota Motor Sales U.S., explained: "We don't sell a Lexus at the same price point as a Toyota. The lowest price Infiniti [was priced] less than the Nissan Maxima and the Acura Integra [was sold] in the Honda Accord territory. The Toyota channel takes care of the volume selling, period, while Lexus aims to be the highest mark of luxury."[68] Nowadays that two-tiered pricing strategy is considered common wisdom in the auto industry. But in 1989, Toyota Motor's gambit looked to be anything but a sure bet. "It is a blank page to be written on," said *Fortune*. "What if Lexus doesn't make an appropriate statement? Will customers put value ahead of ego?"[69] *BusinessWeek* cautioned: "Even with slick cars and soothing surroundings, the Japanese won't easily cruise away with a market that others have been cultivating for decades."[70] And in a follow-up article entitled "Surprisingly Mixed Result for Lexus", *BusinessWeek* noted that Lexus was forced to trim its overly optimistic first-year sales projections from an initial figure of 75,000 down to 60,000 cars. In another inauspicious sign, one California dealer broke ranks with the brand's "Thou Shall Not Discount" policy to clear out excess inventory of ES sedans just months after Lexus made its debut. The dealership advertised 15% markdowns in a short-lived campaign called "The First Ever Lexus Sale".[71] It was indeed the first — and the last— such campaign. How Toyota Motor overcame such unexpected setbacks will be detailed in later chapters.

THE VALUE-ADDED IMPERATIVE

The genesis of Eiji Toyoda's momentous decision to move up market was a simple one. The company needed a successor to its Cressida sedan, which had gone through several model changes since its launch in 1968.[72] By the early 1980s, the car was badly in need of an update. Yet Toyota Motor feared the Cressida bloodline had too little oomph to keep owners loyal, especially as they moved into higher income brackets. And, after a measure of success in 1981 with a technically advanced mid-size sport sedan (sold in Japan as the Soarer — a precursor to the Lexus SC line), many within the company felt ready to take on a bigger challenge. As a preliminary measure, in the summer of 1983 the product planning division drew up a marketing report on what American buyers were looking for in the next Cressida. TMC veterans had seen demand for luxury cars plummet during the oil crises of the 1970s and then recover in the 1980s. It was what newly elected U.S. President Ronald Reagan called "Morning In America" again. Americans were shaking off the hold of a stubborn recession and a strong economic recovery got under way. And Toyota Motor needed a more powerful export model to appeal to Americans in search of greater horsepower at a feel-good time of economic revival. In the early 1980s, Toyota Motor's most powerful sedan was the 2.5-liter Camry. But the company's product-planning coordination committee wasn't interested in the understudy product planning division's finding until Eiji Toyoda expressed an interest in developing a luxury car. "There was a 'do we really need to do this' sentiment among some [at TMC]," said Jim Perkins, a GM veteran who was tapped to be the first general manager of the Lexus division at TMS.

"[But] once the upper management realised this would be Eiji's legacy, there was a groundswell of support.[73] Kiyoshi Matsumoto, a senior managing director in charge of technology and later executive vice-president, was given authorization by the board to set up a study team to pursue the idea. Matsumoto's enthusiasm stemmed from a visit to Europe in 1982 when he drove rented Audi, Citroën, Benz and BMW models up and down the autobahn. The sharp handling and high speed capabilities of these cars, he found, far outstripped anything Toyota Motor had to offer. He knew then that Toyota Motor had its work cut out if it intended to compete in the global market for luxury cars.[74] Most Toyota Motor executives were convinced that the company could succeed and responded with a proposed car that was much larger than the Cressida, with a powerful 3.0-liter V6 engine under its bonnet.

This all stemmed from a desire on the part of Toyota Motor to retain its core customer base and expand into the baby-boomer market.[75] Indeed, Toyota Motor increasingly feared losing touch with these key car-buyers. "The people who had been buying our cars were moving up in life," Eiji Toyoda recalled. "We wanted to meet their heightened needs."[76] As college students in the 1960s and 1970s, the boomers had long loved Toyota Motor's budget-minded, low-pollution, no-frills approach to mass transportation. Trusty Corollas and Celicas were the workhorses of that generation. But as the boomers started earning more and settling down with families, they wanted something different to accommodate their changing needs. Toyota Motor didn't make station wagons. Detroit, for its part, had long written off the compact-car market, leaving it to import brands such as Volkswagen, Datsun and Toyota Motor. To the Big Three, profit margins on compacts were far too low to justify a war of attrition with cheaper cars manufactured overseas. Instead, they focused their attention on larger, more profitable vehicles such as sleek saloons and heavy-duty pick-up trucks (the latter protected by high tariffs on imports). Cadillac, after all, was king. Yet by 1974, half of all cars sold were compact models — mostly imports.[77] Detroit's short-sighted strategy would come back to haunt it in due time, but at the beginning of the 1980s it was Toyota Motor and VW that worried most about losing customers who had "graduated" from their days driving cheap import models.

There was another, less-publicized reason than the changing tastes of potential customers for Toyota Motor to move into the luxury market: trade friction. Toyota Motor and the other Japanese brands were enough of a nuisance to Detroit — an influential political constituency — that even as consummate a free-trader as the late President Ronald Reagan came out in favor of "voluntary" quotas.[78] Those quotas, of course, were voluntary in name only. They were negotiated by the Japanese government — which had many exports other than cars to worry about — in order to placate the U.S. and safeguard the "special relationship" between Tokyo and Washington. What's more, the Japanese trade ministry "wanted to make a point" by forcing Japan's often maverick auto industry to buckle under to government authority.[79] But there was considerable resistance to this from Japanese car-makers. Toyota Motor executives encouraged their friends in the media to take up the cause of free trade, with reports calling Japan's top trade negotiator a "whore for the foreigners" and "Reagan's concubine".[80] In the end, however, the voluntary quotas were accepted under duress. A May 1, 1981 accord called for three-year export restraint, capping exports at 1.68 million cars the first year. It was renewed a year later, before eventually becoming obsolete.

For U.S. trade negotiators, the taste of victory was fleeting. Voluntary quotas were a complete failure. They required absolutely no meaningful restructuring by the Big Three, and simply delayed the taking of greater market share by import brands. It also got Japan's government into the business of "managed trade" of automobiles and turned a blind eye to potential anti-trust violations by the Japanese. Most significantly, it got Toyota Motor, Nissan and Honda thinking about ways of extracting profits from a market with a tight ceiling on export sales growth. One answer the Japanese companies came up with was to shift more production of their cars to the U.S., which gave rise to the Japanese "transplant" phenomenon over the next two decades. But another solution was just to sell fewer, but more profitable, export model cars. "Value-added" became their watchwords. This allowed existing plants in Japan to keep humming along, even as new factories for low-end models sprouted up in the cornfields of Ohio and Kentucky. Thus a protectionist trade accord designed to give Detroit some breathing space turned out to be a boon for Japan's car-makers. It did so by creating a powerful incentive for them to diversify — not only by shifting more production out of Japan but also shifting into new, more lucrative market segments — such as luxury cars.[81]

At the time, at the top of Toyota Motor's line-up in the U.S. was the US$25,000 Supra sports sedan. Engineers at Toyota Motor wanted the company — which had passed Nissan to become Japan's No.1 producer, seller and exporter of cars as far back as 1966 — to test their skills against the best the Americans, Germans and Italians had to offer. In fact, unlike most of Japan's other car-makers, Toyota Motor could claim a certain — albeit limited — heritage in manufacturing high-performance vehicles. In the late 1960s, the auto world sat up and took notice of Toyota Motor's 2000 GT sports car. That car, the spiritual ancestor of the current Lexus SC 430 coupe, is perhaps best known for its cameo debut as a white two-seater convertible (replete with hidden surveillance cameras and a voice-activated tape recorder) racing through the crowded streets of downtown Tokyo in the 1967 James Bond movie *You Only Live Twice*. Toyota Motor never quite forgot this first foray into specialty cars or the warm reception the sporty coupe received overseas. As an internal Toyota Motor history recounts: "Not all early Toyotas were for the masses. In 1967, the company produced a small number of this exotic sports car, the 2000GT; it was the first proof that a Japanese carmaker could compete with the world's established makers of sporting automobiles. The 2000GT won rave reviews in American car magazines. Powered by a 2-liter dual-overhead camshaft 6-cylinder engine and equipped with a 5-speed transmission, it was capable of over 135 mph (217 kph). Racing-style independent suspension (actually similar in concept to that of the LS 400) gave it remarkable handling. It even had four-wheel disc brakes — remarkable in 1967! A racing version, with a special 200-horsepower engine, was campaigned on American road-racing circuits by Australian driver Peter Brock."[82]

To this day, that sporty Japanese convertible has legions of diehard fans around the globe. But only 351 were ever made, the last rolling off the production line in 1970. After that experiment, Toyota Motor reverted to what it did best: the mass production of reliable, if stylistically dull, cars. So it was that in the 1970s and early 1980s Nissan's Fairlady Z fastback models stole the hearts of a generation of teenage boys.[83]

But Toyota Motor's engineers, some of whom had worked on high-performance aircraft engines during World War II, never forgot their roots. Once the company had accrued enough profits to afford the higher costs associated with more limited production models, they were ready to fill the breach. This was more than a matter of pride or intellectual challenge. While they felt they were the equals of their counterparts in the U.S. and Europe and would like to be given the chance to prove it, it was the making of big cars with big engines that had attracted them into the industry to begin with. And it was this that would be the major motivation for getting into work early and for staying late into the night.

For years, Nissan attracted the best and brightest engineers in Japan simply because it offered the chance, however slim, to ascend to the ranks of the elite few who designed and engineered the Z. In their home market, Nissan and Toyota Motor were locked in a battle for the small but prestigious luxury market with vehicles unknown outside Japan. To this day, both companies' top-of-the-line cars — the stately Toyota Century limousine, and the favorite of Japanese CEOs, the Nissan President — aren't sold overseas and can only be glimpsed outside Japan on the compounds of Japanese embassies. In global terms, Toyota Motor's engineers could take pride in their company's hard-won designation as the top maker of fuel-efficient compacts. But, deep down, they wanted desperately to make a "world-class car" that was competitive with the likes of Jaguar, Lincoln and Mercedes.[84]

Toyota Motor's engineers weren't the only ones with something to prove. "Big and conservative, Toyota does not get the respect among auto aficionados that chairman [Eiji] Toyoda thinks it deserves," wrote *Fortune*.[85] And, as noted earlier, the boardroom was anxious to exorcise a demon that had haunted the company for years: its first, little-known foray into the higher end of the U.S. market with the Crown model. When the Crown first went on sale in Beverly Hills in the summer of 1958, the car made history. It was Toyota Motor's first export to the U.S. mainland,[86] and expectations of it were sky-high. After all, the Crown was a success in Japan, where it made its debut in July 1958.[87] But it never had a fighting chance against its American rivals. Featuring a tiny engine and a top speed of about 62 miles per hour (100 kph), it shook violently on California's turnpikes and "tended to overheat when driven over mountains and on long, straight, desert stretches, [such] as between Los Angeles and Las Vegas".[88] Less than two years after its debut, Toyota Motor withdrew the US$2,300 Crown from the U.S. market.

The failure was a setback in more ways than one. A demoralized Toyota Motor exported fewer than 12,000 vehicles to the U.S. in 1961, less than the previous year and even fewer than Nissan.[89] But it learned an important lesson. In the future, all cars sold abroad would be tailored to meet local driving conditions. Never again would Toyota Motor market one of its domestic models "off the shelf" in a foreign market. Significant alterations would henceforth be made after intensive study of native tastes and preferences. When, 30 years later, the first Lexus reached the U.S., it had been built exclusively with American drivers in mind. With it, Toyota Motor would prove its mettle. "Simply put, it was time," said Eiji Toyoda.[90]

The LS 400 stunned the auto world, beating the Benz 420 SEL on aerodynamics, cabin noise, comfort, fuel efficiency and maximum speed. And to cap it all, it was also nearly US$30,000 cheaper. Fifty years after its establishment, Toyota Motor had its first truly "world class" car.

SEARCHING FOR BOBOS

More than a year before Eiji Toyoda gave approval for the *maru-efu* project to go ahead, Toyota Motor engineers were already chomping at the bit. In the early 1980s, Japanese auto-makers were considered a threat globally only at the low end of the market. Those involved in developing a successor to the Cressida wanted dearly to create their first "world-class car", luxury or otherwise. By "world-class" they meant a car that would set an industry benchmark against which all similar rival models would be compared. So once Toyota Motor formally approved the proposal to deliver a full-scale luxury car, the company turned to one of its legendary engineers to lead that effort.

In February 1984, the car-maker's Management Directors Committee appointed as head of the program Shoji Jimbo, who had developed the fourth- and fifth-generation Mark II. [1] That mid-size sedan became so successful in Japan that the media dubbed car-buyers' reactions the "Mark II Phenomenon". Jimbo also worked extensively on the Celica hatchback and the Cressida, two key export models which bolstered his status with the company's American employees. Among his colleagues in Japan, he was known for being academic and meditative. His fondness for 18th-century Baroque and Rococo art was said by some to have been reflected in the structural rigidity and sophisticated looks of the Mark II and Cressida models.[2] Drawing from Toyota Motor's elite Product Development Planning Department, Product Management Planning Department, Design Division and other bureaus, Jimbo selected proven engineers known for their leadership and cutting-edge skills. His 15-member team included engine-unit chief designer Kazuto Iwasaki, color specialist Katsuhiko Shiro, body-structure expert Ichiro Suzuki and his deputy Masakazu Seio, chief exterior designer Kunihiro Uchida, and chief interior designer Tomohide Yamada.[3] Most were of the generation that — much like their target buyers in America — had graduated college during the height of the counter-culture movement in the late 1960s and joined Toyota Motor with a more independent bent than the immediate post-World-War-II generation. By October, all members of the team had reported for duty. Anxious to get away from Toyota Motor's stuffy headquarters in Nagoya, Jimbo arranged for a brainstorming session at a hot-spring resort in Hakone, a popular mountain retreat outside Tokyo. To get there, members rented a dozen top-of-the-line European luxury cars and drove more than 150 miles (241 km) from Nagoya, along the Tomei Expressway and then onto Hakone's scenic, winding roads through thick glades of ferns and cedars. Breathing Hakone's fresh air in the foothills of Mount Fuji, the engineers discussed the finer points of each of the rented vehicles and such matters as what Toyota Motor hoped to accomplish with its flagship vehicle. What were the defining characteristics of a luxury car anyway? The general consensus was that it should be a car that looked equally at home outside a stone-built chateau, the ornate opera houses of European capitals, and the all-glass skyscrapers of modern America. While such remarks might betray a sense of superficiality, they show that the team was heading in the right direction. The cars needed to look the part for those with the "bling-bling" — an affluent lifestyle and the means to support it.

Regardless of the setting, Toyota Motor knew it needed to come up with a vehicle that would revolutionize Japanese, if not necessarily European, design trends. To that end — and after extensive and impassioned debates about the merits and flaws of each of the rental cars — they agreed to use the Mercedes S-Class and the BMW 7-Series, two icons of the luxury market, as the benchmark for the F1 car.[4] It immediately became clear that a mere successor to the Cressida would not be sufficient to compete against the German thoroughbreds.[5] After setting out these broad parameters, the team began researching their target market. Initially, this involved a one-month trip to the U.S. — the world's largest single market for cars and the land of milk and honey for luxury auto-makers — in May 1985 to find out what luxury-car buyers wanted most. In the course of this early research expedition they made stops in several major American cities, including Denver, Houston, Los Angeles, Miami, New York and San Francisco. The purpose of the intelligence-gathering exercise was kept under tight wraps to prevent the competition from getting wind of the still secret program.[6] At the outset of their whirlwind tour, the Japanese visitors were treated by their American colleagues at Toyota Motor Sales — many of whom were oblivious to the purpose of the excursion — to meals at some of the best restaurants in Los Angeles. But fine dining wasn't their primary objective: instead they spent alot of time surveying the restaurant parking lots to take note of which marques were most prominent. They also studied how valets treated their four-wheeled charges and, much to their surprise, uncovered a rigid caste system of sorts. The most exotic and expensive cars were parked closest to the entrance. Less prestigious cars were parked further afield and any jalopies were relegated to the Siberian outer reaches of the parking lot. Another unexpected discovery for Toyota's technicians was the prevalence of ostentatious trims on many of already fancy vehicles — from the occasional set of gilded hubcaps to the ubiquitous vanity plates. "Members of the F1 team who had not visited the United States before had epiphanies while standing in the parking lots of Los Angeles restaurants about exactly how alien American culture was" to them, said one official at Toyota Motor Sales U.S.A (TMS), the company's sales unit based in

Torrance, California.[7] The Japanese delegation visited a range of dealerships on each stop in their tour — both Toyota and non-Toyota — to see how they operated and to observe first hand what kind of car appealed to well-heeled Americans. Other stops on the itinerary included expensive boutiques and exclusive country clubs in Beverly Hills and Palos Verdes.[8] "You can't determine unilaterally what constitutes elegant style — you also have to learn what your customers mean when they say 'style'. To do this, we felt we had to go to America, to get to know our most important customers," said Kunihiro Uchida, the chief exterior designer for the F1. "Buildings, the width of streets, other cars on the road, even the vegetation," he continued, "...all affect how a car looks."[9] To that end, clerks and caddies in the L.A. area were queried on how they catered to the whims of their most moneyed patrons. What came across most clearly was the importance these potential customers placed on personal service at upscale shops. This was something largely absent in the auto business. And, it didn't take long for the team to recognize an opportunity to win over car-buyers. In affluent suburban housing developments, the team took detailed notes on what kinds of cars were parked outside the three-car garages of luxury condominiums and houses. They also studied the reaction of dozens of luxury-car drivers at focus group sessions in each of the cities they visited, which were organized by their minders at the Product Planning Department of TMS.[10]

THE ANTI-YUPPIE

The drivers, unaware of who had commissioned the focus groups, were prodded by a moderator to detail their automotive — and broader lifestyle — preferences. What gave a car prestige? What distinguished an expensive "mid-market" model from a cheap "luxury" car? Was comfort more important than style? What prompted their last purchase of a luxury car? And what kind of car did they plan to buy next? Attending one session in Long Island, N.Y., were six Audi 5000 owners, three BMW 528e drivers, a pair of Benz 190e owners and one Volvo 740 driver. The group's members described what they liked about European luxury cars, using such terms as "classic", "understated richness" and "clean lines with less chrome". American cars — as embodied by Cadillac — earned less complimentary descriptions, such as "gimmicky gadgets", "poor quality" and an "overstated sofa on wheels [too soft a ride]". By comparison, when asked about Japanese cars such as the Nissan Maxima, the group found them "too small and tinny", "(too) busy" and having "no image of success".[11]

Toyota Motor duly noted what was liked and disliked about its European rivals:

	Strengths	Weaknesses
Mercedes-Benz	Quality, Investment Value, Handling, Sturdiness	Too small, Weak style (vs BMW)
BMW	Style, Handling, Functionality	Too many on road
Audi	Style, Space, Affordability	Poor quality, Poor service
Volvo	Safety, Reliability, Quality, Sturdiness	Boxy styling
Jaguar	Most attractive styling	Poor quality, Small interior

Overall, Toyota Motor found that the people it surveyed tended to fall into one of three categories. The first consisted mainly of older consumers without advanced educational degrees and who had come of age during the golden years of Big Three icons such as Cadillac, Lincoln and the Chrysler New Yorker. These buyers placed importance on a comfortable ride, lots of creature comforts and, significantly, the "Made in the U.S." heritage of their cars. Needless to say, they were not the type of car-buyer Toyota Motor thought it would most easily win over. A second group, which was younger and had better academic backgrounds and faster-track careers, favored BMWs. Their definition of luxury incorporated superb engineering, and stiff — but not especially comfortable — automobiles. "They had the sense, reinforced by the advertising for these cars, that they were supposed to suffer a bit for their [cars'] hyper-engineering," said a Toyota Motor official. "And many of them wished this weren't so."[12] But, above all, this group of car-buyers wanted to make a statement to their friends and neighbors, and for that reason they were wary of buying luxury cars without a prestigious brand name. The third group, largely Mercedes owners, were the wealthiest and most established luxury-car buyers. While they too sought out a prestige marque, they were less concerned about impressing the neighbors than with issues such as reliability and maintenance. Their major problem with existing brands was one of *perceived* value — they felt that the high price of a luxury car should mean fewer repairs, less maintenance and better service than was the case for their experience with Mercedes. As a result, more of these owners indicated a willingness to switch brands for better perceived value. This "recession-proof" group was largely composed of baby boomers, but — importantly — not image-obsessed yuppies, who were more likely to go for "Beemers" like the BMW 3-Series cars. And it was this open-minded group, first and foremost, at whom Toyota Motor would later aim its advertising for its own luxury brand. "When we brought our information back to Japan, [executive vice-president Shiro] Sasaki told me not to be too much influenced by the opinion of the yuppies in the baby boomers group," said Uchida. "I'm very thankful for his words."[13] The consumers Toyota Motor targeted are what *New York Times* columnist and author David Brooks would later define as "bourgeois bohemians", or Bobos: "These are the highly educated folks who have one foot in the bohemian world of creativity and another foot in the bourgeois realm of ambition and worldly success."[14] Toyota Motor has another name for them: Lexus buyers. "We saw an opening with the nouveau riche, or the people who are now called Bobos, who live a comfortable life but are less driven by whatever everybody else thinks than [by] what works best for their own lifestyle," said Lexus Planning Division general manager Shinzo Kobuki in Toyota City.[16]

Important though this anecdotal evidence from the focus groups was, Toyota Motor wanted more than its own amateur guesswork on which to base its decision on the type of car it should build. It therefore backed this up with analysis from professional anthropologists and psychologists whom it contracted to study the basis on which most Americans make their car-buying decisions. The experts concluded that luxury-car buyers desired exotic cars and had a highly developed sense of pride in their purchases. But they also tended to view car dealerships with the same displeasure that they did dental offices — and hated having to bring their vehicles in for painfully expensive tune-ups or repairs. These car-buyers were diagnosed as suffering from what social scientists call "narcissistic injury". In other words, the luxury-car owners in this group felt a sense of wounded pride.[16] The results of all this research pointed to five core areas of concern, which Toyota Motor duly took into account when designing its luxury car. These were:
• Status/Prestige/Image
• High quality (or, more important, the perception of high quality)
• High resale/Trade-in value
• High performance (excellent high-speed comfort, handling and stability)
• Safety
The ranking showed Toyota Motor all too clearly that most luxury-car owners tended to place the most importance on "how others perceive him/her. It was not too much to conclude that he/she purchased a luxury car as 'proof of their success'" in life.[17] There was no question that Toyota Motor would have to compensate for its lack of heritage with an irresistible hook such as lower price for the same quality. Key variables such as engine size, dealer's facilities and, notably, sales service were also found to influence the decision to buy one luxury brand rather than another. This class of car-buyer wanted velvet-glove treatment and a sense of privilege. But they felt were not getting it from the marketplace. If Toyota Motor was to succeed in the crowded luxury market, it would need to impress customers with something more than a firm handshake and a decent

car: cappuccinos and black leather armchairs in the showroom would also become a prerequisite for success.

The lessons learned from all of this homework laid the foundation for the Lexus brand's later success. The results demonstrated all too clearly that Toyota Motor needed both a decent product at a competitive price and a first-class network of dealers capable of catering to the rich. Based on these conclusions Toyota Motor realized that "Lexus was not a car to sell in the same showroom [as] — and next to — a pick-up truck".[18] Information from the focus groups also revealed that Toyota Motor would have to overcome the Third World image attached to Japanese cars in the minds of most Americans. "When asked if they would buy a Japanese luxury car, many consumers said they couldn't even *understand* the concept of a Japanese luxury car," recounted one Toyota Motor executive. "They thought the term was an oxymoron."[19] This was especially true with American women, who viewed Japanese cars as being cheap and flimsy. Undoubtedly, the poor image stemmed from the fact that Japan's car-makers had entered the U.S. market from the low end. Underlying this unfavorable impression was a "vague notion that somehow the steel in Japanese cars wasn't quite as thick as the metal in those big German cars".[20] It was clear that Toyota Motor would have an uphill battle convincing luxury car-buyers of its capabilities at the high end of the market. While that wouldn't be easy, the company took heart from the fact that other brands without long track records in the U.S. had managed to capture car-buyers' imaginations. Audi, for example, wasn't very well known among Americans before 1983, when it introduced a luxury sedan called the Audi 5000-S. But despite its lack of track record, it managed to double the brand's sales in one year. Motoring magazines gave the car glowing reviews and, at US$20,000, it was deemed a bargain for a car with all the trappings of luxury but none of the extra cost. Though Audi undoubtedly benefited from having Germanic roots, its U.S. success made it a key case study for Toyota Motor.

LIVING LARGE IN LAGUNA

Once the F1 team had completed its initial fact-finding sweep through the U.S., most returned to Japan in July 1985 to begin rudimentary planning for the car. But five members stayed behind in Southern California, renting a luxurious beachfront home in Laguna Beach, a bedroom community about 50 miles (80 km) south of Los Angeles known for its art galleries, spas and surf haunts with a Bohemian edge. The *New York Times* described the area as Orange County's "crown jewel...set on striking verdant slopes that plunge to the Pacific"[21] — just the kind of privileged perch from which they could best view their research specimens. The team spent the summer driving around in rented European luxury cars to get the feel of the road. That's when they weren't interviewing luxury-car buyers or working with their counterparts at CALTY Design Research Inc., Toyota Motor's West Coast design studio in Newport Beach, which employed about three dozen designers and modelers.[22]

CALTY had begun its operations in 1973 and led Toyota's Celica and small-truck program. Notwithstanding the technical expertise of the staff at CALTY, the F1 team was chiefly interested in absorbing the rarified atmosphere of this part of Southern California. Uchida believed that "because of its scenic beauty, fashions and especially its interesting people," Laguna Beach was "a very good environment for creating this car". He was very familiar with the good life in sunny Southern California, having spent two years at the Art Center College of Design in the mountains near Pasadena in the early 1970s.[23] It was that experience of being immersed in the culture that prompted him to request permission to stay behind with the key operational members of his team.[24] He and his colleagues Shigetoshi Odawara, Tadao Ohtsuki, Masahiko Kawazu and Hisashi Seto, worked closely with Michikazu Masu, a Toyota Motor designer already stationed at CALTY, along with CALTY chief designers Dennis Campbell and David Hackett. The extended visit paid off: Uchida and his associates returned to Japan with a completed design concept, including detailed sketches and one-fifth scale models molded from clay.[25]

What kind of car would turn the head of a 43-year-old American male Mercedes-owner earning over US$100,000 a year? That was the riddle Jimbo's team had to solve in order to develop a car for Toyota Motor's target customer. He had assigned six dozen designers and stylists to the task. As the designers sketched out ideas and the stylists carved clay models, technicians began calibrating their lathes and levels. Some 24 engineering teams were eventually appointed to the project, a total of 1,400 engineers, 2,300 technicians and 220 support workers — more than half the numbers assigned by Boeing to work on the 777 jumbo jet program in the early 1990s.[26]

Back in Japan, the first job was to take apart top-of-the-line models from BMW, Mercedes and others to find out just what they were made of — and how they were assembled. Just as Kiichiro had done 50 years earlier, they dissected everything from the dashboard wiring to the leather seats. The best made parts of the lot were then adopted as the basis for Toyota Motor's own minimum quality standards. To win supply orders, component-makers would have to beat these items in both durability and cost. Because of this exhaustive cataloging, it was easier in some ways to determine what parts were needed on the inside than it would be to make a final decision on what the car would look like on the outside. While focus group research in the U.S. told Toyota Motor the kind of car Americans didn't want — by identifying the chinks in the armor of Mercedes and BMW— the company had only the vaguest notion what the car *should* look like. As early as July 1985, a prototype was built, based largely on the design of the Cressida.[27] But the design would change significantly over the coming months and years. In total, some 450 prototypes would be built at a cost of many hundreds of millions of dollars.[28]

In fact, the exterior design of the F1, which would become the LS model, was one of the few enduring areas of dispute between the U.S. and Japanese sides of the company. In the fall of 1985, Uchida brought three study models to Japan for a preliminary viewing session. These prototypes exhibited a strong, sporty feel, with long, tapered noses and ground-hugging silhouettes. But the Japanese executives in Toyota City weren't impressed. They found them "too American", overly aggressive, devoid of warmth and lacking stature. Instead, they wanted a boxier, taller profile with the distinctive grille of a "classic" luxury car.[29] The Laguna Beach team was stunned by the criticism. But what it boiled down to was the hard truth that much as American and Japanese consumers bought the same Sony VCRs and Nintendo video-game consoles, they had come to expect quite different things from their cars. Even though the F1 had been earmarked for the U.S. market from the outset, Toyota Motor's influential domestic sales operations grew increasingly envious of the time and money being poured into this all too American car. They began to take an interest in selling a version of the flagship model at home and started to weigh in on the design process. As a result of their considerable influence, later versions of the design became progressively more sedate. One early sketch showed a sporty car, "with a long, low grille stretched thin across the front (and covering the headlamps) and a narrow T-shaped badge dead center. It had a low-slung sloping hood, wide body stance, thick tires and uncovered wheel wells."[30] But this was not destined to be. In January 1986, the company's managing director's committee spelt out criteria for the much blander car that it wanted: "A luxury sedan with a sense of intelligence, which excludes gimmick and pursues the essentials."[31] Later clay models looked much more akin to Mercedes-Benz models, sedate right down to the square front end, color tones distinguishing the upper and lower parts of the body and superfluously large rectangular grille. Other proposals incorporated a split grille design framed by wraparound rectangular headlamps, something like those of the Acura. Yet another rendered the grille with a "Volvoesque" T-shaped badge, which protruded above squared headlamps.[32] Such moves angered some American employees at TMS in Torrance, who tried to convince the powers in Toyota City that the conservative tastes of the Japanese market would have no appeal for American buyers. While ordinary compact cars sold well in the U.S., they argued, they sold because they were cheap and not because of their styling. "The first car proposed was a gussied up Crown," said Jim

Perkins, the Lexus division head at TMS. He and others felt strongly that, to compete effectively in the luxury market, Toyota Motor would need a car with a good deal more panache. "[Originally] the front end was youthful and energetic, but [Toyota Motor's] domestic engineers wanted an old man's car. We were much happier with the first designs than the way it turned out," said J. Davis "Dave" Illingworth, a former Chrysler general manager who served as an early head of the Lexus division. "It was very frustrating." His comments are revealing. To this day, the single biggest fault of the Lexus line has been its relentlessly conservative styling, along with a glaring lack of a true sports performance model to help enliven the brand. It would be 15 years after the debut of the first LS model before those complaints would be addressed by Toyota Motor.

Uchida went back to the drawing board with orders to produce revised sketches by the end of the year. Undaunted, his team came up with eight more proposals, which were narrowed down to a pair of finalists — one with an unapologetically boxy shape and the other slightly more aerodynamic. They built full-size clay models of these to take back to Toyota City. But that presentation also failed to lead to any resolution of the matter.[33] In the end, it took eight formal presentations to the board — each requiring a different full-scale clay model — over a 16-month period to settle on a design. The board didn't actually sign off on a final set of blueprints until June 1987, fully three years and four months after the process got under way.[34] In the end, the resulting car was far more conservative than some insiders felt comfortable with. Its harshest critics called it a thinly disguised Benz clone. Indeed, from either side it was the spitting image of a Mercedes 300E and the rear end mirrored that of the BMW 735i.[35] But such imitation was far more than mere flattery; it was a time-honored Toyota Motor tactic used in its home market of Japan where the modus operandi was: better safe than sorry. While Toyota Motor may be a particularly egregious offender when it comes to what's politely referred to as derivative styling, it's hardly alone. The huge investments required made the risk of designing a car too far ahead of its time too high to countenance.

"RETURNING TO THE ESSENCES"

As competing design sketches were traded back and forth 1986, Jimbo made his most critical — and last — decision on the fate of the luxury-car program: appointing a successor. Jimbo was to become managing director and a member of the board, from which he would oversee the F1 program from a distance. Fortunately for Toyota Motor, he chose his successor well.

Ichiro Suzuki, then a 49-year-old engineer, was asked formally in February 1987 by former executive vice-president Shiro Sasaki to: "Make us a car that's a perfect fit for America...[and] don't even look at another Japanese car." "Allow me this honor," Suzuki replied.[36] Suzuki had joined Toyota Motor straight from Nagoya University in 1959 and then worked his way up in the body-engineering section of the R&D shop. He went on to become general manager and was responsible for such landmark vehicles as the 1976 Crown, the 1980 Cressida and the 1982 Soarer (a distant predecessor of the Lexus SC coupe). As chief engineer, he acquainted himself with every facet of his new project, from the engine specifications to the texture of the seat fabric. It was he who came up with the codename "F1" (which replaced *maru-efu*). This he explained, was derived not from any Formula One racing ambitions, but rather from his mandate to create a flagship second to none.[37] To guide and motivate the thousands of engineers under his command, he came up with a set of unprecedented criteria that the car would have to meet. In doing so, Suzuki challenged his team to push the frontiers of automotive engineering. To do so, new technology and equipment would have to be invented. More than once his subordinates objected to these unyielding demands for unprecedented performance. Some carped that the standards he set were too high for anything but a limited production vehicle. But the chief engineer brooked no dissent. His motto was *naokatsu*, a term meaning "never, ever, compromise".[38] The goal was not just to match but to exceed the lofty standards set by Benz and BMW in five key areas: maximum speed, fuel efficiency, quietness, aerodynamics and weight.[39] That meant producing a car which ran faster than 138 miles per hour (222 km/h), went farther than 19 miles per gallon (8 km/liter), weighed less than 3,880 pounds (1.76 metric tons), muted interior cabin sound to below 61 decibels at 62 mph (100 km/h) and boasted a coefficient of aerodynamic drag ratio of less than 0.32 — a number befitting a sports car. Toyota Motor engineers immediately pointed out the contradictory nature of some of these goals. For example, an engine powerful enough to outrun a Benz or BMW would almost certainly have to be heavier, which would add weight and lower fuel efficiency. But Suzuki's stubborn refusal to settle for nothing less than 100% would lead to endless frustration and lost tempers. He was a tough boss. Much like the disciplinarian teacher all high school students love to hate, the engineers realized only later that Suzuki's uncompromising standards would pay off many times over. Despite occasional grousing, he commanded enormous respect. "All he had to do was snap his fingers and his men would come running," recalled Jim Perkins, TMS's first general manager at Lexus. Today, he is one of the few Toyota Motor employees ever to be named *gikan*, an honorary post given to career engineers who perform above and beyond the call of duty. In Suzuki's case, this involved producing a top-ranking luxury car from scratch. "Looking at my targets for vehicle performance, everybody said it would be impossible to meet them," Suzuki reflected shortly before his retirement in 2003, "But I figured that to stand out from the crowd we had to beat the competition by a wide margin."[40]

During the F1 project team's first tour of the U.S. in 1985, Suzuki had taken copious notes, especially about the idiosyncrasies of upper-income car-buyers on the West Coast. Even after taking control of the program, Suzuki personally made several return visits to study his target audience. During one visit in late September of 1987, six months after being appointed to head the program, he led a small team to a mission-style house in an expensive suburb of Los Angeles.[41] The Japanese visitors had never seen such opulence in a private home except, perhaps, on the silver screen. Because of the extreme scarcity of land in Japan's urban centers and the high cost of housing, many Japanese spend most of their lives in cramped one- or two-bedroom apartments. Even the homes owned by top executives in Japan paled by comparison with the tidy estates of upper-middle-class Americans, to say nothing of the palatial spreads of the very rich. Members of Suzuki's reconnaissance team secured access to the living rooms of these conspicuous consumers and took snapshots of everything from the stucco exteriors to the interior décor. They wanted to get a feel for the aesthetic values that resonated with the wealthiest Americans. Nothing escaped notice: varnished wood mantles and exposed brick fireplaces; richly upholstered sofas; glass-topped coffee tables and plush carpeting; eggshell-white walls; the grand piano in the corner and the silver tea set in the dining room; the chandelier in the entrance foyer, and the arched doorway leading off to a bathroom. All exemplified a highly refined taste and understated sophistication. It was a lifestyle utterly foreign to the visiting Japanese and underscored the feeling that they had their work cut out to produce a car that could appeal to such people. Yet these visits also reinforced their commitment to the task.

There was obviously a lucrative market ripe for the taking. But in Toyota City, engineers were scratching their heads to find a way to meet Suzuki's exacting standards. To stir their creative juices, Suzuki had formulated two zen-like precepts which were to guide and inform the whole process. The first was something he called *genryu taisaku*, or what Toyota Motor defines internally as "returning to the essences".[42] In plain English, this meant focusing first and foremost on the core structural issues involved in putting together a large car without thinking about the luxurious frills. That would come later. Only by doing so, Suzuki thought, could Toyota Motor hope to eliminate major engineering glitches which might crop up at a later stage and cripple the program. The other guiding principle was something he obliquely termed the "Yet Ideal", which was similar to his *naokatsu* principle. The concept came to Suzuki when he overheard early F1 progress reports from TMS being translated into Japanese and could only pick up the term "not yet" from the original English. Anticipating the difficulty the team would have meeting his uncompromising standards, he wanted them to get used to hearing him say, over and over again, that their efforts were "not yet" up to the required standard. The yet ideal meant never compromising on one's objectives.[43]

To ensure that these mantras were adhered to, Toyota Motor instituted quality-control teams called "FQ Committees". These brought together a variety of experienced representatives from the company's R&D departments, production engineering staff and factory-floor workers to evaluate each proposed new part and the manufacturing process used to install it. This way, Suzuki reasoned, potential problems could be resolved immediately, rather than waiting for them to occur on the assembly line. Section leaders met quarterly and in person on what later became known as the *obeya*, or "big room", principle which favors face-to-face meetings to foster discussions. Toyota Motor has found that such forums help prevent miscommunication and *obeya* are now common, even for models developed almost entirely in the U.S. Initially, F1 members resisted the forced integration with other departments, but they quickly appreciated the benefits of using collective wisdom and experience in this way. Suzuki had realized that the only way to attain his goal was to break down the walls separating Toyota Motor's warring fiefdoms. He needed to get experts with complementary skills working towards a common goal. So, he created working groups that cut across divisions and appointed team leaders who were directly accountable for the work of their respective groups. He also encouraged staff to contact their superiors immediately to overcome bureaucratic impasses. Working on the project became such a badge of honor that some Toyota Motor employees who were not involved felt they were being snubbed by their preoccupied F1 colleagues.[44]

THE SHAPE OF THINGS TO COME

One of the biggest problems was figuring out how to achieve the elegant, yet aerodynamic, profile that Suzuki wanted. They knew that a car with perfect aerodynamics would look like a metallic wedge of cheese on wheels. Low front-ends and high trunks reduce wind noise and increase fuel economy. But few car-buyers find vehicles with rear ends appreciably higher than the nose aesthetically pleasing. In fact, most consumers tend to consider just the opposite to be ideal: a square-ish, blunt-nosed front end and gracefully declining back end — a look captured best by Jaguar models. However, since that shape has the worst aerodynamics, it inevitably affects performance and handling. Even as Toyota Motor's stylists in Laguna Beach struggled to come up with a bold, yet suitably conservative, design for the LS, Suzuki pushed his engineers in Japan to craft a car capable of cutting the coefficient of aerodynamic drag (Cd) to less than 0.30 to minimize air resistance and, in turn, reducing fuel consumption and wind noise. But such a low Cd was unheard of for a stretch saloon. The BMW 735i and Benz 420 SE at the time were rated 0.32 and 0.37, respectively. Most average sedans had Cd ratios around 0.35. Even Toyota's own Soarer and Supra sports coupes rated no lower than 0.32.[45]

F1 prototypes were subjected to countless refinements to shape their contours for testing in a specially built wind tunnel. But no matter how much they molded the exterior of the clay prototypes, the technicians seemed unable to achieve the required Cd. Various short-cuts were suggested and then rejected as being inappropriate for a luxury car. One such idea was to attach a "spoiler" fin onto the back of the trunk. This would act to force down the rear end and increase vehicle stability in high-speed conditions. But that was deemed too vulgar for a luxury sedan. Instead, Toyota Motor achieved its goal through innovative engineering. First brake and suspension components were mounted on the underside of prototypes to achieve as realistic a reading of wind resistance as possible. Then tests were carried out again and again as the body design was tweaked to improve airflow. More than 50 separate wind tunnel tests were conducted a three-year period, a testimony to the painstaking effort that went into the endeavor.[46]

There were, inevitably, tensions between stylists — who were more concerned with aesthetics — and engineers, who were obsessed with the aerodynamics.[47] But eventually they came up with a shape that succeeded in meeting Suzuki's demands by using a number of novel engineering tricks. To achieve maximum flow, for example, the window glass and door handles were mounted snugly into the surrounding metal to remove any indentations that could trap air. Similarly the rear window was sloped at a precise angle to propel air off the back end. But perhaps the most ingenious stroke was to incorporate a built-in spoiler on the trunk lid so inconspicuous that most people failed to spot the telltale rise. Other innovations included air-deflecting "spats" positioned ahead of the front wheels; a bellypan to divert wind under the nose; spring-loaded sidelights with seamless gaps; and even aerodynamic refinements to the exhaust pipe. While no one of these improvements was sufficient in itself to bring about the required Cd rating, combined they were sufficient to slip under the 0.30 barrier. The F1, or Lexus LS (for Luxury Sedan), became the first U.S.-specification sedan ever with a Cd of 0.29. Remarkably, this was lower than the Porsche 911. In the process, high-speed fuel consumption was also reduced by 17%, while the car's top speed was increased by seven mph.[48]

As the final shape of the LS, the first Lexus model, was hammered out in design studios and the wind tunnel, other Toyota Motor teams began early road testing to assess handling and performance. The first tests under high-speed conditions on public roads took place in Germany in May and June of 1986, with a rudimentary LS prototype called the 237D.[49] Another round was held in the U.S. in September to determine how American drivers would react to the car. LS testing teams traveled to Sweden to gauge the performance of a newly developed traction-control system and antilock brakes in the harsh Scandinavian winter. Meanwhile, Toyota Motor's Technical Centers in Los Angeles and Ann Arbor, Michigan, worked with another F1 team from Toyota City to work out the bugs in the LS steering and transmission mechanisms.

To keep the program secret during public road tests, Toyota Motor used "mules", prototypes camouflaged with hand-made panels welded onto the body to make them look like other Toyota models.[50] Closer to the launch of the LS these elaborate deception schemes were replaced with simpler tactics such as applying black masking tape over the nameplate and emblem. During one trip from Los Angeles to St. Louis in July 1988, Suzuki noticed that an almost-final version of the LS was attracting a lot of attention from other drivers on the road. "Occasionally, we'd be chased by curious drivers," he later recalled. "But I think we'd have been more worried if no one had noticed it!"[51] LS prototypes were put through their paces under a range of conditions to make sure the final product would stand up to the worst that American highways and byways had to offer. Suzuki himself drove one extended trip from Los Angeles to Florida via Chicago.[52] As a result of the repeated pit stops at fast-food restaurants along the way, the monk-like Suzuki — who would normally drink only weak tea or water — became addicted to McDonald's vanilla shakes. In one cross-country drive, an LS prototype carrying TMS product planning manager Chris Hostetter was driven through the crowded streets of downtown Manhattan in broad daylight. Hostetter had taken the precaution of bringing along hundreds of dollars and was fully prepared to buy the film off any camera-wielding by-passer who should happen to snap a shot en route. Luckily for Toyota Motor, the LS escaped undetected. When all else failed, F1 team members resorted to an age-old tactic to safeguard the program's secrecy and throw would-be pursuers off the trail: they lied. One motorist at a gas station in North Carolina who asked about the LS was told: "It's the new Mercedes."[53]

At the same time as these early road tests, Suzuki set up an "anti-ageing" program to test resilience against the elements and rigors of the road. Engineers wanted to make sure the car wouldn't rattle, scuff or handle any differently, even after 50,000 miles (80,000 km)[54] and specified 96 items for corrosion-resistance testing.[55] LS mules were parked in the Arizona desert and near swampland in Florida for months at a time to field-test a newly developed composite coating for stainless-steel body panels. Toyota Motor found that whereas the condition of cars with normal steel began deteriorating almost immediately and worsened rapidly after two months, the coating on the LS Prototype kept its sheen even after three months of exposure to the harshest of climates.[56] Other extreme weather testing took prototypes as far afield as Australia and Saudi Arabia.[57] This intensive testing led to the use of heat-reflection glass for the windshield, and chrome plating was increased by a factor of eight.[58]

In Toyota City laboratories, special micaceous iron-oxide paint was developed for the LS that gave off a richer luster than ordinary colors and contained crystals which made the hue appear to change in different light.[59] Toyota Motor also began field-testing new vinyls and plastics which resisted fading far better than even those advanced materials used in German luxury cars. A key decision was made early on in the procurement process to use a single supplier to manufacture the leather used for dashboards, interior door-panel units and seats. So concerned was the company with ensuring uniformity and consistency in the LS, that it was prepared to break its own longstanding rule requiring the use of multiple suppliers to ensure competitive prices.[60] While the final prototype's exterior looked vaguely Teutonic, the inside replicated American luxury-car staples, such as wood trim and creased leather seats.[61] The interior design team spent two years searching for the most supple leather and examined 24 different kinds of wood to accentuate the cabin before finally choosing California Walnut, sourced from musical-instrument maker Yamaha.[62]

In addition to indulgent interiors, incorporating the latest technology would also become a hallmark of the brand. As far back as 1985, a team of technicians from Toyota Motor and its largest parts-making affiliate, Denso, began work on an instrumentation panel to house the speedometer, odometer and other gauges. One firm objective: to make the needle more visible in the bright light of day and from any angle. They eventually came up with a novel process using a self-illuminating cold cathode tube filled with a mixture of neon gas to produce a "floating" needle visible by day or night. The LS also was to be equipped with the finest in audio technology. In mid 1987, Toyota Motor developed a "Super Live Sound System" that featured seven cabin speakers, a pair of tweeters and a super woofer for extra bass.[66] To ensure that the standard Pioneer audio package or optional custom-built Nakamichi stereo would outperform the premium sound systems offered by competitors,[67] the company fitted these in Cressida models and asked focus groups in California to evaluate them against sound systems installed in several rival vehicles: a BMW 535i with Alpine audio; a Corvette equipped with Bose; and a Lincoln Continental featuring JBL. The company went so far to enhance the listening environment inside the cabin as to install special shock absorbers and reduce the slack between meshing gears to cut "backlash" engine noise in the cabin.[68]

These technical refinements notwithstanding, as driving trials neared completion, there were still differences of opinion over fundamental handling issues. That flew in the face of Suzuki's exhortations to get the basics right before adding bells and whistles. Technicians from Toyota City were convinced that the ultimate path to success lay in mimicking the "soft" ride of American luxury cars. But Americans in charge of U.S. sales begged to differ, arguing that the way into the hearts of luxury drivers and, importantly, the finicky auto press, was to emulate the tighter suspensions of German makes, epitomized by BMW. Because the primary goal was to lure away BMW and Benz drivers who sought tighter suspensions, the case was decided in favor of a slightly stiffer ride. On a final test run, an LS prototype was driven down the East Coast from New York City to Miami, accompanied by a Benz and BMW so that the handling of these models could be compared. The F1 team stopped each night at motels situated well off the beaten path. There, away from prying eyes, they could make necessary adjustments to achieve precisely the right balance.[69] Once this had been achieved, the car was brought back to Japan where Toyota Motor's chairman and president took turns behind the wheel of the final prototype at the company's restricted-access test track.[70] After driving this LS, a Benz 420 SEL and a BMW 735i — at speeds of up to 120 mph (193 kph), the 76-year-old chairman, Eiji Toyoda, declared: "I found when comparing them that our car had a number of quite excellent merits."[71] He was too modest. In fact, Toyota Motor knew it had a winner.

CHAPTER THREE

DEUS EX MACHINA

Unlike many Japanese engineers of his generation, Ichiro Suzuki has no fond reminiscences about American G.I.- laden Jeeps — or any other vehicles for that matter — from his youth growing up in post-war Occupied Japan. He never even toyed with the idea of working for an auto-maker until he began his job hunt in earnest after college. "I wound up at Toyota Motor because the industry was booming, not because I had a thing for cars," Suzuki said. "What excited me most was the opportunity to throw myself into a job and be on the ground floor of a fast-growing industry."[1]

Although Suzuki spent most of his formative years in the countryside, he was born in Tokyo and as a toddler spied more cars and trucks than ox carts or rickshaws. Yet the vehicles rumbling through the big city streets left no lasting impression. His rendezvous with destiny in the automotive world would come years later as a young man. By then all of postwar Japan was abuzz with the clamor of a new mechanized age when skyrocketing demand for consumer durables would fuel the rebirth of an industrial empire.

THE TRUANT

While Suzuki spent his school years in rural Japan, he was born in Japan's largest city, on Valentine's Day, in 1937. That was the year Japanese troops intensified their invasion of China and started down a path that would lead to war with the U.S. As Japan prepared to attack Pearl Harbor in 1941, Suzuki's father presciently packed the family's bags and moved them out of the capital. He headed for the relative safety of his ancestral homeland before the first U.S. retaliatory bombings of Tokyo the following year. Home for the elder Suzuki was the town of Tsushima, on the outskirts of Nagoya, an industrial city which would itself come under intense bombing in the latter stages of the war. Although only 10 miles (16 km) west of Japan's third-largest city, Tsushima was a deeply conservative enclave that had served as a stronghold of the feudal shogun Nobunaga and which had developed around Tsushima Shrine. To the more cosmopolitan and urbane residents of Nagoya it had a reputation as being a backwater country "shrine town". Apart from farming, the only industry of note was its wool-textile spinning business. So when Ichiro Suzuki was growing up, owning a "Toyota" meant having the latest model from Toyoda Automatic Loom Works Ltd. in the living room or work shed. Despite their background as city slickers, young Suzuki and his family were accepted into the clan.

His father took a local job for Toyko-based Nisshin Flour Milling Co., Japan's largest flour-milling company, and Ichiro spent his days at school, doing chores or playing in the nearby creeks and fields. Life was far from idyllic. The Japanese were mobilized for "total war" and beset by shortages of such basics as food and medicine. There was little improvement after Japan's surrender in 1945, which left its industrial base leveled in smoldering ruins and its people hungry and destitute. Suzuki's family didn't face starvation. The fertile plain of the nearby Kiso River produced bounty enough to feed Tsushima's sparce population. But millions of city dwellers were forced to trek miles into the countryside to barter precious heirlooms on the black market for sacks of sweet potatoes. Those big-city denizens lived what was termed an "onion existence": they had to peel the shirt off their backs to survive.[2]

As Japan struggled to recover from the devastation of the war, young Suzuki's foremost problem seemed to be his lack of an attention span rather than any pressing material needs. Unusually gifted in the classroom, he easily mastered his school lessons, particularly mathematics. But he quickly grew bored with the slow pace of instruction and lack of advanced coursework. Even the classes taught by Nobuo Yanai, a young teacher who became a favorite mentor to him in high school, were unbearably dull. "Sure, I liked math class a lot — but go over and over number problems for 40 minutes?! I couldn't sit still for that long," Suzuki later recalled.[3] So playing hooky became something of a pastime at Tsushima High School. His truancy eventually caught up with him, however, and almost cost him his prized spot in the freshman class at Nagoya University. He was absent so much in his senior year that he lacked the requisite number of days to graduate. This could have resulted in his being held back and forced to postpone — and most likely forfeit — his higher education. Had that happened, it would most likely have derailed his ambitions to become an engineer. Unbeknownst to Suzuki, however, Yanai interceded on his behalf. After consulting with Suzuki's mother, the teacher quietly gave his star pupil a pass — and didn't tell him about it until a high school reunion nearly 50 years later. To this day, Suzuki can only marvel at the "What if?" factor. "What would have happened if I wasn't able to graduate? It's hard for me to contemplate," he said. "That's a secret which my mother took with her to the grave."[4]

With that twist of fate, Suzuki breezed through his years at university and in 1949, engineering degree in hand, he was ready for a fresh challenge. Japan Inc., having been literally leveled by the ravages of war and paralyzed by the immediate postwar purges of upper management, was slowly starting to recover. It was a good time to be an engineer. Demand for college-trained talent far outstripped the supply. Companies were gearing up to meet the Occupation government's call to rebuild the country's devastated heavy industry. When war broke out on the neighboring Korean peninsula in 1950, corporate Japan raced to fill orders for goods and war material — from G.I.s' cotton socks to heavy-duty trucks. For Suzuki, it wasn't an especially unusual move for his peer group to choose Toyota Motor, headquartered in nearby Nagoya. But he did so less for any parochial concerns than because of his conviction that the company was poised to become a major industrial powerhouse. He had made that astute calculation after looking abroad and seeing that many of the biggest companies in other, more developed, countries were car-makers. "Even though the auto industry was still in its infancy in Japan, I knew that GM was the No. 1 company in the U.S. and that Ford wasn't far behind. It was the same story in Germany, where Volkswagen was among the very top companies in terms of revenue. So it didn't take much guesswork on my part to realize that car-makers in Japan also had a lot of potential once the country got back on its feet," Suzuki explained.[5] And with postwar Japan lacking an airplane manufacturing industry, an auto-maker was the logical choice for an ambitious young engineer seeking a career at the forefront of technology. At that time, the only Japanese auto companies of any size were Isuzu Motor, Nissan Motor and Toyota Motor. Soichiro Honda, the founder of the eponymous and well-known auto-maker of today, was still selling cheap bicycles outfitted with small engines.[6]

For its part, Toyota Motor was only too happy to take in Suzuki and use his college education where it felt he could do the most good — vehicle-body assembly. Suzuki hated it. He had his heart and mind set on working on engines. It was a big letdown for him to be assigned to the body shop, where brawn seemed to matter more than brains. While other new recruits calibrated piston strokes and calculated horsepower, he was assigned the task of making sure the chassis held together. After a few weeks of skulking about the workshop floor, Suzuki was so disillusioned he decided to ask for a transfer. But he knew better than to bring it up with his immediate boss, who was a lifelong body-assembly man and wasn't likely to have much sympathy for his plight. Desperate for a way out, he made a direct appeal to a managing director, Hanji Umehara. "It wasn't exactly standard operating procedure for a new hire, but I just couldn't take it anymore," Suzuki recalled.[7] The response to his unorthodox appeal to a higher authority wasn't the summary dismissal that some of his peers thought he deserved. But the reply wasn't what Suzuki had hoped for, either. Umehara, a legendary official at Toyota Motor who later worked under Eiji Toyoda on a quality-control campaign that brought the company its first prestigious W. Edwards Deming prize in 1965, struck a deal with his young petitioner. Instead of granting a transfer and forcing the assembly crew to lose face, if Suzuki would put a year of his best efforts into his current job, the company would consider a transfer to another department. Suzuki reluctantly accepted the offer. He had no option, other than to quit; and that was unpalatable at a time when organized labor was being groomed by corporate Japan to accept the trade-offs of "lifetime employment".

Those first few months passed slowly, as he was forced to learn the ropes from the more senior staffers in the shop. These were unlikely *senpai*, or mentors, for him since few boasted university degrees. But then something quite unexpected happened. As a young company, Toyota Motor's departments were more like teams than entirely separate corporate entities. There was a fluidity about the shop such that fostered daily interaction among engineers assigned to various aspects of production. The assembly crew worked closely with the suspension team and the transmission people. They also interacted with the designers — interior and exterior — to figure out how to make the blueprints come to life in crisply welded sheet metal. And the assembly team met regularly with the managers, who set the cost and manpower limits and maintained production schedules. Thus, Suzuki was able to spend a great deal of time with the engine experts he had so hoped to join — and with just about every other department as well. In fact, they started coming to him to ask about such things as the positioning of the engine in the car and the size and weight limits they faced. He soon began to realize that *his* group was the center of attention — not the engine experts. "I found myself in a position of learning a lot from the other engineers — not just about the body panels, but the suspension and the engine and other parts of the car, too," he said years later. "That made the work much more interesting since I was learning about new parts and design aspects all the time."[8] Much as Umehara had expected, Suzuki began not just to tolerate his job, but to like it. He liked it so much, in fact, that he never brought up the transfer request again.

LESSONS OF THE COROLLA

After working his way up through the ranks of the assembly shop, he took on his first big project as a mid-level body expert. Luckily for him, he had the opportunity to serve under Tatsuo Hasegawa, a famed engine maker who had worked on aircraft engines. Hasegawa had been named chief engineer of a compact model designed to sate the growing desire in Japan for a true people's car. Toyota Motor had already begun a successful shift from producing war-duty trucks to mid-sized cars such as the Crown and the Master. But these relatively expensive models were mainly used as taxis or chauffeur-driven sedans for CEOs. In fact, sales of these models began to stagnate and fall by the mid 1960s.

Meanwhile, the market for compact and mini cars was growing apace.[9] As the economy expanded, Toyota Motor realized it needed a mass-production vehicle that was affordable to the upper echelons of a burgeoning middle class. The decision came as Japan was on track to move ahead of Germany in terms of percentage of household spending earmarked for discretionary purchases by 1961. The previous year, Prime Minister Hayato Ikeda had announced his Income Doubling Policy, which was designed to make sure more workers shared the spoils of the postwar economic "miracle". Before long, smaller cars made by competing auto-makers — Honda Motor, Mazda Motor and Mitsubishi Motors among them — were selling well. More to the point, Toyota Motor desperately needed a car capable of competing with the very successful Nissan Bluebird.

Toyota Motor's first answer was the Corona. Rushed into production in 1957, the car was underpowered, overweight and prone to breakdown. The Corona failed, and the Publica didn't fare much better.[10] Later versions of these cars were better received, but none was a huge hit. In 1959, Nissan's output had pulled ahead of Toyota

Motor for the first time in three years. It was up to Hasegawa and his team to produce a winner.

After studying comparable models in Germany and the U.S., Hasegawa went to work fashioning a completely new car for Toyota Motor — the Corolla. "It was aimed at the general user. [But] it had to be a comfortable car as well as a car that people could be proud of," he said.[11] The Corolla would be the first Toyota Motor model to incorporate a MacPherson-type front-suspension package, with shock absorbers and springs that used up less space, weighed less and cost less. But that necessitated a total reworking of the front end, which took more than a year to complete. The car also featured a sportier design, with curved-glass door windows and a four-speed transmission, instead of the more common three speeds. Moreover, on orders from then vice-president Eiji Toyoda, Hasegawa made room for options such as air conditioning and an automatic transmission. In a sign of Toyoda's growing influence, he also approved a request from Hasegawa to install a new 1.0-liter engine, overruling objections from then company president Fukio Nakagawa, who had rejected such a big engine to save on costs.[12] Around this time, it became known that Nissan Motor was developing a 1.0-liter engine for its new model, the Sunny, which prompted Toyota Motor to revisit the issue of Corolla's engine, codenamed the Type K. Despite the fact that production was only six months away, he called on a stunned Hasegawa to scrap the Type K in favor of a 1.1-liter engine. Hasegawa's protests fell on deaf ears and it was Suzuki's job to keep the new Toyota model from coming apart at the seams when placed under the substantial rigors of a newer, more powerful engine.

Despite the demanding schedule, the Corolla made its debut in 1966. Although more expensive than the Sunny — a big gamble for a company that routinely undercut rivals — the car's bigger engine and superior accoutrements made it a smash hit in Japan. The Corolla went on to become Japan's best-selling car for nearly three decades. Its success there and overseas — it was introduced to the U.S. in 1968 — established Hasegawa as a bona fide master engineer in the annals of the Japanese auto industry.

The high hurdles laid out by management for Toyota Motor's

engineers helped distinguish the company from lesser manufacturers. Time and again, that sense of total commitment to the cause — to be the best at whatever it did — would give Toyota Motor the edge over many a domestic and foreign competitor. Its motto was, the bigger the challenge, the better. "In those days, management always set the highest targets for us. But you know what? We always met them," Suzuki said. "The job was never done. But somehow we made the breakthroughs needed to achieve what once seemed impossible."[13]

That seminal experience testing the upper limits of ingenuity honed Suzuki's instincts as an engineer by teaching him to always set the bar higher for those that followed and giving him a well-rounded sense of what went into a well-made and successful car. Indeed, it wasn't *just* the Corolla's more powerful engine that consigned the Sunny to the No. 2 spot. The demands for greater horsepower and torque had to be squared with the structural limitations of the frame, the optimization of the new suspension and exterior aerodynamics. Integrating that package was Suzuki's brief. When he took the helm of the Lexus development program 25 years later, Suzuki brought all that experience with him. He also brought the knowledge that the engine shop deserved no special favors — especially when it came to meeting supposedly "impossible" performance targets.

THE GREAT ENGINE DEBATE

Indeed, from the outset Toyota Motor's ranks were split over a debate about the size of the engine for the LS. Internal records from the 1990s show clearly that this remained the most contentious issue right up to the start of production. Incredibly, engine criteria — usually set out before specifications for almost any other part of a car are determined — weren't finalized until April 1988, just a year before the car was expected to make its debut. As with the first-generation Corolla, the decision on the LS engine came just 13 months ahead of the formal "line-off" ceremony in Tahara, where all Lexus models were to be made.[14] Such a compressed timeframe was unheard of in the 1980s, especially for a luxury car. It was akin to buying a new mattress before measuring the master bedroom.

This 11th-hour decision-making can be traced back to Suzuki's unyielding performance targets for the LS. In addition to unparalleled aerodynamics for a large sedan, for example, the car was to have a top speed of 155 miles per hour (250 kmh), where rival vehicles such as the BMW 735i and Benz 420 SE had a "mere" 138 mph (222 kmh) and 137 mph (220 kmh), respectively. The speed profile alone was asking a lot of his engineers, but Suzuki also called for the LS to have better fuel economy, quieter cabins and a lower overall weight than equivalent or better-class German vehicles. And, to top it all off, the car was supposed to cost thousands of dollars less than the competition.

The key to meeting these goals was the engine, which would have to be like no other the world had seen. But simply recognizing that basic truth didn't make it any easier to accomplish. One big worry stemmed from the inescapable fact that the engine is the most expensive part of any car. While everyone involved in the project knew that a 3.0-liter motor wouldn't be sufficient for a flagship car, significantly bigger engines than that would entail much higher costs. At a minimum, it was agreed, the LS deserved 3.5-liters. But in yet another break with tradition, the F1 project's first leader, Shoji Jimbo, determined early on that the car would have to have a V8 engine. With the exception of the Century, a large, limited-production limousine sold only in Japan, all other Toyota Motor models used fine-tuned inline four- or six-cylinder engines. "Inline" refers to stacking four or six cylinders side-by-side, a method of production that Toyota Motor had refined to an art form over many years. But inline engines, while easier to assemble and less costly to mass produce, don't have the cachet of a classic V8 — an engine with cylinders artistically aligned four abreast at opposite angles. Jimbo knew that having a V8 under the hood was important since almost all sports cars and supercharged sedans are graced with "V" engines. As one Toyota Motor official wrote of Jimbo's decision: "The engine of a car is like the sauce in classic French cooking — it separates the excellent from the merely good."[15]

But also like a thick French sauce, a heavy V8 that was improperly balanced would smother the main course. Toyota Motor was determined to avoid that — hence the importance placed on the sturdiness of the smallest chassis bolt. All the same, some insiders wondered whether even a 4.0-liter V8 would be enough to set the car apart. Others urged caution, worried that too large an engine would increase costs so much that the car would price itself out of the "entry-level" market — a key constituency for developing a loyal long-term customer base. The solution to this part of the conundrum was to offer a sister model to the LS, with a 2.5-liter engine. This, much cheaper, F2 car, a thinly-veiled Camry upgrade, would allow Toyota Motor to attract aspirational buyers who couldn't afford the LS, but who wanted more than a mere Camry. Much as the LS got its name from informal shorthand inside the company for its new "Luxury Sedan," this second Lexus would be named the ES, which was short for "Executive Sedan." Having mollified the auto-maker's money-men with a cheaper Lexus, Suzuki was free to call for a bigger engine in the LS. Just how big became a flashpoint.

Everybody working on the project agreed that the LS needed an engine large enough to compete with European rivals, but the F1 project engineers' enthusiasm was tempered by weight worries: the engine is not only the most pricey part of a car, but also the heaviest. This was a problem because the technicians knew they needed to come up with an engine light enough to avoid attracting the dreaded "gas-guzzler" tax, which took effect for any car that could only muster 22.5 miles per gallon (9.6 kpl) or less. From the project's earliest days, Suzuki outlined high fuel efficiency as an absolute must, and this was to become a continuing headache for the engineers. The tax, instituted in response to the oil crises and gas shortages of the 1970s, was designed to make drivers of vehicles with higher fuel consumption pay heavily for the privilege. Toyota Motor's marketing people realized early on that if the company could manufacture a car that avoided the tax, it would provide a critical marketing edge for the LS over heavier, less fuel-efficient competitors. "While we were confident that our customers could afford the tax, we wanted to meet the engineering challenge posed by creating a car that could reach the speed of 150 mph (241 kph) and still avoid the tax," said Kazuo Okamoto, Suzuki's deputy chief engineer and right-hand man.[16] After much reasoned debate, the F1 engineers offered a working compromise between horsepower and heaviness — a 3.8-liter engine that offered acceptable acceleration and which, critically, cleared the gas-tax hurdle with ease. It was, they figured, better to achieve higher fuel efficiency than to compete directly with the American and European manufacturers on raw horsepower.

Early test drives of prototypes seemed to bear this out. In July 1985, one car fitted with a 3.5-liter V8 engine weighed in at 1,900 kg (4,188 lbs) — and even that model could only muster 20.5 mpg.[17] Reviewing these discouraging results, Suzuki wasn't emboldened to push his team any harder. Still, Yoshihiko Dohi, chief of the second engine department who had joined Toyota Motor immediately after graduating with a master's degree in mechanical engineering from Hokkaido University in 1968, argued for greater firepower on the grounds that a slightly bigger engine would both impress the chattering classes and be efficient enough to skirt the tax. Based on his experiences in the 1970s when he was in charge of developing a twin-camshaft engine that was used in the first-generation Soarer, he proposed that the answer to the LS problem was a 3.8-liter V8. In the spring of 1985, a working model was outfitted in a prototype and field tests were begun on the test track in Hokkaido. By April of the following year, the engine was fine-tuned to the point where it cleared the gas-guzzler hurdle. All was set for a final round of tests before the stamping die for production were finally cast.[18]

TEARING UP THE BLUEPRINTS

But had Toyota Motor pushed itself hard enough? What if longtime rival Nissan Motor, which had been expected to choose a 3.0-plus-liter engine in its new Infiniti luxury sedan, instead installed an engine bigger than 4.0-liters? That would put a 3.8-liter LS at a distinct disadvantage in the marketplace — and for bragging rights in the automotive press. Riddled by such last minute doubts, Suzuki tore up the blueprints and drafted plans for a 4.0-liter engine; powertrain that would have to fit in a car weighing less than 4,000 lbs (1,918 kg) so that the gas-guzzler tax could be avoided. In retrospect, it was a wise decision — for Nissan did indeed fit its Infiniti Q45 with a big engine — a 4.5-liter monster.

The immediate reaction was visceral. "It's impossible," said some engineering team members, echoing the complaints about the Corolla development project a generation earlier. But "impossible" was not a word that Suzuki liked to hear. And, despite the disbelief and voices of protest from the normally compliant team members, he was backed up at the highest levels. Yoshiro Kinbara, an executive director in charge of engine development, conveyed a message from "top management" that this grueling engineering feat was to be accomplished "so we will not regret it later".[19] Engine veterans such as Tetsuya Ito, who joined Toyota Motor straight out of vocational high school and led F1 engine development for the First Production Engineering group, went back to the drawing board. For them, it was the same type of last-minute decision that had driven engineers crazy in 1966, when they were ordered to change the specifications of the first-generation Corolla. Yet that had proved decisive in allowing the Corolla to outsell the rival Nissan Sunny, which was introduced six months before the Toyota Motor vehicle.[20] Ito and his colleagues knew deep down that their boss Suzuki had made the right call.

Moreover, there was no chance to appeal the decision to a higher authority. The back-up order conveyed by Kinbara had come straight from the president's office. Eiji Toyoda, who by 1985 had served as president for nearly 20 years, recognized that the auto world was moving once again toward more powerful engines as the shock of the oil embargoes wore off. He felt that Toyota Motor needed to be at the forefront of that movement and agreed to let Suzuki push for more power.[21] Yet the need to match greater engine displacement with less weight stumped Dohi's team. No one questioned Suzuki's commitment, but his manic perfectionism could sometimes alienate those who worked around him in his quest to make the ultimate driving machine, Toyota style. "Suzuki had a mean streak in him," said one person who worked closely with him during that period. "He's a genius but the car became an obsession."[22] What Toyota

Motor's engineers were being told to do was akin to stuffing a whale into a matchbox. Bigger engines are not only heavier but also require more space to house their girth. That works against fuel efficiency and can make it more difficult to control variables such as noise, vibration and harshness. And yet Suzuki remained unyielding in his demand that cabin noise be kept to just 60 decibels at speeds of 62 mph (100 kph).

Faced with this multi-faceted predicament, the F1 team reached back into history and Japan's success in creating compact, but powerful, airplane engines. After World War II many of the Japanese auto industry's best engineers — men like Suzuki's old *senpai* Hasegawa — had come straight out of factories that built warplanes such as the Mitsubishi-Nakajima Zero fighter plane. In its day, the maneuverability, range and speed requirements of the Zero were the most demanding in the world. Its designers were under strict government orders not to lower one performance target to achieve another. In other words, they had to achieve them all, much as Suzuki would demand of his F1 crew four decades later. On hearing of the reported performance of the Zero, U.S. engineers had argued that such a plane could not be built to such demanding specifications. When it appeared in the 1940s, its 1,000-horsepower engine was considered to be the best anywhere. "The Zero was of Japanese blood, and its design reflects our philosophy of independent thinking," Jiro Horikoshi, the aircraft's Western-trained chief engineer, once said. "We were trying to surpass the rest of the world's technology, not just catch up to it."[23] Squeezing a lot into a little package became the Japanese mantra — something which allowed it to retain its hold at the leading edge of engine design years after the war ended in ignominy. It's perhaps not too much to say, then, that the spirit of the Zero fighter lived on in the F1 project, though Suzuki never held out the warplane as a model. Beyond the incremental improvements of the *kaizen* concept, it meant finding new ways to cut costs or weight while still achieving unprecedented performance. That an example of Toyota's mantra to "squeeze water from a dry washcloth". What was needed, Suzuki realized, was a complete streamlining of the LS. The result would be an engine so lightweight yet so powerful that Toyota Motor later seriously entertained the idea of using a modified version in a small airplane. Indeed, in 1996 it won approval from U.S. aviation authorities to market a propeller-driven engine based on the same powertrain used in the LS.[24]

THE SOUND OF SILENCE

The car would thereafter be known as the LS 400 — not the LS 380 — to reflect its new 4.0-liter engine. The departments responsible for the core engine, suspension, transmission and body each sought to increase the precision and cut the weight of components to levels never before attained in Japan or anywhere else. So exacting were the specifications for totally re-engineered components such as the crankshaft, propeller shaft and vibration-proof engine-compartment panels that Toyota Motor needed to replace its existing armory of machine tools, welding machines and mold presses with custom-made equipment — an expensive proposition indeed for a car with projected monthly sales of about 3,000 units.[25] Nevertheless, the company's board approved the massive outlay needed for this undertaking. Meanwhile, to make sure the LS met its fuel-efficiency target, Suzuki's personal approval was required for anything that added more than a mere 0.35 ounces (10 grams) to the car's overall weight.[26] To reduce weight Toyota Motor decided to cast the engine block and most other key internal parts — the cam covers, cylinder heads, intake manifold, oil pan and pump, pistons, valve lifters and water pump — entirely from aluminum, which brought additional benefits in improved handling and more balanced driving performance.[27] As a request, the car's final overall weight was just 3,759 lb (1,705 kg) — well under Suzuki's 4,000 lb (1,918 kg) limit and the 4,020 lb (1,823 kg) curb weight of Nissan's new Q45 luxury car. The effect of this was to improve the average fuel economy of the LS 400 to 23.5 mpg (9.9 kpl), thus avoiding the gas-guzzler tax, which would have tacked on as much as US$3,850 to the base price.[28]

The German luxury brands simply couldn't keep up with these numbers and were subject to the tax. The BMW 735i could muster only 19 mpg (8.1 kpl), while the Mercedes Benz 420 SE trailed with 18 mpg (7.7 kpl). The Benz's solid but portly design — already nine years old by 1990 — wasn't in tune with the trend toward higher fuel efficiency or improved highway performance. "It feels ponderous, like driving a bank," griped a review of the vaunted but heavy set Mercedes-Benz in *Car & Driver*.[29]

For all of its leanness, the LS lacked nothing in output. The LS engine married double overhead camshafts and 32 valves — four per cylinder — fed by electronically controlled fuel injection with continuously variable valve timing. This gave more power without increasing fuel consumption and emissions or hurting torque. Indeed, the car's powertrain package produced a remarkable 250-horsepower rating. But the roar was kept to a pleasant murmur. One ingenious solution to muffle the engine's noise came in the form of a belt with teeth intertwined with Aramid fiber, which was used to propel the camshafts. Unlike the clanking metal chain-driven camshafts common in European luxury vehicles, the slick belt installed on the LS 400 ran quieter and weighed less. The car was also fitted with platinum-tipped spark plugs, which were designed to last twice as long as ordinary plugs.[30] What's more, F1 technicians cut by a third the amount of space between adjoining engine parts to reduce friction and noise. The starter motor, usually bolted to the outside of the engine, was instead placed inside the "V" to contain the sound produced. The most notable innovation, however, was the "straightening" of the propeller shaft, a spinning bar which transmits power generated by the engine from the transmission, or gearbox, up front to the rear differential, which connects the rear wheels. In most rear-wheel-drive luxury cars, the propeller shaft is angled — bent like an elbow where a joint called the "knuckle piece" connects the two halves of the shaft. But that kink increases friction. By perfecting a ramrod-straight propeller shaft, a painstaking task, Suzuki and his team engineered a way around a major source of noise and reduced engine efficiency. This required the type of precision that only a completely retooled factory could reproduce on a mass scale. In this, Suzuki called upon the encyclopedic knowledge gained from his years in the assembly shop of how parts best fit together. He worked endlessly with his engine team to find other novel ways to trim the "fat" in the front end. This produced a number of breakthroughs, including a lightweight cooling fan which ran off the oil pressure in order to eliminate the need for a fan battery.

At the same time, they made sure the LS didn't skimp on any luxury features. A newly developed four-speed automatic "A342E" transmission offered drivers a choice between "normal" or "sport" modes, which provided extra sprinting power by raising the engine speed before gear switches clicked in. It was integrated so well that the engine's spark plugs were programmed to stop firing for a split second during gear changes to allow smoother shifting. Providing a comfortable ride was of paramount importance. To buttress the LS 400 frame's wishbone-shaped suspension in the front and rear, Toyota Motor replaced the standard rack of steel springs with rubber bladders filled with air. The electronically controlled suspension automatically adjusted to compensate for heavier passengers (by inflating the car's bladders) or high-speed travel (deflating them for a more aerodynamic profile).[31] Altogether, one reviewer said, the LS 400's highly orchestrated mechanical innards "may be the smoothest engine ever put into a production car".[32] This was no accident. It was by dint of more than 900 engine prototypes developed over a six-year period and subject to "countless hours" of testing, by Toyota Motor's reckoning.[33] Indeed, three years after the car's debut, the engine still performed to the highest standards set out by Suzuki, even with the most demanding drivers at the wheel. "Under the skin, after 60,000 miles (96,561 km), our [LS 400] still possessed all the solidity, quietness and refinement it was endowed with when new," wrote *Car & Driver*. One of the magazine's reviewers went on to say: "This car is everything people used to think Cadillacs were. Sleek, smooth-riding, quiet, refined, fast."[34]

While some other luxury makes, including Cadillac, Lincoln and Jaguar, also managed to avoid the gas-guzzler tax, none of these could come anywhere near the 155 mph (249.4 kph) maximum speed of the LS 400. None of them reached even 130 mph (209 kph). Yet the

LS ran smoothly enough that passengers didn't need to shout to be heard above the din, thanks in part to innovations such as fluid-filled engine mounts, a knock sensor and a sheet of sound-proofing nylon resin sandwiched in between the sheet metal surrounding the cabin. At a cruising speed of 62 mph (100 kph), the LS 400 produced 58 decibels of sound and only 73 decibels at 124 mph (200 kph). The BMW 735i and 420 SE Benz, in contrast, recorded 61 and 63 decibels at the lower speed and 76 and 78 decibels at the higher velocity. The LS 400's aerodynamics and interior soundproofing materials cut down on road and wind noise inside the cabin. The shape helped boost the fuel-consumption rating of the LS 400 as well. One night while testing the final LS prototype in Torrance, Lexus division head Jim Perkins told Suzuki that he thought he could hear a slight wind noise on the driver's side of the car. Suzuki strained to hear the noise as the car was driven up and down Crenshaw Hill but to no avail. After several attempts, Suzuki turned to Perkins and joked: "Jim-san perhaps we need *more* engine noise."[35] In a testimony to that rare combination of stealthy soundproofing and raw horsepower, *Road & Track* writer Peter Egan recounted that, during one early test drive with Suzuki, he unconsciously flipped through a number of compact disc titles and selected one while cruising along a stretch of road. A very proud Suzuki, seated in the back, said through a translator: "Do you know what you have done, Mr Egan? You have just selected a disc and programmed the CD player while driving at 125 mph (201 kph)." Egan recalled: "I looked down at the speedometer, which was now crowding 130 mph (209 kph). He was right. It was a first. I had never before made a casual music selection while going more than two miles per minute. A near absence of wind noise and mechanical commotion, along with excellent directional stability made the new LS 400 the calmest, quietest car I'd driven at high speed." He continued: "The Lexus V8 and its nearly vibration-free driveline simply set a new standard for combining horsepower with civility."[36] In a similar vein, *Car & Driver* wrote in a coda two years after the LS 400's launch: "Few new cars have burst upon the world automotive stage as triumphantly — and brazenly — as did the luxury Lexus LS 400 in the midsummer of 1989."[37]

LS 400 vs Q45

As much as the F1 team deserved the warm accolades they received for their work on the LS, the Lexus 400 was denied the privilege of basking alone in the limelight. Toyota Motor was again forced to share the stage with its arch-rival, Nissan. Long known for its prowess in engine technology, the Nissan had delivered once again with the Infiniti Q45, the flagship vehicle for its new luxury line. In one apocryphal account of the 1989 Detroit auto show where both Japanese luxury cars were introduced, Suzuki was reputed to have taken a look under the hood of the Infiniti flagship and smugly declared: "At that moment, I knew I'd won."[38] But the Nissan car's all-aluminum quad-camshaft 4.5-liter V8's horsepower of 278 nosed ahead of the LS 400. More important — at least to auto enthusiasts — it produced a guttural roar when fired up and then assumed an understated soft purr like that of a high-performance racing machine. One specialist motoring magazine noted that the quiet monotony of the LS engine, by contrast, was more akin to a "sewing machine".[39] The Q45 also compared favorably in aerodynamics, with an admirably low Cd ratio of 0.30. A firmer suspension and more precise, BMW-like steering outperformed the LS 400's "magic-carpet style" ride —one so soft that some drivers felt deprived of a true feel for the road. In a pique of perfectionism, *Car & Driver* spent nearly US$3,000 to replace the LS 400's absorbent springs with replacements made by a German specialty manufacturer, and installed high-performance wheels and tires. "The modifications made the LS 400 more a BMW," it said, nonchalantly. "It's an expensive switch — US$2,739 for the works — but if you long for a sportier LS 400, this set up works."[40]

It seemed to some observers that, with the Q45, Nissan might reclaim the crown it had relinquished two decades earlier when the Corolla upstaged the Sunny. At higher speeds, the LS stole some of the Q's thunder due to its better balanced ratio of weight between the front and rear wheels. But the Infiniti zoomed from 0–60 mph (97 kph) in less than eight seconds and reached a top speed of 153 mph (246 kph), which made it the fastest luxury sedan. By many other measures, however, the two cars were neck and neck — and rearing to rock the luxury-car establishment off its foundations. "Millenniums from now, archaeologists will dig down through the layer left by the Automotive Era and when they finish their sifting and sorting they'll conclude: `Wow, 1990 was a showdown year in the car business'," said *Car & Driver*. "Model-year 1990 will be looked back on as the time when competition finally hit the high end of the market."[41]

The Q45 drew ready comparisons to the 5-series BMW, while the more understated Lexus had the feel of an E-class Benz. The exterior of both cars shamelessly mimicked European brands: for Lexus it was the Mercedes-like shape, especially around the front grille fascia. Infiniti took a slightly more Jaguar-esque route to the same destination. Inside, the Infiniti offered a driver-focused cockpit reminiscent of a BMW, while the Lexus, with its plush cabin styling, again took the Mercedes approach. The LS featured a sleek California Walnut dash and easily accessible high-tech gauges which projected warning symbols — such as the ubiquitous engine check light — onto the instrument glass. Nissan's interior designers, however, took the Q45 in an entirely different direction, with controls pointed toward the driver and a look stranded somewhere between the avant-garde and the gaudy. At the centerpiece of the console was an oversized analog clock: a wrinkle in time. These contrasting approaches were mirrored in the marketing and showcasing of the cars as well. Infiniti went for a more abstract approach. Showroom shoppers had to pass through odd, Zen-like, "contemplation areas" in the foyer and a faux-asian décor. And the Infiniti ads eschewed pictures of the cars in favor of what detractors dubbed a "rock and trees" approach depicting iconic scenes of nature. Toyota Motor, on the other hand, took a more practical approach. Lexus ads focused on specific features of the cars, such as the quiet cabins and smooth ride. And Lexus dealerships were designed to be functional yet sophisticated, with luxury appointments such as leather chairs and couches. The décor on the East coast was a chic black, while West Coast showrooms were splashed with modern warm beige. While Infiniti confused its customers with kitsch, Lexus coddled them with creature comforts.

The two cars were similar in price: the Q45 started at US$38,000, which was US$3,000 more than the base price for the LS. In another echo of the earlier Corolla-Sunny war, Toyota Motor had managed to undercut Nissan this time around. In fact, LS options such as an all-leather interior or a moon-roof to let in the light from above, often made their respective final transaction prices almost indistinguishable since many "options" came factory-installed. Either way, the cost was thousands of dollars cheaper than comparable German makes. So what made car-buyers choose one Japanese luxury car over another? First, both the LS and the Q outclassed the flagship sedan offered by Honda's upscale Acura unit, which sold a respectable 142,061 cars the year Nissan and Toyota Motor entered the luxury market. Most Infiniti buyers gave high marks to the Q45's handling and performance. Lexus fans, as a group, had somewhat more prosaic concerns, such as craftsmanship and reliability. Both easily outstripped the foreign competition — cars like the Audi V8 Quattro, Cadillac STS and Jaguar Sovereign — in customer-satisfaction terms. In a 1994 survey of 230 LS 400 owners and 182 Infiniti Q45 owners who had driven at least 10,000 miles, *Road & Track* magazine found the Infiniti and Lexus cars scored highest, reporting that "A whopping 96 % of Lexus owners and 94 % of Infiniti owners rated (service and repairs) either good or excellent. In nearly 20 years of our Owner Surveys, no other auto-maker has come close to matching these numbers…Until this survey, Mercedes-Benz dealers (in our survey of 190-class owners) had held the record with a 77 % good/excellent rating." It concluded that, however alike, "of the two cars, the LS 400 had the fewest problems, though the Q45 was much better than average".[42]

The reason for this was clear. Infiniti and Lexus rated extremely well in a number of categories, beating the competition handily. But in such things as dealer timeliness and the need for unscheduled repairs, for example, Lexus had a slight but crucial advantage over Infiniti. Overall, while the average car in the magazine's initial surveys — going as far back as 1975 — had 12 or more kinks as reported by at least 5% of owners, the Q45 had only eight. But the LS had a record low of three. What's more, while most cars on the road at that time had at least three problems that rendered them inoperable or unable to be driven safely, the Infiniti had two such glitches on average. The Lexus had none. Another — perhaps the decisive — factor separating the two was the lower resale value of the Infiniti. In *Road & Track's* estimation, the 1990 model Q45 suffered a 47% drop from its original base price four years later, whereas the LS only fell 31% over the same period. Ironically, the lower resale price and high reliability ratings made the Infiniti model a better bargain for used-car buyers. But that's not what new-car buyers wanted after paying a base price US$3,000 above the LS 400. When asked to identify the five most serious drawbacks of their vehicle, Lexus owners as a group liked their cars so much they could only come up with four of "any statistical relevance". These results were mirrored in other surveys, such as J.D. Power & Associates' influential ratings. In 1991, the market-research firm awarded Lexus top place in customer satisfaction, initial quality and sales satisfaction — the triple crown of quality.

CAR & DRIVER EDITOR'S RATINGS

	Total	Comfort	Engine	Ergonomics	Ride	Styling	Value
Audi V8 Quattro	26	24	27	20	23	23	26
BMW 735i	27	25	24	23	27	22	24
Cadillac STS	18	27	11	17	13	17	13
Infiniti Q45	30	34	30	32	27	33	28
Jaguar Sovereign	20	22	13	29	16	18	15
Lexus LS 400	34	35	33	34	28	35	32
Mercedes-Benz 420 SEL	26	21	22	24	17	14	15

Source: *Car & Driver* magazine, Vol. 35, Issue 6, December 1989, p.56.

Still, the most influential motoring magazines had some difficulty coming down in favor of one car over the other. *Road & Track* called it a draw. And, out of seven same-class luxury vehicles, *Car & Driver* ranked the Q45 second only to the LS 400. Still, the Lexus scored the highest in six key categories — comfort, engine, ergonomics, ride, styling and value — and won the overall ranking by a wide margin. While noting that its graceless grille and lack of pedigree may not be to everybody's taste, the magazine served up heady praise for the first Lexus: "When the machine comes as close as you can imagine to flawless execution, there's no holding back the satisfaction."[43] In their first full year of sales in 1990, Toyota Motor sold 63,534 LS models and Nissan sold 23,960 Q45 cars. Infiniti never caught up thereafter. Lexus routinely outsold it by more than a 2:1 margin and, by 1998, had even surpassed the annual sales of the more established Honda Acura franchise.

Suzuki, for his part, was sure he had delivered a winner. "If anything, I was guilty of going overboard on the LS 400, of doing too much," he said years later.[44] Toyota Motor was confident of his work, too. It took the unusual step of inviting the auto-trade press to Germany to test drive the LS 400 on the autobahn and compare it with the likes of BMW and Benz on their home turf. This proved to be a masterstroke. These writers — potentially the harshest critics of a Japanese luxury car — would see first-hand how well the LS 400 measured up against the competition. The uninvited German press mocked the test drive as a "Disneyland Tour". The German manufacturers, too, felt that to test drive a Japanese car on German roads was something of an insult. "They're rubbing our noses in it," said Ing Wolfgang Peter, Daimler-Benz's head of passenger car development.[45] But the American press felt otherwise, coming away impressed by the performance and comfort of the LS 400. Their reports went a long way toward allowing Lexus to claim the higher ground in the U.S. Toyota Motor was so pleased with the reaction of the specialist magazines that some of its first print advertisements simply showed the LS 400 surrounded by glowing quotes from them. Yet it's revealing that even in those early days, Lexus loyalists, despite having uniform praise for their cars, felt that their choice was a little unpatriotic. In one survey, LS 400 fans listed the fact that the car was "Made in Japan" as one of the top three negatives of ownership.[46] That heritage would haunt the car well into the decade — threatening its very survival at a critical juncture in the mid 1990s.

■ ■ ■

From Tahara to the World!

On a chilly February day in 1978, with the fierce *Ibuki-oroshi* winds blowing down from the Suzuka mountains and across the Ise and Mikawa bays, a procession of chauffeur-driven cars pulled into a desolate field midway along a slender finger of land anchored by the Aichi plains and extending outward into the Pacific Ocean. Dust devils danced wildly on the sandy swath of reclaimed silt as a delegation of 120 dignitaries solemnly took their places around a square patch of the terrain staked out with string and bamboo poles. In front of the group of onlookers, white-robed Shinto priests in black ceremonial caps bowed repeatedly before a makeshift wooden shrine stacked high with sacrificial rice cakes. The *jichinsai*, or ground-blessing ceremony, cleansed the soil of evil spirits in an age-old ritual designed to safeguard the construction workers who would soon flock to the area and the future occupants of the massive Lexus factory destined to be built there. The purification rites concluded and, after a few words from visiting dignitaries such as Eiji Toyoda and representatives from Toyota Motor's union, the group dispersed, temporarily ceding the area back to wild animals and the wind deities.[1]

Over the succeeding months, an army of workers descended on the site near the old castle town of Tahara and in the shadow of nearby Mount Zao. It was landfill which had been zoned for industry in the 1960s, but it was industrial in name only. Few companies had set up shop because of the remoteness of the area. There were no phone lines and few bridges. Toyota Motor had to hire local contractors to lay a telecommunications cable across Mikawa Bay and build up the area's basic transportation infrastructure before construction work could begin on the factory buildings. In time, the area would be transformed into a massive industrial workshop and become the crown jewel of the auto-maker's global manufacturing operations, turning out tens of thousands of Lexus automobiles each year. But in its earliest days, Tahara was a backwater with seemingly little potential. "I first laid eyes on it from a perch on Mount Zao, since it was too mucky to traverse the site even in a Land Cruiser," recalled former Toyota Motor senior advisor and managing director Kaneyoshi Kusunoki. "The land area was so vast I worried that we'd never be able to find a use for it all."[2]

Tahara would become the first new body assembly factory that Toyota Motor had built in nine years, and it was meant to be the last of its kind in Japan. For the local farming population, it would displace Tahara Castle as the chief attraction in the region. The castle was built in 1480 but has lain in ruins for centuries, the symbol of an age long departed. The keep's most famous retainer was a scholar and scion of the Tahara samurai clan in the early 19th century, Kazan Watanabe, who is best known for drafting a treatise called the *Shinkiron*, which called on Japan's shogunate to abandon its 250-year-old national policy of seclusion and embrace the Western world. Unfortunately, Watanabe, a man many years ahead of his time, was forced to commit ritual suicide at the age of 49 to atone for his treasonous musings. In his native district of Tahara, however, Wantanabe is remembered most fondly for a far humbler act. Before his untimely death, he ordered the construction of what became known as the *Houminsou* — a giant warehouse designed to feed and shelter hundreds of locals during a period of mass starvation in central Japan. While the *Houminsou* of old no longer exists, the factory Toyota Motor built is the industrial age's equivalent of that community center, employing some 8,700 workers and pumping untold millions of dollars into the local economy each year.

Tahara is Toyota Motor's biggest plant by far — producing more than 510,000 cars a year and 450,000 engines — and one of the most automated, with 1,500 robots and a 95% automation rate, centering on the press-and -weld operations. What's more, it has been named the world's most efficient factory for having the fewest defects per vehicle by J.D. Power and Associates, which has awarded it the platinum award three times, most recently in 2002 and 2003.[3] The LS 430 and GS 430 models, both made exclusively in Tahara, have just 63 defects per 100 vehicles, nearly a third less than the top models of BMW and Mercedes-Benz. The factory is so good at what it does that it has attracted admirers from some unlikely corners of the globe. *The Detroit News* lauded it as "the benchmark of benchmarks: Toyota Motor Co.'s untouchable Tahara plant".[4]

Such accolades and honors would not come until many years after the factory's foundation was laid in the late 1970s. The decision to build the mega-factory came in response to the fading memories of the first oil shock. Global automotive demand was picking up and fuel-efficient compact cars — mostly import models from Germany and Japan — once again were becoming increasingly popular in the U.S. Toyota Motor's greatest fear was being caught short of supply. The company wanted to boost annual output to three million cars, but didn't have the capacity to reach that goal. The answer was Tahara. Toyota Motor poured all of its resources into the plant. It would become the auto-maker's showcase factory.

The job of finding a site big enough to build a new factory fell to Kusunoki, the Toyota Motor director who would later head the plant and would go on to reprise his role a decade later as the first president of Toyota Motor's factory in Georgetown, Kentucky . He spent most of 1975 and 1976 scouring various sites in the Nagoya area but settled on Tahara rather than a more developed site inland and closer to headquarters in Toyota City. Tahara was selected primarily because of its ocean-side location. It was built on reclaimed land that could easily be fashioned into a wharf just a few meters (yards) from the factory. Kusunoki was very clear about the merits of a seaside location. "The vehicle models were selected knowing the plant would be built along the coast to facilitate concentration of production for export to North America."[5] But the company's official history puts the cart before the horse: as if the factory's proximity to the ocean was a mere coincidence. "Taking advantage of the coastal location of the Tahara plant, TMC [Toyota Motor Company] decided to make it an integrated plant with emphasis on products destined for export. It built a pier on the four million square-meter plant site for the exclusive use of TMS [Toyota Motor Sales] for shipping overseas."[6] Major steel-maker NKK Corp.'s decision to build an export-oriented plant on a man-made island off the coast of Kawasaki prompted Toyota Motor to follow suit. NKK showed it could be done efficiently and effectively, even without a fully developed infrastructure surrounding the factory. Kusunoki briefed Toyota Motor's then executive vice-president and *kaizen* mastermind Taiichi Ohno, of his findings during a chance meeting on a bullet train headed to Nagoya. Kusunoki noted the strategic location and Ohno quickly signed off on the proposal and laid the groundwork for formal board approval in June 1976. As an export factory, land transportation costs were nil: cars could simply be loaded up on nearby ships. But in U.S. auto circles, Tahara's special designation quickly became a codeword for the Japanese import threat, earning the ire of Detroit's Big Three, American labor and protectionist-minded politicians. Toyota Motor's mercantile ambitions also ran into trouble at home. From its inception, company officials clashed with the government over its reluctance to set up a local customs office in Tahara. The company eventually persuaded the authorities to process customs forms at the plant for the cars shipped directly overseas.[7]

To ensure a steady supply of materials for the plant, Toyota Motor invested heavily in new vinyl resin, aluminum casting and machinery facilities in the vicinity of Tahara.[8] The company also decided to set aside space in the plant for a pilot production line that was purposely shorter and slower than its main assembly line. This was used as a staging area for putting new equipment through its paces before any proposed model changes. The area was also used to test production machinery before it was shipped to factories overseas. Later still, it became the primary assembly line for the plant's first luxury models, which required greater care and handling than mainstay mass-production vehicles.[9]

Before Tahara could produce its first car, however, Toyota Motor had to contend with the quicksand on which the factory was to be built. So soft was the ground beneath the proposed factory, that there was a danger the ground would liquefy under the tremendous weight of the presses and other industrial equipment to be installed in the plant. The company needed to reinforce the land with sediment before construction of the buildings could begin in earnest. The project was also bedeviled by blinding sand and salt storms stirred up by gales that blew in suddenly and with terrifying force. This not only affected construction but forced Toyota Motor to rearrange the very layout of the plant and install special shielding to prevent corrosive damage to the exterior of cars from airborne specks of sand and salt. Nevertheless, construction was completed in just 11 months. The plant began test runs in January 1979 and started production just a few weeks later.

At this stage, the company's biggest headache came in the form of staffing difficulties rather than problems with the plant or with the newly installed equipment. Being situated beyond normal commuting distance of headquarters in Toyota City, Tahara required a mass migration of equipment and personnel. Quite apart from the obvious logistical challenges involved, there were serious morale issues to contend with, too. Many Toyota Motor workers resented having to forsake their homes and neighbors for new jobs in a barren landscape. To motivate them, company officials at first planned to adopt the somewhat defeatist slogan "Everything Seems Hard at First!", but after further reflection chose the more upbeat "Let's Uphold Tradition" and "Tahara Can Do it!"[10] Still, gulag-like living conditions were a major source of complaints. In a sign of where Toyota Motor's priorities lay, the plant began operations two months before the first permanent local housing, a 160-unit apartment building, was even completed. During those early days, workers ate their evening meals and slept at the rustic Hotel Tahara at the foot of Mount Zao.[11] Even after employees began to move into the new dormitories and apartments, their families had to put up with an existence akin to that of a life in exile. One car-body inspector recalled that he would often arrive at the plant on a Monday morning to find spent bullet shells scattered about the parking lot, the debris of hunters who roamed the area on weekends. "When I first saw those bullet casings, I thought to myself 'This is a really rough neighborhood!'" the worker later recounted.[12] Somehow, the impact on workers and their families from the absence of convenience stores, greengrocers or dry-cleaning shops didn't seem to have been factored into the company's forward planning. "There were no stores or regular mail service or even so much as a bus stop," recalled the wife of a Tahara plant official. "It was such a deserted place that you wouldn't even see anybody walking around outside."[13] Things soon came to a head at an emergency community meeting, where the harried wives of employees demanded — and got — a company-run shuttle bus that made frequent runs to shopping districts further inland. Senior management acknowledged that these shortcomings hurt morale. "We had a great deal of difficulty finding the right people because of the [disruption] on the work and home fronts," said Masuo Amano, who served as head of both the main plant at company headquarters and also as the first plant manager at Tahara. He later became a senior managing director and then president of Toyota Motor's affiliate Aichi Steel Corporation, partly in recognition of his efforts at Tahara. Despite all of the new factory's lack of amenities, Tahara did have some things going for it: the company-subsidized apartments — once completed — were spacious by Japanese standards; an oceanfront location made for great swimming and fishing; and Toyota Motor officials tried to make up for the lack of cosmopolitan diversions with a number of company-sponsored events, including a traditional Bon dancing festival every July, family field days in September, and a bowling party in December. Slowly, the community began to come together despite — or perhaps because of — the sense of hardship they shared in adjusting to their new environment. Ten years later, the mistakes and oversights at Tahara would be instrumental in teaching Toyota Motor how to — and how not to — build other "greenfield" plants, especially in the rural American heartland.

GEARING UP FOR GREATNESS

For all the trouble its workers had becoming acclimatized to their new workplace, Tahara wasn't really about them so much as it was about Toyota Motor's adventure into automation. It was to be the workplace of the future, pointing the way to a workerless factory for an age when Japan's labor shortages would render it otherwise uncompetitive in world markets. Computer-programmed welding arms and automated jigs would take the place of sweaty brows and grease-smeared forearms. The thinking behind this was that huge investments in technology up front would be justified in later years when production volumes accelerated and labor costs soared. Capitalizing on Japan's high-tech edge, the DNA of Toyota Motor's *mono-zukuri* ("making things") would be transferred from the calloused hands and mental intuition of seasoned workers into the steel clamps and semiconductors of an automated army that neither sleeps nor slips up nor demands higher wages. But that would come in later years, once the teething problems had been worked out at Tahara. Much of the equipment, in fact, would be designed to make it easier for work to be done by fewer human hands, and more comfortably for those workers than ever before. But at the outset, the company relied on its time-tested model for production using the Toyota Production System, a model in which veterans' experience counted for a lot more than new-fangled gadgetry. The first vehicle produced at Tahara — a four-wheel-drive Hilux light-duty pick-up truck — rolled off the line in January 1979. While that ceremony and early production of the Hilux went off without a hitch, dark clouds were gathering on the horizon for the global auto industry. A second major oil crisis erupted that year, after the overthrow of the pro-Western Shah of Iran and the subsequent establishment of a fundamentalist Islamic republic. At the same time, Japanese car-makers also faced renewed competitive threats in the U.S. market from General Motors' much-hyped X-Car compact and the American government's bailout of a battered Chrysler Corporation. Menacing omens aside, Toyota Motor remained committed to full-scale production at Tahara. Twelve months after the first Hilux appeared, the Corolla joined the factory's line-up — helping Toyota Motor produce its 30-millionth vehicle, one-third of which had been earmarked for export. Yet even as Nissan and Honda bowed to political realities and began construction and production at their first U.S. factories, Toyota Motor's slow-go approach left it investing solely in its domestic network. Eiji Toyoda's response to the challenge of more U.S.-built models from Japanese rivals was to boost output at Tahara. "In light of these developments, [Toyota Motor] took steps, first of all, to bolster its domestic production system," the company's official history reads. "One such step was building a second plant at the Tahara site. This new plant was also to be an integrated facility, featuring the most advanced production technology. For example, transfer presses [for stamping out steel panels] would be used widely in the stamping shop, and three different models would be produced on the same line in the body shop. Also, a total of 87 welding robots were introduced to achieve a high level of automation. In the paint shop, new systems were introduced, such as concentrating the dry ovens. Careful consideration was given in the assembly shop, moreover, to make work operations easier and to eliminate the necessity for employees to work in physically demanding postures by using slat conveyors to raise and lower the vehicle bodies and tilt hangers to incline the bodies at an angle."[14] That second assembly line came on stream in February 1980 and export volumes continued to soar. GM's much-vaunted X-Car turned out to be no match for the Corolla. But just as Toyota Motor's new export factory was gearing up for maximum production, the United Auto Workers' union in the U.S. publicly petitioned Japan's car-makers to reduce shipments from abroad. What they wanted, quite simply, was for the Japanese to open plants in America — instead of exporting from Japan — as a way of leveling the playing field. That suggestion was based on the flawed premise that Japan's ethnic homogeneity or other, supposedly unique, characteristics at home gave it an unfair advantage when it came to producing high-quality vehicles. The leaders of American organized labor assumed — wrongly — that Japanese-run plants in the U.S. would face the same endemic quality and labor-relations problems the Big Three had to contend with. The thinking was that once these Japanese "transplants" were on American soil, they'd be easy pickings for unionization. It turned out, of course, that Japanese workers were no more predisposed toward high-quality craftsmanship than workers in the U.S. were to shoddy work. The difference lay in the joint commitment of management and workers. For the Japanese, the core commitment to making high-quality automobiles was far in excess of anything that passed for dedication in Detroit, where a dispirited and lax labor force was perennially at odds with an out-of-touch and unfocused management. Of course, Toyota Motor, unlike its more progressive Japanese rivals, initially harbored some of the same concerns about American workers. Those fears proved unjustified when it opened a joint venture with General Motors in the U.S. years later. In some ways, union leaders' fears were justified: by 1981, Japan had displaced the U.S. as the world's single largest auto-producer. That was also the year that Shoichiro Toyoda, the son of company founder Kiichiro, took the reins as president of Toyota Motor from Eiji Toyoda, who assumed the title of chairman. The new post gave Shoichiro Toyoda operational control over day-to-day managerial activities. The post of chairman in a Japanese company is a largely ceremonial post, but one from which Eiji continued to exercise enormous strategic decision-making influence for the next decade. And the company needed all the managerial expertise it could muster; in 1981, Japanese auto-makers faced the first of many rounds of U.S.-imposed import restrictions. That was also the year a revitalized Chrysler had just unveiled its compact K-Car, which was designed to take on the Japanese in the American market.

Shoichiro and Eiji Toyoda were undaunted. In early 1982, Tahara added the Celica to its production line-up and the plant had made its 500,000th vehicle. But for the Japanese auto industry as a whole, things were starting to look grim. There was a severe recession in the U.S. which, by extension, affected its biggest trading partner, Japan. For the first time in eight years, overall Japanese auto production fell.

Yet Tahara continued to step up production, hitting the million-car mark by February 1984. That year the plant received high-level delegations from Mercedes-Benz and GM, who wanted to see first hand how Toyota Motor mass-manufactured such reliable cars for export. In 1985, the factory's third assembly line started up, and by July 1986 the plant had pumped out its two-millionth car. Tahara's workers were primed and ready to take on their biggest task yet. In August 1987, Toyota Motor announced plans to create a luxury-car division — one month after Nissan committed to launching its own luxury line. Tahara, which was already producing seven different models, had matured over a 10-year period to the point that Eiji Toyoda felt confident that it could take on production of a flagship luxury car. Annual output at the plant had risen from just 50,000 cars in 1980 to more than 100,000 the following year, and double that number by 1982. As output climbed, workers' wives were asked to work part time to meet production targets. Output almost doubled again in 1984 and reached 900,000 vehicles a year by 1988. That set the stage for a small team of elite workers to begin production of the LS 400 in May 1989. With state-of-the art machinery, painstakingly scientific precision and extreme attention to the tiniest details, the first Lexus was born under proud banners pronouncing: "From Tahara to the World!" But the birthing process did not go as smoothly as hoped. Production in the first month reached only 243 LS 400s, 57 fewer than planned, because of a glitch involving the curing process which resulted in paint smudges on dark-colored cars.[15]

In the run-up to full-scale production of the LS 400, no part was considered too minor to be fine-tuned. Technicians carefully studied the sound of car doors closing and then came up with an ideal sound — a solid, quiet "thunk" — which they perfected for the LS 400. Even the ashtrays and cup-holders didn't escape notice and were designed to glide out gracefully from concealed storage spaces at the touch of a fingertip. Similar effort was expended on the paintwork, with Suzuki's team producing a trio of metallic mica-pigment colors and a brand new dark-green that appeared to change hue under different light. The bumpers and lower-body trim came in seven different colors and, along with the tinted window glass, were carefully coordinated with the paint and interior color schemes.[16] Toyota Motor officials went to extraordinary lengths to ensure that the fit and finish would be acceptable to even the most demanding of car-buyers. As Lexus models rolled out of the factory, nowhere — from the exterior paint to the interior floor mats — was even a scuff, let alone a scratch, visible. While this was standard practice in Japan, even for cheap sub-compacts, it would be taken to an extreme with Lexus. Some of the tactics employed drew on native tradition — such as the custom of removing shoes before entering a home. Townsend Harris, the first U.S. consul to Japan, may have been the first — but certainly not the last — foreigner to commit the faux pas of neglecting to shed his boots before entering Japanese living quarters. He did so infamously when marching into a historic meeting with the shogun in the inner sanctum of Edo castle on December 7, 1857, giving *gaijin* a bad name among housekeepers in 19th-century Japan.[17] Beyond the obvious benefits of reducing dust and dirt carried on shoe soles, the habit also serves as a psychological demarcation line separating the sanctity of the home and from the world outside. Yet Tahara may be the first factory in the world where this tradition is practiced — on its Lexus trim-assembly line. There the *kureenu shiuzu sakusen*, or "Clean Shoes Campaign", works as an elaborate scuff-reduction scheme. Before workers approach the line, they first traverse a sheet of sticky material which, like fly-paper, grabs any particulate matter not scrubbed off by power shoe-brushers installed nearby. Once across that barrier, work boots are exchanged for special white-soled slippers. This not only keeps interiors spotless as workers crawl in and out of vehicles to install glove compartments and cup-holders, but it also reinforces the message that Lexus vehicles are special — and deserving of a "home" which needs to be just as clean as any other.

MINDING THE GAP

Months ahead of the grand "line-off" ceremony that initiated manufacturing of the LS 400 in 1989, Tahara received an infusion of cutting-edge equipment dedicated to the Lexus production lines. This ranged from computer-operated diagnostic stations to a new foundry to cast the V8 engine's blocks. Then, a few months later, a completely upgraded assembly line was installed. The plant's adjacent test track was also expanded so that all of the new LS cars could be tried out immediately prior to shipment.[18] Not all of the changes were finished in time for the first batch of vehicles, however. The No. 4 assembly shop, where all LS, GS and domestic-market Crown Majesta models were later made, didn't actually come on line until late 1991. By that time, the plant had expanded to 40 million square feet (3.7 million square meters), which was roughly equal to 800 ballparks the size of Tokyo Dome.[19]

The piece de resistance of all of this work was an army of advanced robotic welders, which executed tasks with unprecedented precision. And the strength of these welds was 1.5 times greater than on other Toyota models.[20] Robotic arms inserted stamped sheet metal into the jigs, or braces, which were then welded into body panels on a completely automated line. Further down, these sub-assemblies were fused together to form the outer shell of a vehicle by the world's first laser-welders for an extra-smooth fit.[21] These machines, standing some 10 feet (three meters) tall, could weld together up to five sheets of steel of different grades, a process that helps deter rust. Even more impressive: the laser-welded spots were so small as to be invisible to the human eye.[22] A separate process took this one step further by sandwiching sheets of a nylon-resin compound coated with metallic powder between two layers of steel, which cut down on vibration and noise inside the cabin. The Japanese have long excelled at fit and finish — the intangible element that gives their cars an aesthetically appealing and well-integrated look, inside and out. Toyota Motor wanted to enhance that reputation even more with its Lexus line by narrowing and streamlining the often unsightly and uneven spaces between exterior body panels to give them a smoother look. It succeeded in this by reducing the number of panels and increasing the precision with which they were installed onto the car frame. The "zero-gap design" criteria used by the F1 project designers ensured that all glass, door handles and headlights were flush with the surrounding sheet metal. Side-lights were spring-loaded for a tighter fit. And where gaps were unavoidable — for example, around the front hood — they were intentionally tapered near the front and rear to make them look more uniform.[23] But it was one thing for designers and engineers to come up with blueprints — or even limited-production prototypes — that achieved "zero-gap design" and quite another to do that for a commercialized vehicle. Yet the image Toyota Motor wanted Lexus to project most was of uniform excellence on a mass scale. Every car should be as well made as the next. For Lexus, management would have little tolerance for shifting specifications where the space between panels was concerned. Every gap had to be the same size — and as small as possible. These demands were the stuff of Kousuke Shiramizu's nightmares.

Shiramizu, who would later become a managing director, was in charge of the Tahara plant when the LS 400 made its debut in 1989. It was his responsibility to make Suzuki's painstakenly-crafted prototype come to life on a mass scale. Shiramizu, a native of Japan's southernmost main island of Kyushu, joined Toyota Motor in 1963 and, like Suzuki, worked his way up through the auto-body shop as a production engineering hand. He had been involved in the whole gamut of factory work during the early years of his career, from stamping to body assembly to the paint shop. By the time he was appointed general manager of manufacturing at Tahara, he could practically work the assembly lines blindfold. Suzuki described him as "a master of sheet metal...[and] a helpful go-to guy."[24] Shiramizu was named head of Toyota Motor's body-engineering division in 1990, overseeing plants worldwide, and he became a board member in 1992. What he had done to merit those promotions was to succeed at his task of cloning the world's finest automobile.

Shiramizu realized early on that systematizing everything to meet the hand-built specifications of the final LS 400 prototypes was the answer to his problem of finding a way to mass-produce perfection. But this entailed a lot of trial and error. "When we started, it was hard to systemize the way we put parts together. But we developed processes for everything, right down to the way seat leather is cut," he recalled later.[25] The hard work paid off. After developing new techniques — and, where necessary, completely retooling equipment to do it — Shiramizu's team was able to ensure that the LS 400 and its successor models came off the line with startlingly few defects. The key to that success was developing new dies, or molds, to stamp the sheet steel, and advanced jigs, or braces, to hold them together while being welded. Prior to this, Toyota Motor, like other car-makers, stamped out four main components for each side panel. But fitting these together tightly enough to shrink the unsightly gap between panels proved a challenge that no one had accomplished on a large scale production vehicle. Shiramizu and his team developed a die press that stamped out all four components into a single panel and which could be affixed to a car's frame with minimal fuss and frustration. This eliminated gaps altogether in some places. In others, for example, where the side doors fit into the surrounding sheet metal, Tahara's technicians were able to halve the size of the average gap between the body panels. They did this by creating extremely precise casting die, so that when panels came together they fitted almost seamlessly — like giant metal pieces of a jigsaw puzzle. According to Shiramizu, Toyota Motor "went to extremes to rethink the way we made cars — everything from the casting of the stamping dies used to form the car's metal parts to the exterior finish. Previously, our mainstay cars had gaps [between the front and rear doors] of about seven millimeters (0.3 inches). Our goal for the LS 400 was to cut that average in half, to four millimeters (0.2 inches)."[26] And with each new Lexus model, innovation has flowed through to make the production process ever smoother and quicker. Whereas it once took seven months to make the stamping dies for a new Lexus, Toyota Motor slashed this to just two months by 2001. In addition, much of this innovative technology has been spun off to non-luxury models, which has helped to advance the whole development curve. That's thanks to improvements in computer-assisted design (CAD), which makes it easier to transfer innovations from one model to another. As a result, at a time when other auto-makers are struggling to bring their product-development cycle below 20 months, it takes Toyota Motor less than 12 months to take a Corolla-class car from the design table to the factory floor. This gives it a huge strategic advantage over rivals, especially when it comes to reacting to new market trends such as the recent crossover boom.[27]

Each and every day, about 360 Lexus LS 430 and GS 430 vehicles are built by an elite corps of about 400 workers, who spend an average of 2.66 minutes of "tact time" (the time it takes to complete a stage of the assembly process; that is, to install a part or set of parts) on every car at each stage in production as it moves down the line.[28] That compares with tact times of about four minutes in one Benz plant and 3.7 in a BMW factory.[29] But Tahara's workers aren't in any particular hurry; they just do their jobs well. It takes fully nine hours to assemble a Lexus properly. One technical marvel employed to that end is the "transverse conveyor line" which pivots cars up to 180 degrees for easier installation of air-conditioning condensers and headlights. It may be the world's only assembly line where cars move around the workers — and not vice versa. Both U.S. and Japan market luxury models, which carry different badges but are otherwise nearly identical, move down the same conveyor belt in a seemingly random — but actually highly synchronized — fashion determined by real-time reports on market demand. In Japan, where the Lexus brand was not scheduled to be introduced until 2005, the LS was introduced as the "Celsior" in 1989. But all that outwardly distinguishes the Lexus LS series from the Toyota Celsior, or the Lexus GS from its Japanese cousin, the Toyota Aristo, is the side on which the steering wheel is installed and the badge. Plastic I.D. tags attached to the back of roofs and computerized printouts taped on windshields allow workers to distinguish the domestic Toyota Celsior and export Lexus LS versions as they move down the trim line. These indicator bills, or *shiji biru*, avoid mix-ups by clearly spelling out which part goes where. "The indicator bills help prevent any confusion about which parts go on what model," said Yuji Horii, manager of the vehicle-inspection division at Tahara. The *shiji biru* is checked one last time before either a Lexus "L" chrome ellipse or a stylized oval Toyota "T" mark is riveted onto the rear of the car. At the very end of the assembly line is an oscillating machine which looks like a giant treadmill. This test the cars by shaking them violently, as computer diagnostics check for any untoward rattles and squeaks that might signal a loose part or substandard installation. After that, each vehicle moves into a noise-testing chamber where it is driven onto yet another treadmill, this time to make sure the interior soundproofing is up to standard.[30]

Much of the manual labor is concentrated on inspecting the fit and finish. In the Visual Inspection Area, a tunnel of blindingly brilliant fluorescent lights, 11 "checkers" and four "tuners" in white gloves swarm over the cars as they roll off the production line. They poke, prod and polish in search of the slightest discoloration, uneven surface or misaligned knob. Toyota Motor calls this process a "tactile going-over by inspectors with gimlet eyes and trained fingertips". About 3% of cars on any given day fail the inspection and are steered into a separate staging area for remedial work. One pin-sized paint bubble or a single scratch on the underside of the leather seats is all it takes to raise a red flag. The rate of full-blown defects is much lower — just 0.5% of the cars produced. Yet even these problems can usually be fixed with a couple turns of a screwdriver or the expert application of some touch-up paint. Still, Toyota Motor vehicle inspectors note that room for improvement remains since the defect rate for the company's venerable Land Cruiser (also know as the LX470) is only 0.3%.[31] Following the inspections, each vehicle is taken on a 10-mile (16 km) "final exam" on a test track to break it in.[32] From there, the cars are loaded onto specially out fitted ships operated by Toyo Fuji Kaiun Co., a Toyota Motor affiliate, for their journey to other Asian nations, to the Middle East, and to Long Beach, California — gateway to the all-important U.S. market.

RISE OF THE MACHINES

Important though the role of the inspectors is, the real talent at Tahara are the plant's machines, which play their part in the earliest stages of production. For the first LS, Toyota Motor laid plans for an entirely new assembly line at Tahara — No. 4: the Mother of All Production Lines. From the outset, the goal was to greatly reduce the number of workers required through an "exploration of technological frontiers in assembly automation".[33] It would be the sum of all the company's pilot research into the worker-less factory. The new line was meant to push the limits of automation, and to give Toyota Motor just claim to having built the world's most advanced high-tech factory. As it was with the development with the F1 prototypes, so it was for the first Lexus factory: money was no object. One scholarly analysis of the plant concluded in an understated fashion: "Some production engineers admit there was a desire to show off the capabilities of Toyota's production engineering by building a showcase factory; budget constraints were not emphasized. Considering the timing, it is also likely that its plant design was influenced, at least partially, by the assembly automation experiments Toyota conducted between 1988 and 1991."[34]

To witness the manifestation of that goal was to be transported into a futuristic orgy of machinery. Deep in the heart of Tahara, two-storey, 5,200-ton industrial presses stamp out batches of hundreds of identical panels, chassis parts or engine components with uncanny precision. The action then moves to a thicket of machinery visible only from overhead catwalks — there's no need for human pathways below. There, a legion of robots, the bulk of the 400 in assembly shop No.4, fuse together the freshly-stamped panels, the first of 5,647 weld points, aided by electronic cameras and computer-assisted blow torches.[35] Further on, robots wrap around car frames like giant metallic preying mantises and unleash a frenzy of welds as they marry steel plates and add-on components. The machines move quickly in an intricately orchestrated robotic ballet. Skeletal body frames enter the iron gauntlet at one end and emerge as nearly-complete cars on the other side. It's a high-tech wonderland; something more befitting of a semiconductor plant than a car factory. Next up, an automated conveyor belt immerses the cars into a bath of rust-resistance chemicals, after which they receive four coats of robot-applied paint. Further along, metallic arms rivet on the wheels and reach in to install seats.[36] Meanwhile, unmanned parts delivery carts dart about the shop floor like the mindless Death Star droids from *Star Wars*. Their job is to replenish bins with refills from just-in-time delivery bays. Each cart is programmed to "hum" a different piece of classical music as a safety mechanism to alert the occasional worker who happens to walk by of their approach.

The factory was built as a laboratory experiment — albeit one on a grand scale. It sought out — and found — the very limits of automated manufacturing. "Besides introducing a high degree of automation in the new plant, which was difficult to implement in plants already in operation, it also tested many new ideas, including, for example, features to improve the working environment, such as better air conditioning and natural lighting," the company's official history recounts.[37] In some ways, Tahara's automation is the very epitome of a modern factory. "It's one of the most beautiful plants [in the world], and very neat and tidy," said Tokyo-based Credit Suisse First Boston analyst Koji Endo.[38] The air-conditioned factory is light years from the hot, gritty plants of yesteryear. The impression Tahara leaves is akin to a visit to Fantasyland in Disneyland — an air-conditioned Disneyland.

All of this raises the question of whether, with all these robots at Tahara, a totally automated factory devoid of humans will soon follow. This is a question that Toyota Motor has answered, quietly, in the construction of still newer plants built since Tahara was built and augmented. Surprisingly, perhaps, the answer is "No". For all of the "world's firsts" and "world's mosts" and platinum awards it has garnered, the plant has a reputation inside the company as a billion-dollar boondoggle.

The experiment determined that machines cannot replace men entirely. *Mono-zukuri* can't be summed up in a mathematical equation, one involving so many tons of rolled steel and optimum laser welds per minute. These were the important lessons Toyota Motor took away from the hyper-automated plant. "Tahara was actually considered a mistake because it was much too automated," said auto analyst Maryann Keller. "It was not a competitive factory when they built it."[39] The chief problem: Tahara was conceived of in anticipation of a severe shortage of workers brought about by a demographic shift in Japan. With one of the lowest birth rates in the world, the government had forecast that the population would peak in 2006 and decline thereafter. While that's still expected to come to pass, many Japanese — euphoric with the excesses of the "bubble" economy of the 1980s — never envisioned the decade-long slump, rampant deflation and high unemployment that would ensue in the 1990s. Nor did they anticipate the rapid rise of China as an economic power and as a "Workshop of the World" fueled by cheap labor. Odd as it seems now, the conventional wisdom 20 years ago was that the most serious problem facing Japan's economy was that it would overheat from too much demand and not enough manpower.

To meet demand for cars both at home and abroad — and to keep Japan's industrial base intact — automation was considered to be the way of the future. Toyota Motor wasn't alone. Other auto-makers followed suit, though not on the scale of Tahara. From 1990 through 1992, Honda's Suzuka plant No. 3 assembly line, Mazda's Hofu plant No. 2 line and Nissan's Kyushu plant line No. 2 all sought to optimize automation. But all were unable to capitalize on their supposed strengths. Needless to say, not only did that prediction of a labor shortage fail to hold up as the Japanese economy slumped and China emerged as a viable offshore-production alternative, but domestic demand for cars had peaked by 1990. The Japanese auto market would actually stagnate — or shrink — over the next decade. After production was increased to a high of 7.5 million cars a year in the early 1990s, output at Japanese plants fell to 5.79 million in 2002, the lowest since 1986.[40] So it was that the heavy, front-loaded costs for the robots and other cutting-edge equipment came to haunt Toyota Motor and other Japanese auto-makers. "These assembly plants," according to Tokyo University professor Takahiro Fujimoto, a Toyota Production System expert, "suffered from high fixed cost owing in part to assembly automation when Japanese domestic production started to decline because of [the] post-bubble recession and further appreciation of the yen in the early 1990s. It became clear that the Japanese auto companies had to readjust their basic designs of assembly factories, automation and work organizations."[41] The surge in the value of the yen after the so-called Plaza Accord in 1985 made it much more difficult to export cars since it made them more expensive overseas and eroded the value of repatriated profits. Worse, unlike labor costs, which can be controlled through austerity measures such as bonus cuts or even forced retirements, a robotic workforce offers no flexibility. Once installed, their depreciation is the same whether they run 24 hours a day or just 15 minutes. "The Tahara No. 4 [assembly line] became a symbol of Toyota's new-generation factories," Fujimoto added. "After the bubble era ended, however, the plant was criticized for its high capital-investment cost, which was a high fixed-cost burden for Toyota."[42]

Toyota Motor's blind faith in technology failed it in another way, too. To make Tahara work, especially for its luxury cars, machines were needed to cut the metal and affix the laser-welds. But to meet the threshold for true luxury, especially in the fit and finish, Toyota Motor found that it required a worker's hands and cumulative experience. These are things that can't be programmed into any machine. The company realized it had lost something at Tahara. It needed to get back to the essence of what had made Toyota Motor successful to begin with — its workers' total dedication to product. It needed to reclaim its soul. It needed to go back to the handcraft-oriented basics of *mono-zukuri*. "Some argue that the plant was a symbol of Toyota's mismanagement in production engineering," Fujimoto wrote. "For them, Tahara No. 4 is a temporary, but significant, deviation from Toyota's manufacturing tradition."[43] By the time this dawned on the management in Toyota City, it was too late to do anything about Tahara, except to make minor modifications and scrap plans for yet more robots. Workers in Tahara would take a more prominent role where possible.

In light of the Tahara experience, Toyota Motor made a conscious decision not to overemphasize automation. Plants built since then — from the Kyushu factory in Japan to the first American transplant in Georgetown, Kentucky, to the factory in Valenciennes, France — are notable for their minimal use of automation. This hybrid model of "modified automation", however, has proved to be a big success — and one that distinguishes Toyota Motor from its rivals. "Toyota appears to be the only Japanese company that could articulate and implement a new concept of final assembly that explicitly aimed at improving not only customer satisfaction but also employee satisfaction by the mid 1990s," wrote Fujimoto. The newest challenge for Toyota's production model — and luxury-car business ambitions

— is in China, where the company has taken the concept of automation-less production to an extreme.

The company's first mainland plant, at Tianjin on the outskirts of Beijing, started making Vios sub-compacts in October 2002 and produced 49,000 of the cars for the Chinese market in 2003. Although it is Toyota Motor's newest plant, it is one of the least automated, relying heavily on old-fashioned manual assembly, not only because local labor is so much cheaper than imported equipment, but also because workers are encouraged to master their jobs by learning to do them largely by hand or with semi-automated equipment.

As part of their training, Chinese workers were required to put together their own component bins, trolleys and workbenches from kits shipped from Japan. Instead of automated buggies, workers push hand carts and move engines around manually on dollies. Tianjin represents just a foretaste of what's to come. "The Vios factory is just laying the groundwork for us in China," said Yuji Umehara, president of Tianjin Toyota Motor Co. and a former factory head at Tahara in the 1990s. "This is the start of something big. In some countries, we've never been able to reach the quality levels of Japan. Our goal here is nothing less than matching the quality of Japanese factories — or exceeding it."[45]

In August 2003, Toyota Motor reached an agreement with its local partner, the state-run FAW Group, to manufacture 400,000 vehicles a year in China by 2010. Construction is already well under way on a much larger plant in Tianjin, which will make luxury models such as the Crown (now sold only in Japan and currently being made in Tahara's assembly shop No. 4). And like export-oriented Tahara, that newer Chinese factory, with an initial capacity to produce 50,000 cars a year, is built on the Bohai Sea coast alongside a port opening out to the Pacific.

CHAPTER FIVE

THE LEXUS COVENANT

J Davis "Dave" Illingworth, the man who perhaps did more than any other to put Lexus on the map in the U.S., can't ever remember not being fascinated by cars. Daydreaming about them kept him going through four years of high school at a military academy in the Appalachian foothills near Wheeling, West Virginia. The son of a Presbyterian minister, Illingworth was born on the outskirts of Youngstown, Ohio, on September 1, 1943, but spent his formative years across the Ohio River in West Virginia. He was an indifferent student. As a young man, what captured his interest more than academics or field sports was sportscar racing. Illingworth's passion for motor sports was stoked by a trip to the Indianapolis 500 as a high school sophomore to see America's fastest vehicles push the limits of engineering. "My father took me to the '58 Indy 500' and I was hooked," said Illingworth. "I've been back to see it 25 times since then." After an undistinguished academic career at Ohio University, where he majored in sociology, he completed his B.A. in 1966 and enrolled in the army. But unlike many of his peers who were shipped off to active duty in Vietnam after brief stints at officers training school, Illingworth was sent to South Korea, where he spent 18 months stationed along the demilitarized zone (DMZ) near the tense border with communist North Korea. As a fresh 2nd Lieutenant, he was in charge of a maintenance squad for the upkeep of the tanks, trucks and other military vehicles. On completing his tour of duty he returned to the U.S., bought his first car — a slightly used '66 Ford Mustang' — and cast about for something to do. It was his grandmother, finally, who suggested he call a relative who worked in Detroit. "She said: 'You like cars, so why don't you go into the car business?'" Illingworth recalled. So it was that he turned to his uncle, Robert "Buck" McCurry, a sales executive at Chrysler. McCurry provided the key introductions and soon enough Illingworth was on his way to Portland, Oregon for an entry-level position at a dealership. From there, he went on to prove himself as a talented field office representative in Montana, where he married the daughter of a local Chrysler dealer in 1972. Soon after, he was transferred back to the Northwest for a job overseeing regional dealerships in Seattle, Washington.

In those early years in the auto business, Illingworth quickly made a name for himself coordinating marketing efforts and became a trusted liaison between the local dealers and the often-hated headquarters in Detroit. His skill as a problem-solver for Chrysler won him early recognition and paved the way for rapid promotion to assistant regional manager at the San Francisco office. In 1979, at age 36, Illingworth was appointed general sales manager for the Northeast Ohio region, a key post in an important market. He was the youngest person ever to hold the job. As a rising star in Chrysler, he could look forward to a bright future at one of America's biggest companies. But after years of mismanagement at the very top, Chrysler was teetering on the edge of bankruptcy. Poor quality vehicles, terrible labor relations, deteriorating factories and chronic inefficiency were finally catching up with the weakest of the Big Three. The second oil crisis which erupted that year would be the tipping point that pushed the company over the edge. Just two weeks after Illingworth accepted his promotion, Chrysler decided to close his Cleveland office in a last-ditch restructuring effort. The brash new president of the company, former Ford Motor chief executive Lee Iacocca, made the announcement after summoning all regional managers to an emergency meeting. At 7:30 a.m., Illingworth and dozens of other managers from across the U.S. filed into the Green Room at the K.T. Keller building at Chrysler headquarters in Highland Park, Michigan. But this was to be no pep rally from the new leader. Iacocca was upset Chrysler dealers weren't offloading more cars from a ballooning inventory onto a rapidly shrinking customer base. And he let them know it. "He spent half an hour chewing us out and using every swear word in the book. He told us that if we couldn't do our jobs the right way that he knew of plenty of people at Ford that could," said Illingworth. After this tongue-lashing, Illingworth knew the time had come to part ways with Detroit once and for all.[1]

He headed to Los Angeles and, for a second time, called upon Buck McCurry, who had quit Chrysler the previous year and taken up with a distributor selling Toyotas. McCurry, 20 years Illingworth's senior, had been a top sales executive at Chrysler, but, upset over the direction in which the company was headed, had quit months before Iacocca arrived.[2] McCurry then moved to Baltimore to become general manager of a private distributor of Toyota models in six Mid-Atlantic States. By 1982, he had been tapped to head Toyota regional sales operations in Los Angeles. Before long, he was asked to run the show from Toyota Motor's American unit, TMS, as executive vice-president under Yukiyasu Togo. Illingworth, encouraged by what he heard from his uncle about working for the Japanese, decided Toyota might be the right place for him, too. He followed up on contacts provided by McCurry and landed a position in sales at TMS. On his first day, at a meeting of general managers, he was surprised to see Japanese executives listening patiently as sales chiefs from field offices around the country identified problems in marketing and distribution and offered suggestions. Impressed by the very un-Detroit style of give-and-take between the sales force reps and top executives, Illingworth threw himself at his new job with a renewed confidence in his choice of profession. In time, this mediocre co-ed in his college years would become a visionary for the company.

A New Franchise

Like McCurry, Illingworth eventually became a trusted member of Toyota Motor's inner circle in the U.S. This brain trust was composed mostly of former auto industry officials who had opted out of the navel-gazing culture that prevailed at the Big Three. Other key members of the group of disillusioned Detroit veterans included Jim Perkins and George Borst of General Motors and Jim Press of Ford Motor, all of whom would one day head Lexus sales operations in the U.S. Each of these men believed that Toyota Motor had more to offer than the insular and bureaucratic companies they left behind in Detroit. The fast-growing Japanese presence in the U.S. gave them a veritable *tabula rasa* upon which to rewrite their careers. For its part, Toyota welcomed the institutional wisdom about the U.S. market that these men brought with them. Input was not a dirty word. McCurry and Yale Gieszl — a former Pricewaterhouse accountant who joined Toyota in 1970 as corporate controller and served as TMS executive vice president when Lexus was launched in 1989 — were instrumental in putting the company on a solid footing in the early 1980s. They helped come up with "Toyotathon" sales events and memorable taglines like "I love what you do for me". That allowed Toyota to pull ahead of Nissan and Honda in the U.S. market. Once Toyota Motor had firmly established itself in the heart of the American market with cars such as the Camry and the Cressida, these American executives pushed tirelessly for bigger, more powerful car which could compete with Ford's Lincolns and GM's Cadillacs. Even though Toyota Motor had decided to enter the global luxury-sedan market in 1983, the F1 project proceeded quietly in Japan and unbeknownst to most of the company's American officials. It wasn't until December 1986 that half a dozen TMS officials, including Illingworth, who was named to help orchestrate Lexus operations in the U.S., were briefed on the program. "All I was told was that it was going to be a separate division [from Toyota dealerships] and that my job was to make it work," said Illingworth.[3] But, in fact, these weren't the first Americans to be briefed on the F1 program. McCurry had been told of the "flagship" project two years earlier in meetings in Japan, just a few months after being hired by Togo, who had been appointed president of TMS in October 1983. "When Togo and I went to Japan, Eiji Toyoda told us they wanted to build the best car that was ever made. That was in early 1984," said McCurry. "(Shoji)Jimbo and his group never made mistakes. We knew all we had to do was set up a marketing program and leave the product to them."[4]

It was at this time that Toyota Motor's F1 team members were making their first round of surreptitious visits to the U.S. to research the luxury-car market. McCurry and Togo, a former car racer who learned English working as an orderly for a U.S. Army Lieutenant after World War II, were excited by what they heard in Toyota City. But each soon came to the conclusion that the existing sales network wasn't up to the required standard. Something was needed to distinguish the proposed new cars from Toyota's run-of-the-mill models. The two men worked hard to promote the establishment of a sales channel independent of the existing network of Toyota showrooms. TMS felt that a completely new franchise was needed to sell the world's first luxury Toyota. But the leadership at Toyota Motor wasn't convinced of the need for this. The board was split down the middle. Overseas-product planning chief Hiroshi Okuda, later to become president and then chairman of TMC, and Iwao Okijima, the board member in charge of North American operations, convened 10 separate board meetings to try to forge a consensus on the matter.[5] Dissenters argued that as the car had been created on the basis that it would be the whole company's flagship vehicle. Not selling it at existing Toyota brand dealerships might send the wrong message — both to car-buyers and the company's loyal U.S. dealers. Moreover, a new channel would complicate contracts with the existing dealers, who had contractual rights to sell any Toyota model. Togo and McCurry, however, insisted that a separate dealership chain was needed to do the car justice. "We knew that wasn't the way they'd do it in Japan, but we wanted a [separate] single line to give a select group of dealers control over the facilities and product," said McCurry. TMS insisted that it was imperative for the brand to overcome the prestige barrier a Japanese luxury car was sure to face. Eventually, though, it got its way. "Originally, it was to be sold under the Toyota name," said Junzo Shimizu, a Toyota Motor board member who oversaw the F1 project at its inception. "Then we learned that if we wanted a prestige product, we needed a separate dealer channel." "In the end," added Okijima," we realized that you can't sell a boutique product in a supermarket."[6]

To win the argument, Togo and McCurry had cashed in on some of the chips they'd earned with Toyota City for turning around U.S. operations. In the early 1980s, due to the combination of a rising yen — which had forced up prices in U.S. dollars — and the onset of import restrictions, sales sputtered. But the two men succeeded in quickly reversing that slide by creating a customer relations department, overseeing the successful U.S. market launch of the first front-wheel-drive Camry in March 1983 and improving feedback from an expanded dealer network. By 1986, TMS was back on track, having become the first import brand to sell one million cars and trucks in a single year.[7] It was against this background that TMS Chairman Eiji Toyoda and President Shoichiro Toyoda deferred to TMS on setting up a new franchise. As McCurry remembers it: "At the last meeting we had on this in Japan with Dr [Shoichiro] Toyoda, Togo said that if the luxury dealerships didn't work out as advertised, he would resign."[8] That final session settled the matter in late 1985. Thus, the LS 400 wouldn't be sold next to the lowly Tercel. Illingworth said that this "was the single most contentious issue outside of the decision to make the car itself".[9] But there was one proviso: the American sales unit would have to set up the new network of dealerships using proceeds from local sales and by persuading new dealers to provide most of the necessary funds. No special subsidies would be forthcoming from Japan. "We had to fund out of our own profit the money for research and establishing the brand in the U.S.," said Yale Gieszl.[10]

THE LEXUS COVENANT
The task of actually building this new franchise would fall to Chevrolet veteran Jim Perkins, the first head of the Lexus division, and his right-hand man, Dave Illingworth. "The car had to be more competitive than anything we'd ever done," said Perkins. "The main thing for us at first was maintaining the security. Very few people were informed

about it." They were excited by the peeks they got of the F1 in regular visits to Suzuki's workshop in Japan to comment on the development of prototypes. "We liked what we saw," Illingworth recalled, "but had some suggestions on things such as how the front end should look."[11] They also suggested an upgrading of the wheel design, which Illingworth and other American executives thought did not look sophisticated enough for the car.[12] Despite these quibbles, TMS officials knew that they were being handed an incredible product on whose development no expense had been spared. It was their job to make sure it sold. Because Toyota City had decided to start small — with only 100 new dealerships — TMS could afford to be choosy in awarding them. Most of the those selected boasted the largest showrooms in their respective areas, ranked high in customer service and already had experience with one other import-brand franchise, such as BMW or Benz. Lexus dealers were to be the cream of the crop. TMS wanted to make sure its customers felt they were dealing with seasoned professionals, not pushy novices. At the same time, the dealers knew that if a car with as much going for it as the LS 400 failed to sell, they'd have only themselves to blame. "The only ones that could [possibly] screw up are the damn dealers," said Danny Davidson, general manager and owner of a Lexus dealership in Riverside, California. "We have the best product and the best people to work with, so there's no reason we shouldn't always be No.1."[13] The customer-first philosophy that drove Lexus in the U.S. was codified by Illingworth in August 1987 in a document called The Lexus Covenant. Every dealer was required to sign this code of conduct as part of their contract with TMS. It was derived from a set of 10 principles in a "Flagship Constitution" drafted in Japanese a year earlier by Tatsuro "Ted" Toyoda, a TMS official who was the second-born son of company founder, and co-authored by TMS senior vice-president Takao Kawamura.[14] The Lexus Covenant, later carved into a 6.5-foot (2.0-meter) tall black granite block standing in the atrium of the Lexus headquarters building in Torrance, laid out the law for employees and dealers. It read:

The Lexus Covenant
Lexus will enter the most competitive,
prestigious automobile race in the world.
Over 50 years of Toyota automotive
experience has culminated in the creation
of Lexus cars. They will be the
finest cars ever built.
Lexus will win the race because:
Lexus will do it right from the start.
Lexus will have the finest dealer network
in the industry. Lexus will treat each
customer as we would a guest in our home.
If you think you can't, you won't…
If you think you can, you will!
We can, we will.

No fan of clever wordplay, Illingworth's pat mantra for the new luxury marque reflected a more simple wisdom: under-promise and over-deliver. That philosophy carried over to much of the marketing strategy at Lexus. Although the brand's sales and marketing organization considered customer satisfaction to be the top priority, Illingworth made sure that it was never mentioned explicitly in early advertisements. Instead, the brand's reputation for excellent service — before and after the sale — would rely solely on word of mouth. Illingworth felt that personal testimonials were a far more powerful way to spread the message. This conviction was confirmed by outside consultants, including top service-industry companies such as the Ritz-Carlton hotel chain. They reported to TMS that being openly boastful about a commitment to service only seemed to encourage people to doubt the claim and test it out—by complaining more. Internal research by TMS seemed to confirm that few consumers took such self-promotion at face value.[15] If a company had to make such a pledge then, chances were, the service wasn't all that good. By the same token, the thinking was that Lexus shouldn't *need* to remind people. In time, good service would become synonymous with the brand name.

But that didn't mean there wasn't a pressing need to spread the word about all the new features that the car itself had to offer. The company asked its longstanding advertising agency, New York-based Saatchi & Saatchi, to assign a creative group to a secretive new account. In order to safeguard confidentiality — and to more clearly distinguish the two brands — Saatchi & Saatchi informally set up the special unit in the spring of 1986. It wasn't officially established, though, until November 1987, at which time it took on the name Saatchi & Saatchi Group One. A similarly named (but unrelated) film production company in the area complained, however, so this was changed to Saatchi & Saatchi Team One. Later still, the prefix was dropped altogether in favor of the more succinct Team One.[16] It had one client: Toyota Motor's luxury division. Initially, the advertising group worked in a walled-off area of Saatchi & Saatchi's office in New York. But staffers not working as part of Team One account resented the locked doors and confidentiality of the new Toyota account. TMS officials in Torrance also disliked having to deal with people constantly flying back and forth to New York or, worse, confusing the two separate brand campaigns. Before long, Team One relocated to the West Coast. "I made them move to California," said McCurry. "We didn't want them to mix up what they already were doing for us with Toyota."[17] While Ted Toyoda wanted Team One to set up shop in Beverly Hills — for prestige reasons — Team One chose El Segundo, California, just a few miles from Torrance, where TMS had established its head office in 1982.

A RELENTLESS PURSUIT

The momentous decision to set up a distinct sales channel for the LS 400 and ES 250 had been made, but it still wasn't clear whether the name "Toyota" should appear at all in the marketing for the cars or at the new dealerships. Research by Team One showed that Honda Motor's efforts to introduce its luxury line-up in 1986 with the tagline "Acura, a new luxury line from the American Honda Company" had backfired. The phrasing damaged the image of non-premium Honda Motor models such as the Accord, and proved ineffective at positioning

Acura as a top-flight luxury brand. What's more, when focus groups were asked what they thought about a luxury car from Toyota, their reaction was equally negative. Oddly enough, Team One found that the name "Toyota" meant "trucks" to many Americans. The link between Toyota and trucks stemmed from a major marketing push in the 1980s to expand the company's share in the U.S. light pick-up truck market. While "voluntary" export restraints limited Toyota Motor's shipments of cars to the U.S., there were no such limits on the number of trucks the Japanese could sell. So, although cars represented two-thirds of the company's sales in the U.S., it was spending 60% of its advertising budget on trucks. TMS executives were even encouraged to trade in their company cars for trucks.[18] That might have been good for overall sales goals but the blue-collar appeal of pick-up trucks clashed with the more up-market image desired for a new line of luxury cars. Team One's Scott Gilbert was among those in a delegation to Toyota City which had the unenviable task of telling the septuagenarian chairman Eiji Toyoda, president Shoichiro Toyoda and other members of senior management that the company-cum-family name just wouldn't do for the new luxury line.

The seating plan for that meeting in Toyota City in June 1988 had been worked out a month in advance to prevent anyone from unwittingly breaking the unwritten rules of corporate Japanese protocol by taking the wrong chair. Gilbert, for one, wasn't keen on attending in the first place because it meant missing his first wedding anniversary to travel to Japan. "It was pretty weird to have to tell a guy who's last name is Toyoda that his family name wasn't good enough for a luxury-car line," said Gilbert, who had won the company's good graces for his earlier advertising work establishing Toyota Motor as a leader in the pick-up truck market. "The [Japanese] guy who was translating what we were saying actually broke out into a sweat."[19] Luckily, Team One was backed up by persuasive arguments from Illingworth and some pre-meeting *nemawashi*, or networking, by Ted Toyoda . In the end, Eiji Toyoda gave his blessing without so much as a peep of protest. A distinct brand name would be developed, one that was to be unique to the luxury-car line. If nothing else, a new name would clear TMS from any lawsuits filed by dealers invoking their contract rights to sell any "Toyota" branded model. But Eiji Toyoda noted the gravity of the decision and the importance being placed on the project by Toyota Motor. "Before the meeting ended, Eiji Toyoda made a point of telling us to treat the new vehicle launch like it was our first-born daughter getting married," said Gilbert. "By putting it in such incredibly human terms, it sank in that this was something special."[20]

Finding an appropriate name proved to be a difficult exercise. It had to be elegant, but not effeminate; classy, but not prissy; bold, but not brazen. And it had to be unique. The matter was addressed in a meeting of TMS, Lexus and Team One officials in October 1986. A master list of 219 potential names had been compiled by New York-based consultancy Lippincott & Margulies. From that raw data, 10 finalists were selected. Then, after further debate, it was narrowed down to five: Alexis; Calibre; Chaparel; Vectre; and Verone. The only name that everyone in the room seemed to agree on was the first, Alexis. But the chief argument against it was that it sounded like the name of a person, not a car. Worse, "Alexis" had acquired something of an infamous connotation as the name of the femme fatale in a popular television serial. "I remember sitting up and saying, 'Isn't Alexis the name of the crazy woman in [the TV show] *Dynasty*?'" said George Borst, then a manager in charge of sales and marketing at TMS. In the end, from some creative doodling by John French, a TMS project manager and chief liaison with Lippincott & Margulies, the name Lexus was born. French scratched out the "a" and, after a little discussion, the group then replaced the "i" with a "u". "When John suggested the name, we all agreed right then and there that it sounded pretty good," said Borst.[21] Next came the Lexus logo — the letter "L" enclosed in an imperfect ellipse. Official TMS lore says it was perfected according to a precise mathematical formula over a six-month period — and with the help of no fewer than three design and advertising agencies. It then won out over five other competing designs and made its public debut at the Los Angeles auto show in January 1988. In fact, Perkins contacted an old acquaintance with some experience in this area who actually came up with the winning design. Molly Sanders, owner of Molly Designs Inc., crafted the distinctive oval and "L" over a three-month period in 1997. That replaced the previous favorite, which was a stylized "L" made to look like a seagull's wings and without an enclosing circle. "That was too whimsical. I felt it needed to look like jewelry. I wanted the edges to be crisp like a Movado watch," said Sanders. He initially had the logo etched on a piece of titanium, and then cut, filed and polished it. "Everybody's eyes lit up and said: 'That's the one'" when he showed it to TMS officials, he said.[22]

Meanwhile, Gilbert and other Team One executives were in Japan being briefed on the status of the LS 400 project through many hours of meetings with two dozen different engineering groups working under Suzuki's leadership. Suzuki wanted to make sure the car's representatives in the U.S. knew it almost as well as he did and had arranged for the Japanese head of each of these teams to memorize presentations in stilted English and lecture for their distinguished guests. While fascinated, Team One officials had to struggle to absorb all of the minutiae. "They showed us not just every rivet, weld and seam," said Tom Cordner, Gilbert's colleague and chief creative consultant, "but the thought that went into every rivet, weld and seam."[23] Despite Suzuki's best efforts to turn them into crankshaft experts and piston professionals, it was all they could do to distinguish the carburetor from the clutch. Yet, as it turned out, some of what they dutifully jotted down in notebooks and journals during these study trips proved useful in subsequent advertising campaigns. For example, some Team One members took notice when Toyota Motor technicians explained that the sensors they used for the car's airbags were gold-plated to prevent corrosion. To hammer home the idea that the LS 400 was assembled from the finest materials known to man, Team One created advertisements that played up the use of this precious metal. A subsequent television commercial had a voiceover which cooed: "Every Lexus features airbag terminals plated in gold. Of course, we might have used a less expensive material. But it wasn't money we were interested in saving". An airbag deploys tellingly in the final frame. But what the ad didn't say — and what Team One members didn't know until later — was that gold-plated sensors are standard on almost every car.[24] However, few in the viewing audience seemed to notice and it served its purpose by reinforcing the notion that Lexus was synonymous with quality of the highest order.

More intriguing than the stiff lectures was what Team One staffers saw going on around them in the secretive prototype workshops at the Toyota Motor design center. "We walked past one of the rooms and saw a Mercedes-Benz in pieces on the floor," said Gilbert. "Another had an LS 400 engine which was literally glowing red to test its endurance at high RPMs." As Tom Cordner recalled, "It looked hot enough to cook meat on the manifold."[25] But what impressed them more than anything was the fanatical devotion of Suzuki and his team. While many of the technical details from the briefings washed over them, it was patently obvious that the LS 400 would be a very special vehicle indeed. They saw first-hand that Toyota Motor was building a car that would clear all current benchmarks, one that would stun car enthusiasts with its agility, grace and superior quality. "It really felt to us like those guys were not only making a car but making history," said Gilbert.[26] Cordner seconded those sentiments: "The engineers were relentless," he said. "It was made clear to us beyond any doubt that they wanted to beat Mercedes-Benz, BMW and Jaguar."[27] The two furtively dubbed Suzuki as Toyota's "Japanese leprechaun", the sobriquet a reference not only to the magic he worked on the F1, but also to the glint in his eye when he spoke of the project as if he was a proud parent.

On the trip back to the U.S. after his first encounter with Suzuki, Cordner thumbed through a dog-eared notebook with his musings from the trip and let his mind drift. Team One had yet to come up with a snappy tagline, one that would prompt car-buyers to sit up and take notice. The key, he figured, was to encapsulate the tremendous energy and devotion that went into the making of this car — in five words or less. He began jotting down random words and phrases reflecting the raw dedication that characterized Suzuki's team. They were certainly fanatics; he and Gilbert had never seen people so wild-eyed about a work project. But more than that, Toyota Motor's engineers had demonstrated an almost Zen-like zeal to achieve perfection, as defined by Suzuki. Even down to something as seemingly insignificant as a key, the team had done their homework and had come up with what they determined to be the world's best. Cordner marveled at their pursuit of...perfection. It was truly...relentless. He had a tagline. When their plane touched down in Los Angeles on a Sunday evening, Gilbert and Cordner headed straight to the office. There they worked until the early hours of the morning, having been bitten by the same bug that had gotten to Suzuki's people. Energized by what they had seen in Toyota City, Team One was determined to create a vision worthy of the LS 400. Over the course of the next few weeks, the subject of a tagline came up at internal meetings at Team One. After listening to half a dozen possibilities presented by other staff members, Cordner offered the line "The Relentless Pursuit of Perfection". Everyone in attendance knew immediately that this was the refrain they were looking for. Focus-group testing confirmed that view: people said it piqued their curiosity in a positive way. The only problem, it turned out, was selling the idea to Toyota City.

Neither for the first time nor the last, Toyota Motor let it be known to Team One that it was extremely sensitive about its public image. With emotions raw about Japanese auto-makers' inroads into the U.S. market in the late 1980s, the company felt a lot of pressure to be politically correct by biting its tongue in its advertising. TMS executives in the U.S. were even more concerned about this than their bosses in Toyota City. That meant restraining boastful talk and making any criticism of competitors so oblique as to render it meaningless, at least in the minds of many at Team One. The concept of a relentless pursuit seemed to TMS executives to be a little too aggressive. They would have preferred a tagline that spoke of a rigorous pursuit of perfection or, perhaps, a thorough quest for quality. "The word 'relentless' was the key," said Cordner. "The big rub against it was that it's a kind of chest-pounding message, not exactly an 'Oh-What-A-Feeling' tagline" — a reference to the Toyota brand's feel-good motto.[28] In the end, after much persuasion, Team One's argument for "relentless" carried the day. But the debate over the direction of the advertising campaign had only just begun.

GETTING THE WORD OUT

Well ahead of the launch, Team One had Lexus display the LS 400's all-aluminum V8 engine, accompanied by fuzzy drawings of the still secret exterior design, at the 1988 Chicago, Los Angeles and New York auto shows. The intention was to whet the appetite of the trade press and build up a buzz in automotive industry circles. Attendants at the Lexus booth handed out flyers with some of the LS 400's performance specifications in return for a survey which asked about the interested person's name, age, address, income level and current car model. The list of 15,000 names collected in this way was then combined with a larger catalogue of names, obtained from third-party vendors, of people who owned competing cars to create an 800,000-name master list for advertising. Toyota's own existing customers, including owners of the top-of-the-line Cressida model, were considered off limits for Lexus mass mailings to avoid cannibalization between the brands.[29]

A stealth-advertising campaign for Lexus began in early 1989 after the car's debut in Detroit. One teaser ad in motoring magazines showed only the underside of the LS 400, to play up the aerodynamic qualities of the car — an ad so successful that it would be remade for Lexus 15 years later. Phase one of Team One's strategy was to focus on anecdotes that highlighted specific advantages of the brand. The basic concept was to show the LS 400 where it was strongest — stellar performance, advanced technology and high quality — in a series of ads that introduced car-buyers to the brand. It was decided early on to focus tightly on the product instead of resorting to the more predictable devices such as using leggy models, macho drivers or gorgeous backdrops. The idea was to lure buyers into showrooms by breaking up the car's many performance features — such as its ultra-quiet cabin or smooth yet powerful engine — into easily digestible bites. Getting the word out about why Lexus was so special would also help buyers come up with an easy-to-grasp rationale to "defend" their purchase against any criticism from skeptical family members and friends. TMS didn't want to force buyers to rationalize their purchase on a daily basis. "We wanted a buyer's aunt who lived half-way across the country or the friend at a cocktail party to be able to understand why he just spent US$35,000 on a Japanese car," Gilbert explained.[30]

The strategy worked, as even rival auto-makers acknowledged. Richard Collins, who had been appointed to head Mazda's stillborn Amati luxury-car division, said: "If you belong to a country club and you're sitting around after a round of golf and say you've just bought a [Nissan Infiniti] Q45, you're going to have to justify that decision. Lexus buyers don't have to. It has become the cult car for the mass market."[31] Whereas Nissan's Infiniti brand took a more metaphorical approach in its advertising using abstract images, Lexus would beat potential buyers over the head with its outstanding characteristics. The goal was to steal the Mercedes-Benz tagline — "engineered like no other car in the world" — right from under its nose. Importantly, it was decided early on not to play up the car's Japanese roots. This, too, was a big difference from Nissan's Infiniti campaign, which focused on the Q45's "Japaneseness" in ads which spotlighted rock gardens, leaves in a stagnant pond, a solitary tree enveloped by mist, flocks of geese in a yellowed sky and waves washing up on a deserted beach — but no more than a glimpse of the car itself. One post-modern Infiniti print ad that did feature an actual vehicle showed a rusty-red pick-up truck. This was placed as an attention-grabber next to a short essay on how traditional Japanese lacquerware is made by tapping the *urushi* tree for its sap. These ads seemed to confuse more car buyers than they inspired.

This unorthodox campaign had all started with a question posed by Billy Heater of the Hill, Holliday, Connors, Cosmopulos Inc. advertising agency, a copywriter Nissan had contracted for the account. "Why do we need to show the car [at all]?" he asked. "It does kind of get in the way," his art director agreed.[32] Those words would haunt the Infiniti brand for many years to come. Infiniti's dealers had problems with the artsy campaign from the very start. "They're selling nature," complained one showroom owner in Northern Virginia. "You've got to show the car [to sell it.]"[33] What is now known derisively as the "rocks and trees" campaign in auto-industry circles was nothing if not memorable. Market research showed that the televised spots ranked No. 3 in the top 10 most-remembered ads aired in the fall of 1989; but that didn't translate into bringing more buyers into Infiniti showrooms. "[The Q45] is one of the best cars on the market, but people don't know that from pictures of cows scratching themselves on trees," sniped the president of an Infiniti dealership in Oklahoma City, Oklahoma.[34]

Lexus, by contrast, homed in on the nitty-gritty of the LS 400 — and skipped the Zen motifs. "We never considered the Japan angle," said Gilbert. "In the 1980s, the Japanese weren't known for style and design."[35] To add a sense of sophistication, Lexus ads used voiceovers by Jim Sloyan, whose slightly stuffy, smoky, psuedo-European timbre conveyed a vague sense of refinement to many American ears. But not all. *The Wall Street Journal* would later snicker at the "faux-lofty tone of a Lexus commercial."[36] Nevertheless, Sloyan became "Mr Lexus", the permanent spokesman for the flagship Lexus model. Team One opted against using celebrities or models to promote the brand, although the idea was entertained as late as February 1988, on the grounds that it would distract attention away from the product.[37] Many of the most interested potential Lexus customers in the focus groups were far from the cheese-eating, Bordeaux-swilling dilettantes of the popular imagination. In fact, Team One members were surprised to discover how average many of the target buyers turned out to be. "Just because they had money doesn't mean they had class. They were disheveled pigs," was how one official involved in the project indelicately put it.[38] The first big Lexus television campaign began with a "full buy" on the August 21, 1989 broadcast of Monday Night Football.[39] A wave of print, radio and television ads followed in a wide range of lifestyle magazines and television programming. The idea was to create a sensation among the chattering class, to get the neologism "Lexus" rolling off people's tongues and into the pages of Webster's dictionary. This didn't mean Lexus had limitless funds to spend. Officials in charge of the program say that, after an initial flurry of ads to coincide with the car's official launch at the Detroit auto show, they were kept on a tight leash when it came to buying air time and newsprint pages. "We had to fight for every nickel and pick up the crumbs [left over from the Toyota brand budget]," said Illingworth. "We would have liked to have had much more advertising."[40] Yet press accounts at the time estimated that Lexus and Nissan's Infiniti division each spent some US$50–$60 million on advertising in the first year of sales alone.[41]

To ensure that Team One's messages were in line with the Toyota Motor program, the wording of early advertisements had to be vetted for accuracy by engineers in Japan: whatever claims were made had to be able to be backed up with hard data. Team One also was under direct orders from Toyota City not to antagonize Detroit or the Germans. "Toyota was anxious to avoid poking the competition in the eye," said Gilbert. "They told us not to embarrass Cadillac or Lincoln and not to make the Germans look stupid."[42] One of the proposals that was rejected was dubbed "The Last Supper". The plan was to shoot a long procession of German luxury cars snaking up a winding roadway leading to a castle. An interior shot of the castle would follow, showing a *fin-de-siecle*-type party, with rich German socialites mindlessly mingling. It was to be a spectacle of over-the-top debauchery. "It was [going to be] a Fellini-esque party with ice sculptures and everything. It was to show them celebrating [oblivious to] the end of their dominance" of the luxury market, said Cordner.[43] The proposed punchline, to be read in a Mr Lexus voiceover, was: "The Europeans have dominated high-performance cars for 58 years. They now have 30 days left to enjoy it."[44] Another hard-edged pitch along the same lines that never made it off the storyboards was one intended for major newspapers. The idea was to show the logo of each of the European luxury brands —the Daimler star, the BMW crest, the Jaguar hood ornament — on successive pages followed, on the last page, by the Lexus "L" logo. Underneath that, the proposed caption would repeat the television commercial's punch line about these brands having only 30 days longer to enjoy their lock on the market for up-market sedans.

While those ads for a national audience were nixed, greater leeway was allowed in advertisements commissioned by regional dealerships. The dealers were used to playing hardball with the competition and they pressed TMS for more aggressive, comparative ads. For them, Team One produced a few brass-knuckled commercials. In one, a parody of a Mercedes-Benz ad, a Benz, BMW and LS are shown hovering side by side over a lake. Slowly, the two German models begin to sink until totally submerged, leaving only the Lexus above water.[45] TMS tacitly backed these dealer-commissioned ads. While they didn't want to stir up controversy, they were aware that Honda's troubles expanding its upscale Acura brand in the U.S. resulted in part from too docile a PR campaign.[46]

STIR THE SOUL...AND NOT MUCH ELSE

Despite the various creative and cost constraints under which Team One worked, it produced a trio of highly successful ads that launched Lexus into the consciousness of many a luxury-car buyer. The first of these, aptly named "Ball", showed a ball bearing rolling slowly and evenly along the seam in the bonnet of an ES 250 to highlight the sliver-thin narrowness and uniformity of the gap between its panels. The voiceover said: "Every sports sedan is supposed to do well in the fast lane. But what about these lanes?" — a reference to the smooth seams. Another ad, dubbed "Noise", showed an LS 400 zipping around the lake at the Vanderbilt Mansion in the Blue Ridge Mountains. In one version, as an LS 400 makes the rounds, the sound of the wind, engine and other extraneous noises gradually disappear until only the stereo can be heard in crystal clear form. Sloyan's voiceover intoned: "At Lexus, we didn't just suppress the engine noise. We suppressed the gear noise; the exhaust noise; even the wind noise. And all that was left was the perfect environment for you to create a little noise of your own." Another version of the same ad dropped the voiceover altogether in favor of just the disappearing sounds. The commercial ended in total silence with the words on screen: "Because we believe a luxury sedan should be seen...Not heard."

But the Lexus ad that really captured people's attention was dubbed "Bounce" internally. It showed a pyramid of 15 motionless champagne flutes stacked on the bonnet of a humming LS 400, which was on a treadmill going more than 140 mph (225 kph). This trick was the brainchild of TMS official Dick Chitty, Lexus vice-president for parts and service, who liked to impress visiting sales teams.

He would place a glass of water on the roof or hood of an LS 400 propped up on blocks so that its wheels couldn't touch the ground. Then the engine would be revved up to full speed — well into the tachometer's RPM "red zone". Yet not a ripple could be seen in the glass, a testimony to the smoothness of the engine. Chitty came up with the idea after recalling visits to state fairs during his childhood in Iowa. There, lubricant salesmen would rev up cars on blocs to demonstrate how throaty an engine could sound with a drop of "magic formula".[47] It wasn't long before enterprising TMS officials repeated the water glass stunt at a briefing for the auto press on the technical specifications of the car in the summer of 1989. Upon seeing it, the assembled journalists reportedly broke into spontaneous applause.[48] As a result, what could have been construed as a minus — the lack of a masculine engine roar like that of the Infiniti Q45 — became a sign of engineering refinement.

When Cordner and Gilbert heard about the trick, they immediately grasped its significance as an advertising gimmick and decided to rework it for a commercial. They overcame objections from Toyota City that it would be "too circus-like" with a touch of class — by using champagne flutes instead of water glasses. Jim Sloyan's voiceover for the ad simply said: "Even at the equivalent of 145 miles per hour, the LS 400 is designed to stir the soul…and not much else." To prove real glasses were being used — and placed in the order shown without any tape or glue — a video tape was made of the making of the commercial. This defensive move was made in the wake of criticism lodged against Volvo for a commercial that appeared to show one of its cars emerging unscathed after a monster truck climbed over it. Volvo was forced to admit the stunt was staged by reinforcing the frame of the car. When the LS 400 ad appeared in January 1990, it caused a stir among the viewing public. Critics such as populist activist David Horowitz challenged Toyota Motor to furnish hard evidence and TMS provided a copy of the tape. Still incredulous, the television personality attempted to recreate the procedure for his nationally syndicated show. "Horowitz called our bluff, but we brought him in and proved it," said Gilbert.[49] Much to

THE LUXURY DIVISION OF TOYOTA

Design sketch of LS 400 prototype used in early press materials. Notice the flowing contours and sporty look absent in the actual production version.

Photo courtesy of: Lexus, a division of Toyota Motor Sales, USA, Inc.

The LS 400 "champagne glass" advertisement, which played up the car's smooth engine and helped spread the word about Toyota Motor's new brand.

Photo courtesy of: Team One Advertising

The LS 400 engine, designed to beat
all same-class rivals.

*Photo courtesy of: Lexus, a division of
Toyota Motor Sales, USA, Inc.*

The 1990 LS 400, the original flagship
sedan of the Lexus brand.

*Photo courtesy of: Lexus, a division of
Toyota Motor Sales, USA, Inc.*

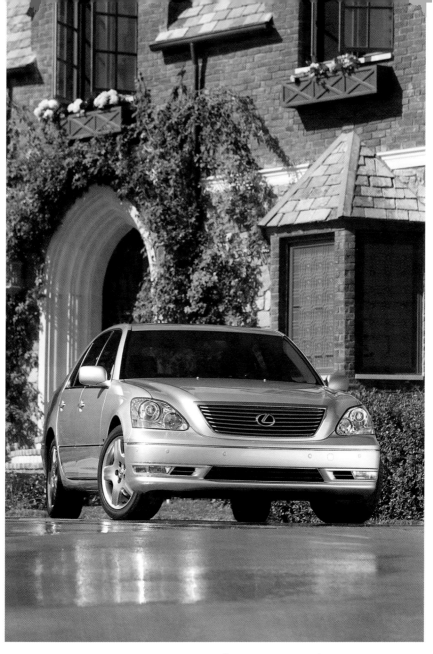

The 2004 LS 430, the latest version of
the standard-bearing Lexus model.

Photo courtesy of: David Dewhurst Photography

The 2004 RX 330, the update to the popular SUV that allowed Lexus to pass Cadillac and Mercedes-Benz as the best-selling luxury vehicle brand in the U.S.

Photo courtesy of: David Dewhurst Photography

The 2006 GS 430, the first production model to showcase an all new look for Lexus. Note the low-slung front grille and grooves on either side of the hood.

Photo courtesy of: Guy Spangenberg,
Spangenberg Photography

The 2006 GS 430 interior console.
The cockpit design accents the brand's
effort to seamlessly blend advanced
technology and luxury refinement.

Photo courtesy of: Guy Spangenberg,
Spangenberg Photography

The Lexus 2006 GS 430 will offer a keyless SmartAccess system that allows the driver to lock, unlock and start the car simply by touching the door handle (with a key fob in pocket) and then simply pressing a push-button to start.

Photo courtesy of: Guy Spangenberg, Spangenberg Photography

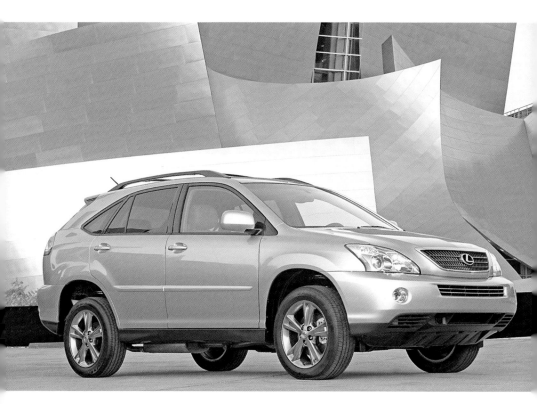

The RX 400h, the world's first luxury
hybrid SUV.

*Photo courtesy of: Guy Spangenberg,
Spangenberg Photography*

The 1992 SC 400 was designed in the
U.S. and offered the ultimate in
performance and luxury.

*Photo courtesy of: Lexus, a division of
Toyota Motor Sales, USA, Inc.*

The HPX Concept, with the front grille
showing off a bold new
styling direction for the future
of the Lexus line-up.

Photo courtesy of: Guy Spangenberg,
Spangenberg Photography

Horowitz's surprise, the stunt worked as advertised. Lexus reaped the rewards of all the publicity.

These commercials ran on top-rated U.S. network television shows, but the battle to win over public opinion was just beginning.[50] To spread the word further among wealthy car-buyers, the campaign was extended to include sponsoring events such as golf tournaments, ballet openings and orchestral performances. Notably, Lexus received top billing for underwriting a black-tie dinner for the L.A. premiere of "The Phantom of the Opera" and the 1989 U.S. Polo Association Open Championship. In an early example of guerilla marketing, theater-goers might find themselves presented with a glossy but tasteful goodie bag courtesy of Lexus with a token gift item inside. Toyota Motor officials were careful not to go overboard.[51] They wanted to provide just enough name recognition to get people talking about the brand, but not so much that they felt inundated with it. At the heart of the effort was Illingworth's dictum: under-promise and over-deliver.

POURING THE FOUNDATION

TMS had no trouble attracting dealers for the launch of Lexus. The success of Toyota brand cars led many to think that, no matter how long the odds seemed, the new luxury-car might well be successful. Having taken note of the disorganized and haphazard approach Honda Motor experienced to launch its Acura division, TMS, on orders from Toyota City, decided to limit the initial number of dealerships to just 100 (of which, only 73 were ready to open by September 1989 when sales were scheduled to commence). To attract a good mix of prospective dealers, TMS bought full-page ads in the leading trade publications — *Automotive News* and *Ward's Auto Dealer* — in the summer of 1987. The wording marked a departure from Toyota Motor's usual modest proclamations. It read succinctly: "Lexus is looking for the finest dealers to sell the world's finest motor cars."[52] More than 1,500 dealers beat on TMS's door to apply. The qualification criteria set out by Lexus required a high ranking on independent customer-service index ratings, consistently above-average sales in the region in which the dealer operated, proof of experience running a high-profit business, a successful track record in implementing personalized service, and a commitment to investment and sales-force training commensurate with a top brand.[53] TMS asked applicants to put up anywhere from US$3–$5 million for the initial investment in facilities and training. While this was fairly standard for a new dealership in the U.S., the Lexus dealers also had to agree to continue operations for three to five years — even if they were losing money.

In addition, Toyota Motor would not permit "absentee" owners who outsourced day-to-day management by requiring general managers of showrooms to have at least a 25% stake in the dealership.[54] Dealers were even required to refer to their garage mechanics as "diagnostic specialists".[55] TMS micromanaged right down to the fabric for the curtains, the thickness grade of carpets and the leather upholstery for the showroom chairs. "We dictated the styling of the showroom and even had the furniture picked out for them," recounts Illingworth.[56] The two-story model dealerships designed by CALTY and the Miller Zell architectural firm contained a dome-like ceiling, enough space to showcase four or five cars and a backlit large scale "media wall". No gaudy banners were to block the view from the windows. Desks for sales people were banned in favor of low coffee tables, which were perceived as more approachable by customers.[57] The dealers also had to install windows from which customers in the showroom could see their cars being worked on in the workshop. This came in response to focus-group research that showed that owners of European luxury vehicles didn't like the fact that they couldn't see what mechanics did to their cars. What's more, TMS officials traveled to every one of the finalists' proposed sites to make sure the designated area had appropriate traffic flow and demographics to keep the showrooms full on weekends. Toyota Motor wanted to be in each of the top 50 markets, so it placed a premium on geographic diversity. But apparently it was not interested in racial diversity. None of the 100 dealers who were appointed were African American, in a country where minorities make up a growing percentage of the population.[58] The first batch of successful applicants was announced in May 1988. One dealer that TMS was keen to sign up was former 10-time Indy 500 champion driver Roger Penske, whom McCurry had encouraged to buy a Toyota dealership in 1985. To persuade Penske to make the leap to Lexus, TMS flew him to Toyota Motor's Shibetsu test track in Hokkaido in 1988, where he became the first American to take a spin in the final LS prototype.[59] Impressed with the car, Penske became one of the first Lexus dealers.

While Lexus eschewed any overtly Japanese touches in its advertising and showrooms, Nissan's Infiniti struck out in the opposite direction. Instead of unparalleled service, these dealerships became known for faux-Oriental theme-park touches such as stone floors, waterfalls and sliding paper screens. Infiniti went so far as to commission original modern Japanese sculptures for the "contemplation areas" in the foyer of its dealerships. And the brand's mechanics sported tunics with patches meant to resemble feudal Japanese family crests usually found only on kimonos. "They want the dealership to be Japanese-looking," complained one Infiniti dealer, unhappy with the company-mandated décor of his dealership. "In all of my years [with the Nissan brand], one thing they did not want you to do was to look Japanese."[60]

Lexus dealers were different from German dealerships in important ways, too. Something that set them apart from, say, Mercedes-Benz showrooms was that the city or town where Lexus showrooms were located had to appear clearly as part of the name. That was meant to help prospective customers find them in phonebook listings. To augment sales and service, TMS linked its dealers with headquarters via satellite. That way the company could offer repair and maintenance advice while, at the same time, keep track of any problem patterns that developed. The system also gave dealers access to a complete repair history — something like a portable medical chart — for every vehicle sold. "We wanted Lexus buyers to get the same service anywhere, even if they were traveling half-way across the country," said TMS vice-president Kawamura. "Our policy was that each customer should be treated as if they were a guest in our home."[61] Lexus backed up its products with a comprehensive warranty, a toll-free hotline for dealers and emergency assistance for problems that dealers couldn't remedy. It even despatched veteran mechanics from Torrance to deal with the trickiest repair jobs. The company also set up a nationwide roadside-assistance program, one of the industry's first and most comprehensive.[62] What's more, an operations manual was written up and distributed to the dealers which provided the basics for such things as how soon to follow up on a sale and how to set up local focus groups for feedback.

In late 1988,TMS hosted a forum for showroom owners and general managers at its CALTY design center in Newport Beach, giving them the opportunity to take their first test drives in LS 400 and ES 250 prototypes and to be briefed by Suzuki's engineers. The dealers responded positively, sending their sales people back for training at TMS "boot camps".

The connection between Lexus buyers and the company didn't end with the sale of a car and routine after-service. With the encouragement of TMS, Lexus dealers also provided all sorts of little extras to leave a lasting impression with customers. Lexus showrooms boasted everything from free coffee and car washes to complimentary weekend breakfast buffets and mini putting greens to keep customers coming back. TMS benchmarked itself against Mercedes, Nordstrom and Ritz-Carlton for customer handling and satisfaction. The system worked so well that 10 years later, when computer microprocessor manufacturer Intel set about developing its own benchmarks to improve customer service after a product recall, it sent a special team to study the operations at Lexus headquarters in Torrance.[63]

Even though TMS and Team One had done everything they could think of to set the table for the sales banquet that was to kick off in September 1989, they grew uneasy as the date approached. Unlike Suzuki in Japan, who was supremely confident his car would sell, Lexus Division officials in the U.S. wondered whether the standard package would be enough to entice car-buyers. Overall car sales were trending downward that year and with the dollar sinking below 150 yen, Toyota Motor seemed unlikely to make a lot of money on the LS 400, which was priced to start at US$35,000. With the addition of leather seats and an optional Nakamichi sound system, the price easily drifted US$10,000 higher. Worried Lexus might lose its oft-touted status as a bargain, Illingworth forbade dealers from pre-ordering LS 400s priced at above US$40,000. "At the time, Toyota's most expensive model [the Cressida] was US$16,000 and yet the LS 400 started at more than double that base price. Price was a big concern for us," said Illingworth.[64] He knew that price wasn't a problem for BMW and Benz, which only sold luxury cars and didn't suffer from a mass-market tag. Lexus dealers could only hope Toyota Motor's reputation for low-end cars wouldn't spoil the LS 400's party. Luckily, the average annual income of the first group of customers to make their way to the shiny new showrooms was a quarter of a million dollars. And fully 25% of these early movers were CEOs or company presidents — just the sort of big fish Lexus had hoped to hook[65] — among them Microsoft founder Bill Gates. The dealers were ecstatic with the early response because TMS had built in a 20% margin between the dealers' wholesale cost and the price offered to customers. As a result, it wasn't unusual for a dealer to earn US$6,000 per car.[66] Shipments of the first LS 400 and ES 250 models started to arrive in showrooms on August 2 and although the formal launch was slated for the first Tuesday after Labor Day — the first weekend in September — Illingworth, not wanting to turn customers away, gave approval to dealers who opened their doors early.[67] By December 31, Lexus had sold 16,233 cars, well above TMS's target of 16,000 cars for the debut year.

CHAPTER SIX

ZEN AND THE ART OF AUTOMOBILE MAINTENANCE

At six o'clock on the morning of New Year's Day 1989, the phone rang in the dark at Tadashi Arashima's childhood home on the outskirts of Nagoya. He had arrived with his family the previous day to spend a week's holiday. Woken by his elderly mother, Arashima stumbled to the phone and picked up the receiver. At the other end was his boss, Ted Toyoda, calling from TMS headquarters half a world away. Coming just days before the start of the annual Detroit auto show where Lexus was scheduled to make its global debut, Arashima knew the call couldn't be good news. It wasn't. The very next day, he was on a Northwest Airlines plane bound for Detroit, preoccupied by the news of a court injunction against the use of the name Lexus. "I usually drink a lot on those long international flights, but that time I didn't touch a drop," Arashima recalled.[1]

For the company, the court order was a worst-case scenario come to life because so much work had been done already — and so much money had been spent — to promote the new brand name. The concept models were all set for display and the pre-printed materials ready to be handed out to the thousands of journalists expected to attend the show. Dies, or molds, with the name had been cast in Tahara. At an emergency gathering in Detroit of the most senior TMS staff, it was decided, reluctantly, to cover any promotional signs and keep pamphlets mentioning the name out of sight until the case was resolved. For the purposes of the show, the brand would simply have to be known as "the luxury division of Toyota Motor". It was back to square one: no buzz; no distinction from the regular Toyota brand name. "If the issue wasn't somehow resolved, we made up our minds to buy masking tape to cover the word 'Lexus' spelled out on the cars' rear ends," said Arashima.[2]

The catalyst for these desperate last-minute measures was a motion filed by Miamisburg, Ohio-based Mead Data Central (MDC), a unit of Mead Corp. The data-processing company, which owned the computer database search engine Lexis/Nexis, wanted TMS to desist immediately with its use of the word "Lexus", deeming the term to be uncomfortably close to its own registered product name. The alternative for Toyota Motor was to hand over US$100 million plus other royalties over a 15-year period. MDC (which was purchased by publisher Reed Elsevier in 1994) also wanted a prominent disclaimer in every Lexus advertisement, disassociating its data subsidiary from the car brand.[3] Responding to these fears of a "dilution" in the Lexis brand name, on December 30 — just four days before the opening of the auto show to the world's press — a Federal judge in the Southern circuit of the U.S. District Court of New York banned TMS from using the name "Lexus". The timing couldn't have been worse. And the judge who made the ruling, David N. Edelstein, was reputed to be ill-disposed toward corporate giants. The last judicial appointee of former U.S. President Harry Truman, Edelstein was a champion of the "little guy". He had earned his reputation by presiding over the U.S. government's 43-year antitrust case against IBM. Nor was he particularly well disposed toward Japanese. Things did not look good for Toyota Motor. "[The judge] had a cultural bias which was pretty evident," said Jim Perkins, then a TMS senior vice president and first head of the Lexus division. The company's own legal counsel gave a blunt assessment of the outlook, saying privately, according to one account, that in his opinion Edelstein was "the worst Federal Judge in New York, perhaps anywhere..."[4] On hearing this, a normally tranquil TMS senior vice-president, Katsumi Usuda, blurted out "Jesus Christ!", surprising his American colleagues as much with his profanity as with his evident alarm. Toyota Motor executives back in Japan couldn't understand what all the fuss was about. After all, the company had dutifully vetted the name before lawyers and had received assurances that Lexus wouldn't infringe on any copyrighted words. The lawyers reasoned that the two companies operated in completely different industries with little overlap. Yet fully eight months before the December court injunction, MDC had filed its legal brief against Toyota Motor in New York. TMS had been formally served notice in October, but officials in Torrance, confident they would prevail in court, smugly went about their business promoting the brand.[5] Immediately following service of the injunction, Toyota Motor protested the ruling, arguing that consumers could not possibly confuse the two names. But the court decided MDC would have its day in court. Assembling a team of some 30 lawyers, TMS pleaded at the very least for a reprieve in the restraining order until the end of the month — in other words, until after the Detroit and L.A. auto shows. A panel of three judges for the U.S. Court of Appeals in New York granted that motion at the last moment, sparing TMS the embarrassment of having to break out the rolls of masking tape.

But the grace period was effective only at the auto shows, not in any nationwide promotion. The larger issue remained unresolved and, if it remained so, as of February 1, the division would be effectively nameless. If Toyota didn't win its argument on full appeal then it stood to lose tens of millions of dollars. Court documents revealed that TMS "had planned to spend US$18 million to US$20 million" for marketing the new brand name. Recasting the molds used for the tail badge alone would force at least a six-month delay in production at Tahara. TMS had already begun an extensive direct mail campaign using the name Lexus, targeting wealthy consumers culled from lists obtained from American Express and MBNA. What's more, dozens of Lexus dealerships faced the prospect of having to rename their showrooms and re-order everything, from outdoor signs to doormats and business cards. Neither was there a rich crop of alternative names from which to choose a suitable replacement. Among the possibilities considered by TMS were Lexia, Lucidia, Luxel and Luxul.[6] Then there was the negative publicity which threatened to overshadow the car's release.

Ted Toyoda himself would have to testify in the case before it was resolved. But in a welcome turn of fortune, in a hearing on March 8, the trio of judges on the appellate court found unanimously in Toyota Motor's favor. "It was a slam dunk," said then Lexus division chief Perkins. The court rejected MDC's claim of dilution, noting that "among the general adult population, Lexis is recognized by only one percent of those surveyed". Everyone at TMS was overjoyed — and not just because MDC had to pick up Toyota's US$30,000 legal fees. A huge cloud had been lifted. Spirits soared. Word spread quickly. More than 300 journalists gathered outside the courthouse steps to cover the court's decision. The flip side of what had seemed to be a wave of negative publicity in January was that Lexus now had much greater name recognition than it would ever have had without the court case. Ted Toyoda heard of the good news during a brief business trip to Toyota City. On the return flight to the U.S., a Nissan Motor official seated nearby asked, half in jest, whether the court battle with MDC had been staged to give both companies millions of dollars worth of free publicity.[7] Toyoda had to bite his lip. Whatever the dire predictions by the cynical media just a few weeks earlier, Lexus had dodged its first bullet.

But a second shot was fired from a most unexpected quarter. Jim Perkins, who had helped revamp the Toyota Motor brand in the U.S. and had led the Lexus project from early days through its long-awaited debut in Detroit, made a big announcement of his own on January 15. "I'm sorry to say this to you," he told Ted Toyoda, "but I've got to leave Toyota's U.S. operations by the 20th."[8] Perkins was going back to GM, his former employer, this time as head of its Chevrolet division. He had been lured back not only by the prestige associated with serving as top dog — something then reserved for Japanese at TMS — but also by GM's agreement to triple his yearly earnings, mostly through stock options. "Toyota never understood why I left," said Perkins. "But having started my career at the lowest rung at Chevrolet [in 1960] and then having a chance to go back and run it was pretty appealing."[9]

For Toyota City, the announcement was tantamount to a stab in the back. Perkins had become a defector — and an embarrassing one at that because his resignation came so soon after the Lexus launch. "It was a big shock," said Tadashi Arashima. "[Toyota Motor president] Shoichiro Toyoda's secretary called me at home on that Sunday [after Perkins had given notice] and asked me how much Perkins earned. I didn't know and had to ask Yale [Gieszl], who told me it was US$350,000."[10] While that wasn't pocket change, neither was it a great deal of money for someone with Perkins's skills and institutional wisdom. The so-called wage gap between Japan and the U.S. had existed for years, as former Big Three employees accepted smaller pay packages from Japanese car-makers in exchange for a form of lifetime employment and the promise of greater responsibility and a more creative environment. But job satisfaction only went so far. Everyone assumed there was a glass ceiling when it came to how far any American could rise in TMS, let alone headquarters in Japan. "Could (an American) have been president (of TMS) at that time? Probably not," said Perkins. What's more, the Japanese were considerably behind most U.S. companies when it came to executive compensation. None of the TMS managers was poor, of course, but Toyota Motor had long resisted the "localization" of pay scales. Toyota Motor, which didn't offer stock options even to its senior executives in Japan, certainly wasn't about to match GM's offer to Perkins. One reason for Toyota Motor's reticence was the problem of squaring "fair market value" in the U.S. with wage scales back in Toyota City, where big pay packages were unheard of. As a trade-off, all but the most menial part-time jobs were considered secure for life (or at least until the minimum retirement age was reached).

This so-called lifetime employment system had sprung up in the postwar years in reaction to blue-collar labor unrest about job security at Toyota Motor and other major manufacturers. In time, company-specific unions (as opposed to industry-wide trade unions) became fully integrated with management, and "rights" such as seniority-based pay and guaranteed jobs for life spread to the white-collar professions as well. While employees may not make much more during the fat years of an industrial cycle, neither did they stand to suffer major base pay cuts — or dismissal — during a cyclical downturn. Bonuses were used as a fulcrum to spread the wealth or pare back, depending on a company's profitability. With shareholder rights all but nonexistent in Japan, stakeholders split most of the gains from a bumper crop of profits and shared some of the pain when profits shrank. Labor mobility was limited by virtue of the big companies' aversion to headhunting and mid-career hires, which made it very difficult to change jobs. Another major disincentive was that, unlike the 401K-type personalized pension plans now common in the U.S., corporate pensions for employees in Japan have never been fully portable. This meant that switching jobs was more than likely to entail forgoing hard-earned retirement money. The more senior the manager, the more difficult it became to consider moving. So although a Japanese senior manager might transfer to the U.S., his (such top jobs were limited to men at Toyota Motor and other top companies) base pay matched that of his company peers back home in Japan. This was designed to both ease re-integration once an overseas work stint ended and to prevent the prospect of better wages from coloring transfer decisions by the powerful (and highly politicized) personnel office. The cost of living benefit paid to Japanese working abroad was considered enough of a perk. Most Japanese expatriates enjoyed living in homes of a type they could never afford in Tokyo. Besides, the wage gap was never an issue when the Japanese occupied most of the top positions at TMS. As more and more Americans began moving up in the pecking order, however, the wage disparity with Detroit and promotion limits became much more of a problem. But it was always just beneath the surface. Or had been until Perkins left.

It was a painful lesson for Toyota Motor's most senior executives, who took such transfers as a form of personal betrayal. Of course, money wasn't the only issue involved, despite what the boardroom officials in Japan might have thought. Some TMS officials from that period have noted that Perkins appeared to have worn out his welcome with other top staff in Torrance. He was said to have pulled rank well above his pay grade. "Jim kept forgetting that Toyota owned the company and that Ted's name was on the door," said one official familiar with the issue.[11] For his part, Perkins said: "There were some Americans on the staff that might have felt threatened." McCurry, in particular, who was executive vice-president of TMS, was said to have felt intimidated by the ambitious Perkins, a group vice-president and general manager of Lexus. While TMS and Toyota Motor went to great pains to show a unified — and perennially smiling — façade, personnel issues at the Lexus Division were more complex than publicly acknowledged. Perkins's departure was one of the first examples of disharmony at the highest levels over pay and chemistry. There would be others; and the fallout from these internal battles would have big consequences for the Lexus brand.

DAMAGE CONTROL

A third round in the chamber which had the name "Lexus" etched on it was fired eight months later — and just two months after the start of sales in the fall of 1989. It all started when Lexus Division headquarters in Torrance got a troublesome field report from a San Diego dealer who had called the service hotline in late September. According to a salesman at the dealership, an LS 400's cruise control had malfunctioned during a test drive, kicking into overdrive and roaring ahead even as a potential customer slammed on the breaks. The quick-thinking salesman was able to override the system by disengaging it manually, but it had been a close call. It fell to Dick Chitty, chief technical liaison with the dealers in charge of parts and service support, to deal with the matter. And Chitty took it very seriously. "We knew right there and then that if we didn't handle this properly that Lexus was finished," he recalled.[12] He informed Dave Illingworth immediately. Their first order of business was to get a detailed report from the dealer and to send the faulty cruise-control switch by express mail to Toyota City for an automotive autopsy. Time was of the essence: if it was determined that a recall was needed, the company would have only five days before it was required to notify U.S. regulators. And if Toyota Motor couldn't tell the National Highway Traffic Safety Administration exactly what had happened by then — and how it intended to fix it — the fallout among the public at large could be disastrous for the new brand.

The analysis showed that a flaw in the machining process of the cruise control's actuator switch had caused the problem. There was still a possibility that this was simply an anomaly, a one-off event unlikely to crop up in other LS 400 cars, but Chitty didn't want to take the risk of having it happen again. He asked Lexus Division staff to try to trigger the malfunction on purpose. They were able to do so, with the same result. Luckily, no other customers had reported problems. But the faulty activator switch wasn't the only problem. Almost simultaneously, Lexus Division was made aware of complaints about the car's wiring. One involved a loose clamp on a battery wire attached to the alternator, which had caused the car's electrical system to fail. In another, unrelated, incident an LS 400 owner in Texas reported that an overheated brake light on the inside of the rear window had melted the black plastic housing of the unit. While executives at Toyota Motor were not pleased with these developments, they didn't set about finding a scapegoat or assigning blame. Instead, Eiji Toyoda decided on an immediate recall of all the cars. All parts were to be replaced free of charge.[13]

This seemed like precisely the wrong move. It would be a logistical nightmare to carry out on a mass scale. And this essential admission of guilt was sure to give the American press a field day questioning the brand's claims to superior quality. Nevertheless, on December 1, 1989, Toyota Motor issued an unconditional recall of its flagship car. "My first reaction was, 'Oh my God, here comes trouble'," said Ken Meade, owner of the Lexus dealership outside Detroit.[14] What prompted this all-out effort to assuage customers, however, was the knowledge of what could happen to an import brand that failed to take remedial action.

At first blush, the LS 400's problems appeared to mimic a malfunction that had plagued the Audi 5000-S about three years earlier. That car had appeared to widespread acclaim in 1985, but less than 12 months afterwards it was being tried in the court of public opinion for an inexplicable acceleration problem. The car was apparently predisposed to lunging forward when shifted from drive mode into park or reverse mode. No mechanical explanation was ever detected and Audi was quick to lay the blame on incautious drivers. But a zealous New York Attorney General, Robert Abrams, stepped into the case after complaints from several 5000-S owners. The dogs had been unleashed. Soon enough investigative television show "60 Minutes" was in on the action, interviewing an Ohio woman who hit her own son with the car — and blamed it on the mysterious defect. An Audi Victims Network was created to pressure the company into readdressing the alleged problem. Overnight, Audi's name was tarnished. Worse, the company compounded its problems by resisting calls for a nationwide recall. In one of the dimmest public relations moves ever demonstrated by a major auto-maker, the company continued to point the finger at apparently innocent victims. Audi insisted that drivers were simply mistaking the gas pedal for the brake. Furthermore, it had the temerity to claim that the problem wasn't unique to the 5000-S model. In other words, Audi was calling its own customers too stupid to know the difference between the brake and the gas pedal. Not surprisingly, the tactic backfired, alienating the company's core customer base and leading to a belated recall almost a year after the complaints were first lodged. Audi then embarked on a massive goodwill advertising campaign, offering incentives of up to US$5,000 per vehicle and pledging to make up for falling resale values. It was too little, too late. Audi sales plunged across the board — dropping 69% from peak 1985 levels to just 22,943 cars by 1988. Some analysts suggested the company might be forced to retreat from the U.S. market. Ironically, that year Audi was cleared of any wrongdoing in the case filed by the Ohio driver. Shortly thereafter, the governments of Canada, Japan and the U.S. determined that the acceleration problem stemmed from driver error: there was no mechanical glitch in the 5000-S. But the damage had been done. It was a self-inflicted public-relations wound. And it would be more than a decade before Audi could reclaim its good name among the car-buying public in the U.S.[15]

Eiji Toyoda's decision to deal with the brand's first big product crisis by replacing all the parts posthaste was not only magnanimous; it was masterstroke. Instead of trying to defuse a bomb that had already gone off, Toyota Motor would acknowledge the error, take the loss and move on. Chitty and the others at TMS heartily concurred with this strategy. So it was that on Friday, December 1, Toyota Motor notified the U.S. government of the apparent defects. An emergency conference call connected Lexus Division senior staff in Torrance — led by Togo and Illingworth — and all of the principle owners of Lexus franchises nationwide (one dealer was reached while sailing on a yacht off the Florida Keyes).[16] The dealer network was briefed on the nature of the problem and the planned response by Toyota Motor. Chitty and Illingworth knew that quick action and total cooperation were paramount to success. Meanwhile, headquarters staff set off around the country to explain the recall to shop mechanics about the problems and to ensure that all 8,000 LS 400 owners nationwide were personally informed about the recall. The deadline for contacting the car owners was the close of business on the following Monday. TMS wanted them to find out before they received a strongly worded official notification letter, which was due to start arriving in mailboxes that Wednesday. The letter, written according to strict U.S. National Transportation Board standards, warned LS 400 owners not to use their cruise-control switches until they could be replaced. But the language it employed was vaguely alarmist and implied that continuing to drive the car could lead to an accident. The prompt response from sales teams to their clientele meant that Lexus Division headquarters fielded fewer than 10 calls from worried customers in the first few days after the recall announcement.

Chitty wanted the installation of the new parts to be completed by Christmas — which meant within about 20 days, no easy logistical feat.[17] To make up for the inconvenience this necessarily entailed to their customers, Lexus dealers made loan cars available on request and volunteered to handle pick-up and delivery of the LS 400s so that the replacement parts could be installed as quickly as possible. In Japan, newly made components poured off the production line and were air-freighted to the U.S. on a daily basis. As a result, 95% of the cars sold were outfitted with the new parts by the deadline, compared to an industry average of 50–60% for recalls. Basically, the only cars that weren't retrieved had been re-exported outside the U.S. or been torn apart by rival auto-makers who wanted to see how the LS 400 worked. "The only reason it wasn't a 100% completion rate is that GM, Ford and Chrysler had bought several of the cars and had them dismantled [for study]," said Chitty. "We couldn't believe they bought that many."[18] Lexus headquarters made sure that each recalled car was returned scrubbed, waxed and with a full tank of complimentary gas.[19] In the end, the adroit handling of the episode seemed only to burnish the brand's reputation. Lexus had done it again by snatching victory from the jaws of defeat. "Zen and the Art of Automobile Maintenance", quipped *Time* magazine. "Up against the industry's pedigreed names, Lexus has created virtually instant brand loyalty, a feat unprecedented in the luxury auto market."[20] The dealers, too, were impressed with the all-out efforts of Toyota Motor and its Lexus Division. "The company didn't run and hide," said Detroit dealer Ken Meade. "They stepped right up to the plate."[21] Underlying all of this was the Lexus Covenant, which had held the dealers and TMS together despite a crisis that threatened to poison the brand's chief selling points: customer service and quality. "That was the defining moment for many of us," said Chitty. "It proved to everyone that Lexus was everything we had said that it should be at the very beginning."[22] Lexus had emerged from a potential pile-up unscathed and, remarkably, with its reputation enhanced.

A FALL FROM GRACE

The legendary status the Lexus brand was starting to earn, however, was undermined by a tragic flaw in one of the tale's lead characters. The LS 400 had made its entry in pretty much the form Suzuki had envisioned and it was his total dedication to the car that had made it all possible. But the staff at the Lexus Division knew that that devotion cut two ways. On the plus side was Suzuki's determination not to leave a single stone unturned in his pursuit of perfection. But the obverse of this was immediately recognized by anyone who crossed him. He wanted to have a say in everything and wouldn't countenance opposition. He was driven by some inner demon to create the perfect car. Seemingly, he could do no wrong. Without exception, whenever engineers had grumbled that what Suzuki wanted couldn't be accomplished, he had been proved right. At some point in the long journey toward completion of the LS 400, however, Suzuki crossed the line from constructive devotion to unhealthy obsession. He had developed something of a maniacal attachment to the car and felt no compunction about belittling those he didn't think worthy. Some felt he had a mean streak that was damaging to morale.

The usually freewheeling Team One staff went on high alert whenever Suzuki was around. While they admired his engineering prowess immensely and sought his help to showcase the LS 400's technical highlights, they also strove to keep him at arm's length where possible. They knew he did not suffer fools gladly — among his own staff or others involved in the program. "I'm sure he ruffled some feathers," said Tom Cordner. "He was very intense and you could tell immediately that it was his way or the highway."[23] It was that very intensity that would lead to Suzuki's luck running out.

It happened during a test drive of his beloved car at 10:25 on the morning of August 31, 1990. Suzuki, then 53, was at the wheel, cruising along at top speed through a slalom course set up on the Toyota Motor test track in Shibetsu. As he cleared one cone and began a sharp arc to take the next, he lost control. The car slammed into the guard ropes ringing the track, spun out of control and flipped over. Suzuki and a colleague strapped into the passenger seat walked away with only light injuries. But Osama Ogawa, who had been sitting in the back, did not. The accident resulted in a severe neck injury.[24] Shocking as it was, the high-speed accident was neither the first nor the most serious to take place at the track during Suzuki's watch. A little over two years earlier, an LS 400 prototype driven by a 32-year-old Toyota Motor driver spun out of control in a brake test and hit another employee, Takayoshi Ono, who was on the side of the track. Ono was rushed to Shibetsu General Hospital where he died two days later from trauma induced by the tremendous loss of blood.[25] Though Toyota Motor never officially assigned blame nor publicly reprimanded Suzuki over either incident, following the second accident he was in time transferred to tiny TMC affiliate Toyota Auto Body Co. Ltd. It is not unusual for a chief engineer to move on after an assignment is completed, especially one as demanding and successful as the LS 400. But it was clear to all those who knew the workings of Toyota Motor that unceremoniously despatching Suzuki to an affiliate company marked an undeniably ignominious end to his career at Toyota Motor. A price — however token in nature — had to be paid for the LS 400's blood debt. But Suzuki's time in the wilderness would be relatively short-lived. He was too valuable an asset for Toyota Motor to allow him to simply fade into legend. After a period of penance, he was quietly brought back into the parent company fold in 2000, honored with the title of *gikan*, or executive advisory engineer, and spent the rest of his career serving as mentor to a new generation of Lexus engineers, before retiring in 2003.

Even as Suzuki's star faded, the Lexus brand to which he had served as midwife truly began to thrive. Having come through the recall with flying colors, the LS 400 and its sister model, the ES 250, attracted more and more car-buyers with their unique combination of value and quality. In mid 1990, the LS 400 reached Britain, where most of the 700 cars earmarked for Europe were sent, with the remainder heading for Switzerland.[26] Lexus may have taken on the Germans in the U.S. and, to a more limited extent, in the U.K., but doing so on their home turf was an entirely different challenge — and one Toyota Motor wouldn't relish or rush into. Still, U.S. sales climbed steeply, leaving Nissan Motor's Infiniti Q45 and entry-level M30 in their wake. In 1990, sales more than quadrupled, to 63,534 cars, and then rose again to 71,206 the following year. While this figure was less than the 75,000 Toyota had initially hoped to sell for 1990, it wasn't bad considering the brand's difficult birth.[27] "We

expected a lot of red ink that first year and it never happened," said
TMS's finance man Yale Gieszl. "There are a lot of successful Toyota
brand dealers who turned down the opportunity [to own a Lexus
showroom] and are still kicking themselves today."[28] Indeed, no one
was happier than the Lexus dealers, who were ringing up fat profits
on fully-loaded LS 400 models and trying desperately to keep enough
of the cars in stock. Even the once-nonchalant Germans — who were
still preoccupied with launching sedans such as the 5,000 lbs (2,268 kg),
US$143,333, 11.0 mpg (4.7 kpl) Mercedes-Benz 600 SEL — were
seriously worried by 1990, and for good reason. Over the previous
three years, BMW and Mercedes-Benz sales dipped 29% and 19%,
respectively, costing each an estimated US$1 billion in lost revenue.[29]
In 1991, Benz sales fell a further 24% to 58,869 cars — down from a
peak of 99,000 in 1986. Some blamed the recession in the U.S., but
the company's American market sales had barely budged during a
much more severe recession a decade earlier.[30] "Two years ago —
back when Lexus was just a name, not a car — there were doubts
that a Japanese sedan could ever sit at the head table with Mercedes
and BMW. Doubters are now as rare as Iraqi sympathizers," *Car and
Driver* remarked dryly. "Toyota shouldered its way into prestige
territory the old fashioned way — with a better product."[31]

THE GOLDEN YEARS

But it wasn't just the winning product that was selling. The service
at Lexus dealers won kudos too. One columnist at *Road & Track* noted
the subtle genius of the brand's exhaustive efforts to keep customers
happy and build brand loyalty. "One factor I think is having an effect
in the Lexus success story may seem rather trivial on the surface:
Each Lexus employee is responsible for calling four buyers every
month to ask what they like or dislike about their Lexus. Now that
is not terribly difficult when you don't sell millions of cars — in fact,
total Lexus sales since the year-ago introduction are some 60,000 cars,
including the ES 250. But it says a lot about the philosophy of the
management and their style of marketing."[32]

Indeed, Toyota Motor had much to be proud of, and nowhere more so than in its Lexus Division. The impressive results were a far cry from the fall of 1989 when first monthly sales came in below expectations. To boost morale, Illingworth had challenged headquarters staff to motivate dealers enough to sell 16,000 cars in the next three months. As an added incentive, he vowed to indulge them in a round of *karaoke* if that goal was met. While this might not sound like much of a concession for a manager at a Japanese-owned company, where late night singing sessions are a rite of passage, Illingworth had hated singing all his life. He found the spectacle of crooning in front of colleagues silly and demeaning. Yet when the final tally came in for 1989, Lexus Division sales were exactly 302 cars above target (11,574 LS 400 models and 4,728 ES 250s). Illingworth said nothing more about his pledge until one morning in March 1990 when, most unusually, he called in sick. He left word with his secretary that someone would be filling in for him, but didn't say who. Later that day, a stranger wearing sunglasses and a black fedora strode regally into the spacious, two-story atrium of the Lexus Division building in Torrance, followed by a three-man band. Before anyone realized what was happening, the sound of Illingworth's shaky voice rang throughout the building, belting out an off-key version of the Elvis Presley hit and karaoke standby "Hound Dog". He had fulfilled his part of the bargain, semi-incognito.[33]

In 1991, a third model joined the Lexus family: the SC 400 (SC for Sports Coupe). Originally codenamed the "F3", at US$37,500 it was priced between the ES 300 and LS 400. But it bore little resemblance to its Lexus siblings. Unlike most coupes, which are simply two-door versions of four-door sedans with a minor sheet-metal makeover, the highly sculpted exterior of the SC 400 marked it as a car in its own right. Many of its internal parts, such as the air-cleaning unit, were also specially designed for it. About the only thing it shared with the LS 400 was its powerful engine — and even that was adjusted for additional torque. While the ES 250 and LS 400 were angular and square-jawed, the two-door SC 400 was curvaceous and rounded. But its ground-breaking style — with details such as embedded headlamps, years ahead of their time — immediately vaulted it into the ranks of the industry's most aesthetically innovative cars.

Credit for the SC 400's avant-garde styling goes to a pair of CALTY designers; Dennis Campbell, who had worked previously at both Ford and Chrysler, and Erwin Lui. Instead of sketching designs in the usual way, they used plaster-filled balloons to create flowing shapes which were then photographed and manipulated to render a final design concept. The product of this three-dimensional doodling was a car with a blunt nose, elongated hood line, abbreviated trunk deck and fluid roof lines. "The new Lexus SC 400 coupe is as rounded and slippery and slick as a caplet of Extra-Strength Tylenol," wrote *Car & Driver*. "The big difference is that this baby will *cause* headaches. Imagine that your house payments and your kids' new shoes depend in some way on sales of Mercedes-Benz or BMW or Cadillac or Lincoln…the migraine will kick in as soon as your customers see this *real* coupe from Lexus, the brand that can do no wrong in the four-door market."[34] Nor did the designers economize on the interior, which featured standard luxury appointments such as bird's-eye maple trim on the dashboard and door, along with plush leather seats.

Launched in the U.S. market at the Fairmont Hotel in San Francisco in June 1991 (it had gone on sale in Japan from April as the Soarer model), the rear-wheel-drive SC 400 boasted a 4.0-liter engine capable of taking it from 0-60 mph (0-97 kph) in 6.9 seconds — 1.5 seconds faster than the LS 400.[35] "Passing slower cars isn't just an ability with the SC 400, it's an avocation," commented *Road & Track*.[36] To add to its sporting image, chief engineer Seihachi Takahashi had fine-tuned the car's exhaust to give it a throatier, guttural sound as it shifted gears. What made the car notable — other than its design — was the fact that essentially it had a market all to itself. The closest competitors to the SC 400 were the cheaper, front-wheel-drive Acura Legend Coupe on one end, and the huge BMW 850i priced well above it. A slightly down-market version of the car, a sports coupe called the SC 300, was unveiled with a 3.0-liter inline six-cylinder engine. Both models proved to be hugely popular, with 9,374 SC 400s and

2,401 SC 300s selling through the end of 1991. In the first full year of sales, 12,695 SC 400s and 7,982 SC 300s were sold. "That car was an absolute home-run right off the bat," said Yale Gieszl. Among the buyers was Hollywood actor Harrison Ford.[37] Team One created another memorable ad for the launch of the SC 300/400, again using the power of silence to drive home the point. It showed an SC 400 being driven up to a red stoplight, at which point the picture fades to black as the words "How Do You Want to be Remembered?" appear on the screen. As if in the blink of an eye, the next frame shows the light turning green and the car sprinting off down the road.

Though the launch for the Lexus Division was big, the SC 300/400 was not all that TMS had in store for its upwardly mobile customers. In September 1991, the woefully underpowered and stylistically challenged ES 250, which had been assembled from the Toyota Camry parts bin, finally bowed out. Its replacement, the ES 300, offered a 3.0-liter engine and a roomier interior, with an extra three inches in width and five inches in length on the ES 250. From the start, Toyota Motor had viewed the first generation ES 250, called the Windom in Japan, mostly as a place holder to make the brand seem bigger than just the flagship LS 400. "Nobody in the company was especially happy with the ES 250, but we took what we could get until the ES 300 arrived," said former Lexus Division product planner Tadashi Arashima.[38] "We underestimated the potential for the ES 250 when we first introduced it," Gieszl said. "At the time of its initial release, it was more of a stop-gap measure than anything else."[39] *Car and Driver* gave the remake a hearty welcome in an article entitled "The Camry Clone Gets the Broom".[40] The ES 300 was a more worthy sibling in many ways, though it was still ill-equipped to deal head on with the likes of the BMW 3-Series. Team One didn't let that lack of heritage stop it from introducing the newly styled car with advertisements mocking the Germans. In one, rendered in a creepy Germanic accent and read against a background of pagan chants, a voiceover hisses: "I am Autobahn, Lord of the Highways. Do you think you have what it takes to tame me? Do you? *Try me.* I dare you!" At that point, Jim "Mr Lexus" Sloyan's familiar tone chimes in to take up the challenge. As an ES 300 appears from out of nowhere and streaks down a stretch of the ink black pavement headed toward a sign marked "Munich", Mr Lexus is heard saying: "The all-new ES 300. The road is calling. Answer it." As the taillights of an ES are filmed zooming away triumphantly into the distance, the voice of the Germanic fiend returns, with the weak riposte: "Come back! I *let* you win that time…"

Far fetched as that scenario may have been, it seemed to strike a chord with American luxury-car buyers. Some resented what they perceived to be the German brand's haughty attitude toward its customers. Another set of ads for the new ES was shot in familiar parts of America, including New York City's Park Ave., Wall Street, the Brooklyn Bridge and an isolated part of Highway 50. Each used a voiceover to pitch the car as worthy of the snootiest, richest, rudest or most rural places in the country. An R-rated version of the Brooklyn Bridge ad even used profanity to sell the car. In it, an ES 300 is shown cruising over the bridge, as a man with what can only be described as the accent of a cynical Brooklyn cab driver says: "Yo! Down here. Where the f*** you lookin'? I'm 'da Brooklyn Bridge. You think you could take me? You wanna piece of me scumbag, eh? Let's go. You an' me. Right now. I got your f***in' fancy suspension right here!" Whether or not these ads were responsible for drawing people into showrooms is unclear. But what's indisputable is that the Lexus Division under Illingworth was doing something right. By the end of 1991, sales had hit 71,206 cars and grabbed a 7.1% share of a one-million-car luxury market, up from just 1.5% in 1989. Sales of the ES 300 eclipsed those of its (increasingly pricey) elder brother in 1992, with 32,561 LS 400s being sold compared to 39,652 ES 300s. Lexus became the best-selling luxury-class import brand, beating out even Mercedes-Benz and BMW. "Before Lexus came along," wrote *Car and Driver*, "the Germans were riding a reputation of design and engineering infallibility stretching back to the '60s, a myth they leveraged into a monopoly of the luxury-car trade. But as happens with monopolists, they became arrogant and complacent, raising prices to nose-bleed altitudes with impunity and getting by with incremental upgrades of their cars from year to year rather than keeping them up to date with timely redesigns. In effect, they were telling their customers: 'Hey, if you're going to quibble, go somewhere else.' Then along came Lexus and there was somewhere else. The Japanese company forced the German auto-makers, Mercedes-Benz in particular, into painful reforms that ended careers and buried long-held illusions of invincibility."[41] More impressive than topping the Germans in annual sales was the hat trick Lexus pulled off — an industry first — in topping the J.D. Power & Associates ratings for best in customer satisfaction, initial vehicle quality and sales satisfaction. The brand had become such a runaway success that Toyota Motor eased up a little on the value-for-money aspect. Cars were built loaded up with more and more expensive extras. The price of LS 400 models was above US$45,000 by early 1992 and it wasn't unusual for it to exceed US$50,000. This was a far cry from the bargain-basement pricing strategy used in the car's introductory year. And it was the first sign of what would become a troublesome trend, especially as the Japanese yen rose steadily against the U.S. dollar, forcing the price still higher.

THE GERMANS STRIKE BACK

Toyota Motor made some cosmetic changes to the LS 400 model in September 1992. These included slight modifications to the front grille and a few minor alterations, such as adding a standard passenger-seat airbag and more seat-positioning controls. The facelift boosted the base starting price to US$46,600.[42] But fewer buyers seemed to think the car was worth the extra cost. Sales dropped from 42,806 cars in 1990 to 36,955 in 1991 and just 32,561 in 1992. In a bid to stem the decline, TMS president Togo felt the best strategy was to appeal to the Lexus base and keep people who had already bought LS 400s coming back. He himself appeared in an unintentionally comical pitch taped for a direct-mail video that was sent to the homes of thousands of potential buyers. In it, his central line was: "It's not a car. It's an invention." But unfortunately, he fluffed the pronunciation and the phrase came out sounding like: "It's not a car. It's an invasion."[43] That wasn't quite the impression the Lexus Division wanted to give to potential customers in an environment of increasing trade friction over Japanese exports. The drop-off in sales of LS 400s notwithstanding, the brand as a whole continued to trend higher — thanks mostly to strong sales for the more down-market ES 300. For the year, Lexus sold a total of 92,890 cars, for a healthy 9.5% of the luxury market.

Shortly thereafter, TMS and the Lexus Division underwent a major changing of the guard. Togo was replaced by a newly arrived Japanese manager, Shinji Sakai. And Illingworth, who had shepherded the Lexus brand's growth through its earliest and most crucial years, handed over the reins as Lexus Division chief to George Borst. This came just ahead of the introduction of another member of the Lexus stable: the sleek and sporty GS 300 sedan. Sold as the Aristo in Japan, the car featured the same inline-6, 3.0-liter engine as the SC 300, and extras such as walnut trim on the center control panel. But what made it more notable was an exterior that seemed to blend the best elements of the LS 400 and the SC 400/300. The specialist magazines noted approvingly that this was the work of the renowned designer Giorgetto Giugiaro's boutique design studio, Ital Design. The GS 300, like the LS 400, was made in Tahara — unlike the ES (manufactured in Toyota Motor's Tsutsumi plant) and the SC (which was outsourced to affiliate Kanto Jidosha at its Kanji plant). The manufacture of the newest Lexus showcased Toyota Motor's automation drive at its height. Just eight of the spot welds used to make its body were undertaken by human hand, with robots taking care of the remaining 4,200. Other sections of the car were pressed meticulously to avoid welds and seams altogether. "From one piece of steel, a 5,200-ton press creates the entire side-member outer panel of the GS 300. No seams. No welds," reported an awe-struck *Road & Track*, which went on to give an upbeat review. "A car that packs all the luxury of the LS 400 into a smaller, sportier package. A car we wish American car companies would study. And build, for that matter," the magazine said.[44] *Car and Driver* concurred, noting: "Driving the GS 300 was as smooth as we expected, almost too smooth for a car that aspires to displace the BMW in the hearts of driving enthusiasts."[45] Yet despite the generally favorable commentary by car enthusiasts, the GS, released in March 1993, failed to spark the sales boom that Toyota had hoped for. The reason for this was that it was merely on par with same-class rivals such as the Jaguar-inspired Infiniti J 30 and the Volvo 960, rather than demonstrably better, as the LS 400 had been in its peer group. It didn't help either that the car cost US$3,000 more than comparable BMW 525 models.[46] The GS 300 was, in fact, designed to take over the early price point abandoned by the LS 400. But it didn't have the heft, the automotive gravitas, to pull it off — or anything special like an optional manual-transmission or a V8-engine version. Sales of the GS 300 peaked at 19,164 in 1993 and quickly slid to 13,939 the next year and half that number by 1995. More ominously for the Lexus Division, it wasn't just the new GS 300 that was faltering. The entire division's growth curve flattened out demonstrably after three years of surging sales. An unremitting rise in the value of the yen against the dollar forced Toyota to make the difficult choice of raising prices again and again in the U.S. or sacrificing profit margin in Japan when those dollar sales were repatriated into yen. The base price of the LS 400 crept up to US$51,200 in 1994, further eroding the comparative advantage it had once had over the Germans. While the list price of the 4.5-liter V8-powered Infiniti Q45 was US$52,400, the 4.0-liter V8-tooled BMW 540i started at just US$47,500. (*Road & Track* noted admiringly that "this solid German performance sedan is still a benchmark at the US$50,000 point."[47]) By the mid 1990s, Benz and BMW had begun to realize that Lexus wasn't going away. The Germans' response was to slash prices on their vehicles, extend their product range to block the Japanese advantage point by point and overhaul quality and finishing. "What a difference three years makes," wrote *The Wall Street Journal*. "Mercedes, BMW and even the much-maligned Jaguar, now owned by Ford Motor, are roaring back after learning two important lessons from Lexus — keep prices low and increase quality."[48] The debut of the Mercedes entry-level C-Class put a big dent into Lexus sales, particularly in the opportunity cost for the ES 300, which simply couldn't match the prestige for the money. "In the past, [Mercedes] vehicles would be priced for the European market, and that price was translated into U.S. dollars," said Joe Eberhardt, a Mercedes official in charge of marketing in the mid 1990s. "Surprise, surprise, you're 20% more expensive than the LS 400, and you don't sell too many cars."[49] So Mercedes also cut the price on new versions of its E-Class and S-Class models and included more features (such as cup-holders) geared toward American car buyers. Lexus itself faced a long lull in the product pipeline. No new models — other than a remodeled LS 400 — were slated to be unveiled before 1996. That product gap proved particularly untimely given the rapid introduction of competitors' models, such as BMW's revamped 3- and 5-Series.[50] "By 1992 or 1993, the Germans had woken up," said George Borst. "And in 1994 they hit us with a blitz of products. The Germans were cutting prices as fast as we were raising them and our pricing advantage just disappeared."[51]

After lavishing attention on its luxury division for several years, Toyota Motor had taken its eye off the ball. Money was being diverted to other programs, such as an ambitious — and ultimately very successful — sub-compact 1.0-liter car strategy designed to reverse a slow decline in market share in Japan. But that had left the Lexus Division exposed to a renewed German threat. "Lexus had got an awful lot of attention from Toyota [Motor], but then it focused on other areas. There were limited resources and it had seemed that Lexus was doing well enough," said Borst. "But we got hammered."[52]

THE BLACK HOLE

Individually, none of these factors represented a tipping point, but altogether it was a triple punch — the yen, the renewed German assault and not enough new product — that overwhelmed the Lexus Division. It was the beginning of what TMS insiders now refer to as the "dark years" or "black hole" for the brand.[53] Suddenly, Toyota Motor, TMS and its Lexus Division seemed to have lost their magic touch. Growth was no longer a given for Lexus. The division was in a rut, with no easy way out. Complicating matters further was a flood of used Lexus vehicles coming onto the market. These trade-ins and used cars had been built so well in Tahara that they were giving new models a run for their money — for a lot less money. To deal with this threat to price stability and to burnish the brand image, TMS pioneered a concept that's now become standard practice for luxury-car makers: the certified pre-owned program. The Lexus pre-owned program started up in November 1993, partly to soak up the bumper crop of trade-ins. To this day, it's one of the most successful businesses around. By offering an inspection, a "reconditioning process", an extended warranty from the manufacturer and "the prestige of the Lexus ownership experience", the Lexus division has kept prices for these trade-ins higher than they would otherwise be — thereby applying a brake to the rate of depreciation. This goes a long way toward explaining why Lexus cars have the highest resale values year after year. Another reason, of course, is tremendous quality of product. The original LS 400, for example, registered the highest ever score — 179 points out of 202 — in J.D. Power and Associates' Customer Satisfaction Index. Yet by this stage Toyota Motor was well under way with a program to replace its flagship model with something designed to be even better. This project was led by Kazuo Okamoto, Suzuki's successor as chief engineer of the LS program, and chief exterior and interior designers, Makoto Oshima and Michikazu Masu. The final prototype for the second generation of the LS 400 was codenamed UCF21 and came out of an exhaustive process at CALTY involving 20 competing one-fifth scale clay models.[54] Yet the new car's styling was highly derivative of the original LS. Of the top three finalists in the design stage, one was almost identical to the original. The other two designs were only slightly more adventurous. The thinking was to do something evolutionary instead of revolutionary. "We needed to carry over and deepen the LS 400's identity," said Okamoto. "A tradition cannot be founded if you reject the first generation."[55] Yet critics said that the car looked stuck in a time warp. One of the few key differences was in the front grille design. The new façade protruded more and had chamfered corners. Headlamps and turn signals no longer wrapped around the side of the car. Similarly, the rear window was kept focused squarely to the rear instead of curling around the back pillar, where the trunk meets the cabin, as on the first LS 400. A higher beltline wrapped the sides of the car, connecting the front fenders to the trunk deck at the rear. As a 1995 model released in November 1994, the new LS 400 featured a slightly redesigned 4.0-liter V8 engine with greater torque and less weight. Oddly, although the car's wheelbase was 1.4 inches (3.6 cm) longer than the original, the overall length, width and heights were exactly the same. Yet the car did provide an extra 2.6 inches (6.9 cm) of legroom in the back. Notwithstanding these modest improvements — and a positive nod from *Popular Science* magazine as the "Best of What's New" — the car was deemed a failure against the high standards set by the first generation LS 400. "Looked at from the traditional luxury marketing position it attacked so well, the new LS 400 remains a tough act to challenge," said *Road & Track*. "So what's the weak spot? Ho-hum styling."[56] *Car and Driver* weighed in on this as well, writing in an article entitled "Lexus LS 400: Remodeling the Temple of Tranquility": "The more things change, the more they stay the same. That's certainly how it seems with the 1995 Lexus LS 400. In profile and shape, this new luxury car is so familiar that you could drive past one and not give it a second glance."[57]

In listening too hard to the effusive praise heaped on the first generation F1, Toyota Motor became deaf to the need to innovate to keep customers coming back. "We got burned with the second-generation Lexus LS 400," said Toyota Motor executive vice-president of production engineering and former Tahara chief Kousuku Shiramizu. "We tinkered with it. We asked Lexus users what they wanted, and we got a lot of opinions…[but] in the final analysis, the second-generation car can't be called a smashing success compared to the first Lexus. It was too much a carryover from the first."[58] That much is clear from the disappointing LS 400 sales, which fell from 23,783 in 1993 to 22,443 the following year. A breathtaking US$50 million Team One advertising campaign (double the cost of BMW's marketing push for its new 7-series) was launched to revamp the brand. The money was spent filming commercials featuring scenes of yachts sailing along the rock-strewn coast of Maine and red-orange sand dunes in the desert of sub-Saharan Africa. This was paired with an advertising blitz in 78 major magazines and a direct-mail campaign targeting 400,000 people who had bought Lexus cars. By far the most expensive marketing effort since the launch of the original LS 400, it paid far fewer dividends to the brand than hoped. The metaphor-heavy television spots marked a clear break with the feature-driven emphasis of earlier Lexus campaigns. In a weird throwback to the first Infiniti ads, the new LS 400 commercials lingered so long on majestic sand dunes they didn't even show the car until it raced by at 130 mph (209 kph) in the final few frames. Yet there was a method to the "mod"-ness. One of the reasons for the stylistic switch was that the Europeans had caught up on quality and price. By the mid 1990s, Lexus had less to brag about. Scott Gilbert said at the time that "the differences between cars are narrower now. We can't just talk about the ride and comfort."[59] Toyota insiders blame fierce internal struggles over the direction of the brand and product advertising campaigns following the departure of two pillars of the Lexus establishment: Togo, who left on December 7, 1993, and McCurry, who departed a year earlier. The affable Togo in particular was sorely missed by his American staff because of his key role in bridging the culture gap between Torrance and Toyota City. (After his retirement from TMS, Togo embarked on an 89-day trip around the world, piloting his single-engine Cessna from Long Beach, California to Nagoya, via Europe.) Togo's distant and less-personable successor, Shinji Sakai, was a stark study in contrast. Sakai and a few new staff from Japan quickly reasserted control over most aspects of brand building, marketing and sales strategy that Togo had been happy to delegate to others. Blunt and argumentative, Sakai developed a reputation for preferring to put more power into the hands of distant managers in Japan. He wasn't comfortable ceding authority to local employees in the U.S. — at least in the minds of his American staff members. Because of that perception, he was reviled by many of the people who worked for him, including senior aides. "He was awfully opinionated — his opinion, not ours," said Jim Perkins, who worked closely with Sakai before leaving Lexus. "Sometimes it got a little ugly."[60] Team One was especially unhappy with Sakai and his minions, among them senior aide Riichiro Chikuma, who served as a senior vice-president from 1993, because they took so much time to decide on campaign themes and storyboards. This left little time to meet actual production deadlines, a constant source of friction between Team One and TMS. "Let's just say that Sakai was no Yuki Togo," said Tom Cordner. "It was not a good time."[61]

THE TRADE WAR

Unfortunately, Toyota City didn't fully realize until 1996 that the reshuffling had poisoned relations with so many local employees. By then a lot of fingers were being pointed about what had gone wrong with the Lexus brand. A blame game ensued. No one wanted to take responsibility for the plateau in sales. The squabbling in Torrance wasn't particularly helpful at a time when many dealers were growing upset. They needed reassurance from Lexus Division headquarters at precisely the time when it was least forthcoming. Dealers were keenly disappointed by the slow start for the newest LS 400. That the car failed to impress as much as its predecessor was disillusioning for dealers who had grown accustomed to the LS 400 practically selling itself. Total sales at the brand declined from a record high of 94,677 in 1993 to 87,419 the next year, which was well below Toyota Motor's five-year plan for brand sales to top 100,000 cars a year by that stage.[62] In 1995, sales hit a nadir of 79,334, and nearly two-thirds of those were of lower-margin ES 300s. The Lexus Covenant's commitment to "the finest dealer network in the country" was under severe stress. Some dealers stopped providing loaner car equivalents to the vehicles under repair or in for a tune-up. Others let service slide in more subtle ways. The primary cause of their irritation was clear: they no longer had a product mix that brought car-buyers into showrooms ready to make a deal. One J.D. Power & Associates survey in 1994 showed that fewer than two-thirds of Lexus dealers thought the product line was sufficient, down from 79% the previous year. Tellingly, TMS detected a drop in interest in Lexus as an auto franchise among dealers. That came as a big setback for a company which once seemed to have a license to print money at its top-of-the-line dealerships.[63] In response, TMS curtailed a planned expansion of the dealer network. The original plan was to increase the number of dealers from the initial 100 to 160 by 1993 and then to 190 by 1995. Instead, only four new "companion" dealerships were built. These were essentially cross-town service-heavy franchises operated by an existing dealer. "We had to stop the expansion. Why did we need more at a time like that?" said Borst.[64]

Despite being in the doldrums , the outlook for Lexus didn't seem hopeless — at least not until a storm, in the shape of a trade war, began to truly shake the brand's foundations. The old auto-trade pressures that had softened with the voluntary quotas and transplants of the early-to-mid 1980s, had begun to build anew in the late 1980s and early 1990s. By then, the last of the "voluntary" quotas had expired and the Japanese had begun feeding ever-higher on the auto food chain — right into the heart of the luxury-car market. At the same time, Japan's own car market remained almost devoid of foreign cars, which accounted for less than 3% of total sales.

Following the awkwardly worded and not entirely successful Market-Oriented Sector-Specific (MOSS) U.S.-Japan trade negotiations of the late President Ronald Reagan's second administration, the next major outbreak of trade friction over autos came amid the Structural Impediment Initiative (SII) of U.S. President George H.W. Bush. This clumsy attempt to engage Japan in a number of trade issues sputtered out in the early 1990s. Yet the Bush Administration was under pressure from Congress, which had passed the 1988 Trade Act, a thinly veiled jab at Tokyo requiring the White House to list "unfair" trading partners. Washington sought to gain leverage over the Japanese by invoking the specter of sanctions based on the so-called Super 301 section of the Trade Act. Bush decided to intercede personally to win trade concessions from Japan. This culminated in an embarrassing summit meeting with Prime Minister Kiichi Miyazawa in Tokyo in January 1992. In a ham-handed attempt to show he meant business,

Bush arrived with a high-powered delegation of Big Three executives in tow. The President departed with a mealy-mouthed accord whereby Japan pledged to make it easier for foreign car-makers to sell there and Japanese auto-makers agreed to buy more U.S.-made parts. But the most lasting impression from the visit was less of a trade victory than of Bush getting sick in the lap of his host at a televised state dinner.

The bilateral trade relationship soured further with the incoming Clinton administration, which pledged a tougher, "results-oriented" policy vis-à-vis the Japanese. Abandoning the alphabet-soup approach of using acronyms such as MOSS and SII to identify trade policy, Washington created a "Framework Agreement" for negotiations with Japan — essentially another basket of simmering trade issues, including autos — in July 1993. These talks went nowhere until the spring of 1995 when U.S. Trade Representative Mickey Kantor, a leading Democratic fund raiser and well-connected lawyer, upped the stakes by openly threatening to impose 100% tariffs on Japanese luxury cars by a June 27 deadline. Such sanctions would severely hurt sales volumes of these cars and cost the Japanese up to US$5.9 billion a year. Notably, of the 13 cars subject to the penalty, five were Lexus models. The price of the LS 400, for example, was set to rocket overnight to US$62,000 for a basic model and to US$100,000 for a fully loaded car.[65] The tariffs not only targeted buyers of these models after the June deadline but also applied retroactively to anyone who had bought one after May 19. Worse yet for the Japanese, surveys showed nearly three-quarters of all Americans supported the imposition of sanctions.

Panicked, Lexus Division officials asked Toyota Motor to cut back production. They also began to discuss emergency subsidies for the dealers by underwriting some of their fixed costs. TMS even considered scaling back the brand's marketing campaigns, an essential catalyst for drumming up showroom traffic and sales.[66] One stop-gap measure that would come back to haunt the brand was the decision to start fleet sales of the struggling GS 300 to car-rental agencies. While that helped offload inventory, it tarnished the brand's prestige among buyers.[67] TMS head Sakai flew to Toyota City for urgent consultations with board members on June 2. There, he asked for subsidies for Lexus dealers and — unbelievably — even proposed selling some ordinary Toyota brand models, which would not have been subject to tariffs, in chic Lexus showrooms. Chairman Shoichiro Toyoda reacted to these suggestions with a deafening silence. One senior official present at the meeting explained: "From the standpoint of Toyota Motor's financial wherewithal, we can take the loss of revenue [from any sanctions]. But what we can't take is the torpedoing of Lexus' carefully-constructed reputation as a luxury brand."[68]

Meanwhile in Torrance, TMS was busy drawing up contingency plans and fighting a pitched public-relations battle in the media focusing on the plight of Lexus dealers and American consumers' rights to buy imports. "Lexus rallied the troops," said Bryan Bergsteinsson, a TMS official who headed the Lexus division in the late 1990s. "Dealers and [sales] associates played a key grass roots role by expressing their concerns to local media and politicians."[69] By mid June there were signs of a compromise in the offing that could head-off the sanctions. Japanese car companies, including Toyota Motor, began "voluntarily" releasing detailed plans to purchase more U.S.-made parts and step up investment in their growing network of U.S. factories. Just hours before the deadline, following intense negotiations in Geneva, the outlines of a vaguely worded deal were announced by both parties.

Although hailed by both sides, the accord was something of a Rorschach test in that Tokyo and Washington each walked away with a different take on exactly what had been agreed to. The official U.S. government press release included a list of detailed targets, such as a 50% increase in Japan's purchases of American auto parts over three years, and 1,000 dealers selling U.S. cars in Japan over five years. But the Japanese government press release contained no such numbers, only blanks for Japan's car-makers' own "voluntary" plans — which didn't commit Tokyo to anything. "This agreement is specific. It is measurable. It will achieve real, concrete results," said President Clinton. But hardline Japanese Trade Minister Ryutaro Hashimoto claimed the U.S. had blinked. One of his senior aides in the trade ministry, Hisashi Hosokawa, beamed: "This agreement is a rejection of numerical targets."[70] About the only thing the U.S. and Japan seemed to agree on was the need for further talks to review the issue periodically — and avoid triggering retaliatory sanctions. To most observers, the two sides had papered over their differences. Trade experts were split on the significance of the brinkmanship. Former U.S. Ambassador to Japan Michael Armacost, who served President G. H. W. Bush, commented later that it was much ado about nothing. "The auto/auto parts issue proved to be more intractable than many knowledgeable observers had anticipated," he wrote. "The agreement was not necessarily a bad deal, but neither was it a big deal. It was laced with sufficient ambiguity for both governments to declare victory."[71] But some academics disagree with that neutral analysis, saying that the trade talks wound up doing more harm than any demonstrable good. Leonard Schoppa, a political scientist at the University of Virginia, wrote: "All in all, the framework talks produced little to justify the tremendous expenditure of time, energy and political capital that had been poured into the talks over two long years."[72] And Brookings Institution scholar Edward J. Lincoln, in a book published four years afterwards, argued that though the accord was of "central importance to bilateral trade relations in the 1990s…by not imposing the retaliation, the [Clinton] administration furthered a Japanese view that this American bargaining tactic was only a bluff."[73] In fact, the accord had no lasting impact on sales of American-made cars in Japan. Even Japan's imports of U.S. parts, after a spurt in the late 1990s, began to decline after 1999.[74] Lincoln went on to say that: "What is most interesting about the modest outcome of the negotiations, however, is that the threat of punitive tariffs had become necessary to achieve this outcome, [which is] indicative of the depth of the opposition to change in this industry in Japan."[75]

In the end, TMS provided no direct subsidies to Lexus dealers, and, despite a fair bit of grumbling, they dutifully resisted unauthorized discounting. The Lexus Covenant had withstood an acid test. "Some of the dealers had begun to wonder if Lexus had just had a good run [that was ending]. In some cases, it took a lot of persuasion [to keep them loyal]. I had to be a cheerleader," Borst recalled.[76] Indeed, despite all the things going wrong for the brand, Lexus still managed to take top honors for customer service in J.D. Power & Associates surveys. But had the sanctions been imposed, it could have been a very different story for Lexus and its dealers. Yet some saw the sanctions as an opportunity rather than as an obstacle, regardless of the potential fallout for the entire U.S.-Japan bilateral relationship. Their reasoning was that 100% tariffs would winnow the field of the weakest players and, ironically, force richer Americans to pay a premium for a standard of luxury many had grown used to from the Japanese. "We were convinced that had the tariffs gone through, Infiniti would have folded because they were in trouble and Nissan couldn't support it," said Team One head Scott Gilbert, who was in charge of the Lexus advertising account at the time. "So we thought Lexus would have some short-term trouble, but would come through stronger."[77] In fact, Nissan was in dire straights, reporting operating losses in 1994 and 1995. Knocking a long-standing rival out of the U.S. luxury market might well have been a tempting consideration. But there's no evidence in the public record to suggest that senior executives at Toyota Motor in Japan concurred with that line of thinking. Still, it could have affected Toyota Motor's controversial decision to continue shipping Lexus models to the U.S. right through the darkest hours of the trade crisis. It was Japan's only luxury-automobile maker to do so.[78]

CHAPTER SEVEN

SOMETHING WICKED THIS WAY COMES

By the mid 1990s, Toyota Motor had realized that its prized Lexus Division was in a rough patch. Sales were sagging, the morale of its dealers was at a low ebb and the product line was wilting under the competitive heat of luxury rivals. Worse, the overall market was shrinking as luxury-vehicle sales in the U.S. declined, from 1.14 million in 1990 to just 1.03 million in 1995. The Lexus market share had dropped from a high of 9.5% in 1992 down to 7.7% three years later. It came as no surprise to many in the auto industry when Mercedes recaptured the crown as top luxury import brand from Lexus in 1995.

Yet, despite the gloom, TMS officials felt that the brand's best years were ahead of it. Lexus had only to recapture its golden touch with a combination of great service, unprecedented quality and revamped vehicles. Although the immediate threat of sanctions had passed by the summer of 1995, Toyota Motor was already well on its way to developing a new, tariff-proof product should the specter of sanctions ever come back to haunt the brand. A core element of the contingency plan was to simply sell fewer luxury cars and more luxury light trucks — in other words, sports utility vehicles (SUVs) — which were unaffected by the narrowly targeted luxury-sedan tariffs. Doing so would also address another key weakness in the import brand: a change in the tastes and buying patterns of the baby boomers. While the company had managed the transition from cheap compacts to luxury sedans successfully, it was still losing many one-time customers to competitors who offered a wider selection of vehicles. TMS could not help but notice that many suburbanite Camry or Corolla owners were switching to more testosterone-fueled vehicles such as the Chrysler Jeep Grand Cherokee, the Ford Bronco and the Chevrolet Suburban. Even Toyota's own rugged Land Cruiser line, once the sole preserve of forest rangers and weekend fur trappers, was increasingly in demand in the suburbs. The gas-guzzling vehicles of the 1980s had begun to develop family-friendly street credibility with affluent car-buyers a decade later. With fuel prices hitting record lows in inflation-adjusted terms and highway road rage on the rise, the SUV became the sensible second-car choice for two-car families. Hollywood actor Arnold Schwarzenegger made GM Hummer a household name after ordering a US$100,000 commercial version of the U.S. military vehicle of Gulf War fame. The likes of the Chevy Blazer and the Ford Explorer proved very successful for Detroit. It was only a matter of time before the super-sized, luxury-trimmed GM Denali and Ford Excursion made their debut. Concerns about fuel efficiency dropped out of the public debate and onto the back pages of *Consumer Reports* magazine, which had become the forum for a SUV safety campaign that fell on deaf ears. Before long, SUVs became the cars of choice in gated communities across the U.S.

It didn't take long for Toyota Motor to realize that if it produced a few options-laden, up-market sport utilities of its own for Lexus, fewer high-end customers would defect to rival auto-makers. By transforming Toyota brand vehicles into Lexus models, TMS would get a quick fix to the problem of a stagnant product line-up. Yet relatively few of its upscale competitors recognized the potential in the SUV market at this early stage.

As early as 1993, the corporate planning department staff at TMS had noticed that Lexus was starting to lose momentum in the sedan market. Corporate planning vice-president Arashima and then Lexus Division corporate marketing manager, David Danzer led a study team to develop the first Lexus SUV. They identified a trio of products from Toyota Motor's existing stable that could be readily upgraded for "Lexification": the 4.5-liter, inline six-cylinder Land Cruiser; the mid-size 3.0-liter, V6-powered 4Runner SUV; and the 2.4-liter, diesel engine Prado, a 4Runner twin sold outside the U.S. "We figured those three would be the easiest to convert into a Lexus," said Arashima.[1] The team presented their findings to the brass in Toyota City, who decided to go with adapting the Land Cruiser — which traces its lineage to the 1951 Toyota Jeep BJ — by adding some trim and christening it the Lexus LX 450. But what had really given urgency to the effort was the saber-rattling on the trade front. Getting a sanctions-proof vehicle out to dealers became a top priority and the development of the LX 450 was pushed up accordingly. Since technically SUVs were categorized as trucks, the LX would not be subject to sanctions targeted at luxury 'cars'. "The LX was a direct result of the [threatened] sanctions," said Yale Geiszl. "It was one of the things we could do in the short-term to cope."[2] While this first Lexus SUV was essentially a re-badged Land Cruiser, Toyota Motor made it more plush by adding luxury touches such as dual air bags, leather seats and fancy wood trim on the dashboard and door panels. The company also gave it antilock brakes and tinkered with the undercarriage to soften the ride and soundproof the cabin. But under the hood, the US$47,500 LX 450 couldn't hide its true parentage. It carried the same engine as the Land Cruiser, which sold for less than US$40,000. The LX 450 wouldn't have the V8 engine befitting of a truly up-market SUV — and one costing nearly US$8,000 more than a Land Cruiser — until its second generation, which was rolled out on an accelerated schedule in late 1997. Early on, some insiders worried that the LX 450 might actually hurt the brand because of its all-too-apparent relation to the Land Cruiser. "I was nervous," said Chris Hostetter, then corporate manager for strategic planning at TMS.[3]

To announce the LX 450's arrival and play up its credentials as a luxury vehicle, Team One developed advertisements that showed a Lexus going where none had gone before: driving vertically up the side of a skyscraper. When the LX 450 made its fast-forwarded debut in January 1996 — as the first new Lexus in nearly two years — the response was encouraging for Lexus dealers starved of product. In that first year, some 7,528 LX 450s rolled out of showrooms, completely selling out its inventory and outpacing North American sales of Britain's 4.0- and 4.6-liter Land Rover by more than 700 vehicles. What's more, the old Lexus expertise in damage control and early response to problems was still intact. When dealers complained of excessively noisy fanbelts in some of the first LX 450s to be sold, TMS immediately contacted TMC unit Araco Corporation in Toyota City, where production of the SUV was brought to a complete halt until the problem had been isolated and resolved. "The vehicles didn't leave the port until the belts had been replaced. No one in the process [was] saying 'Just get the vehicles here and we'll fix the belts later'," said Jim Press, the Ford veteran who had joined TMS and was appointed head of the Lexus Division in 1995. "The reward for that kind of full-scale attention to detail? We've been under a 10-day supply [of the LX 450] all year."[4] The LX 450's strong showing proved critical in stopping the slide in overall sales — especially amid the continued rapid decline in sales of the original GS and SC models. It marked the end of a long drought for the brand. "There was no disease eating away at the foundation; just a few speed bumps in the road," recalled Press, who was later appointed as chief operating officer for TMS. "The logical step for us to take was to expand the line-up because we knew the fastest way to revitalize ourselves was to appeal to a broader cross-section of buyers."[5] Indeed, the first Lexus SUV kicked off a major product blitz over the next three years, one that redefined the term "crossover" and put Lexus back on top in the luxury league after three long years as runner-up.

THE LEXUS "BAD BOY"
To get there, TMS would make changes at the top of the Lexus Division to inject some fresh thinking into the brand after a trying period. Borst stepped aside as head of the division in April and handed over

the luxury division to Press, who had been a senior vice-president of corporate planning at TMS. The new boss was determined to put Lexus back on track for growth and he dismissed criticism that Japanese luxury cars were a passing fad. "It was important at that time not to let short-term pressures cause us to deviate from the equity in the brand that added up to high desirability," said Press. "The first chapter was very successful. The pundits couldn't see the second chapter."[6]

In his first few months on the job, Press wrought a number of changes to put an end to what he saw as self-inflicted damage to the brand's image. The first of these changes was stopping GS sales to rental fleets — to the tune of some 10,000 cars a year. He also marshaled all of TMS's marketing know-how to showcase the debut of the new ES 300 in September 1997. The third-generation ES was introduced to the public by Hollywood actress Sharon Stone at a gala reception on Rodeo Drive in Beverly Hills. The chief styling difference in this version was a slightly more buxom bonnet and sleeker profile. But its most potent weapon in the brutal luxury-car wars of the mid 1990s was its price. At US$29,900, the car not only undercut the outgoing ES 300 model by US$2,500, but also undershot the pricing of rivals such as the Cadillac Catera — a reworked Opel Omega from Europe introduced around the same time — by US$250. Six months later, Lexus was selling more ES 300s each month than Catera had sold since its launch and had only a five-day supply of the car on hand, compared to a 66-day inventory for the Catera.[7] Lexus dealers breathed a collective sigh of relief. Sales of the ES 300, still the brand's top-selling model, jumped from 44,773 in 1996 to 58,430 a year later.

In November, the ES 300 was joined by a second-generation GS, which came in two versions: the 3.0-liter inline six-engine GS 300, priced at US$36,800; and the 4.0-liter V8 engine GS 400 — at US$44,800 (an optional dashboard six-CD player added an extra US$1,050), well below the price of comparable BMW and Mercedes-Benz models. Sales of the old GS had fallen so far, so fast, that Toyota Motor had seriously considered dropping it from the Lexus line-up altogether. Instead, the company decided to go ahead with a major makeover. This took place over an 18-month period starting in mid 1994 under the direction of chief engineer Yasushi Nakagawa and chief designer Akihiro Nagaya. Working in close consultation with TMS, they conducted extensive focus-group sessions in the U.S. to test consumer preferences. The resulting second-generation GS answered many of the criticisms about the original's dearth of power and trunk space. Moving the gas tank under the back seats, rather than behind them, created 15% more storage space in the boot. Even though the new car's overall length was actually shorter than its predecessor, the short overhangs and longer wheelbase increased the cabin room — offering more space to stretch out than either the BMW 5-series or Benz E-class.[8] "It took just 5.8 seconds to convince us that the new V8-powered GS 400 is nothing like the previous GS 300 was," cheered *Car and Driver*. "That's the time it takes the GS 400 to hit 60 mph [97 kph] from a standstill — quick enough to confirm that this car is more of a BMW 540i and Benz E420 predator than it is an innocuous middle-child model like the old car was."[9]

The car's somewhat controversial design was previewed as a concept car under the codename HPS at the 1997 Detroit auto show, 10 months before its commercial debut. There, its facelift received a mixed reaction. The most striking feature was its vaguely menacing front grille squeezed between two pairs of trapezoid-shaped headlights. The new GS also had something of a hunched look, like a cat ready to pounce. Inside, a new auto-dimming Opitron backlighting system for the instrument panel glowed an eerie silver-blue at start-up. The sport sedan boasted a 300-horsepower engine and a silky-smooth five-speed automatic transmission — enough to finally give Lexus dealers something sporty to brag about. "The GS was a breakthrough car for us and the world's fastest sedan," said Press. "It started to change the mold at Lexus."[10] Indeed, the BMW 540i required 6.3 seconds to reach 60 mph (97 kph), while the Mercedes-Benz E420 took 7.0 seconds to get there.

Altogether, the new GS made quite a statement — and one vastly different from the understated elegance of its predecessor. Team One's ad campaign sought to highlight these differences, making the GS the risk-taking black sheep of the staid Lexus line-up. "We were looking to position the GS to be the 'bad boy' of the Lexus family," said Karen Smith, an executive producer at Team One. "We wanted to exploit the car's dark side."[11] They did this with a series of ads with the tagline "Something Wicked This Way Comes". One showed a silver GS racing through an apocalyptic and yellow-hued landscape — strewn with broken down and seemingly haunted BMW and Benz models — toward the safe refuge on an Oz-type metropolis on the horizon. The female voiceover, read as if by a Salem witch and in pseudo-sophisticated babble, cackled: "Where once these ancient nameplates ruled, now each of them succumbs. Where paradigms doth shift, when something wicked this way comes."

"Something wicked" worked. Combined sales of the two versions of the GS more than quadrupled, from a paltry 7,718 cars in 1997 to 30,622 in 1998. Nor was it a one-shot wonder like its predecessor. Sales of the new GS stabilized, hitting 31,884 in 1999 and 28,079 in 2000. Better still, in March 1998, Lexus dealers had a third new model to ply — the LX 470, a 4.7-liter V8-powered successor to the LX 450. The model change involved much more than a new engine. Inside, the top-of-the-line SUV was more like the fancy LS 400 than the bare-boned LX 450, thanks to an ultra-quiet cabin, deluxe wood trim, and fluorescent gauges in the dash. The LX 470 made the extra US$10,000 premium over a Land Cruiser seem like it really was worth the extra money. It clinched first place in a *Car and Driver* rating of five same-class large SUVS, including the Cadillac Escalade, the Lincoln Navigator, the Mercedes-Benz ML 430 and the Range Rover 4.0 SE, winning accolades for its grace under pressure off road and for its creature comforts in city traffic.[12] The big SUV soon developed a loyal following among leading lights in the world of business and entertainment — from billionaire businessman Bill Gates to actors Calista Flockhart and Nicolas Cage and a variety of big-name sporting personalities. "Lexus has become the trendy brand that appeals to every flavor of celebrity," reported *Fortune*.[13] Yet the LX 470 was only a prelude to the most successful Lexus ever, a product that would more than double the brand's sales in three years: the RX 300.

CHARIOT OF THE BABY BOOMERS

After a long day of product planning meetings in the spring of 1993, a small group of TMS and Toyota Motor executives decided to finish deliberations over dinner at Patina, a fancy East Hollywood restaurant known for its Californian French fare and decadent cheese cart. They piled into their cars at the "Country Club" — a nickname given to TMS's sprawling headquarter complex in Torrance, replete with tennis courts and an Olympic-size swimming pool — and headed north onto the 405 expressway from Torrance. In the lead car, Press and Akihiro Wada, then Toyota Motor senior manager and later executive vice-president for research and development, noticed the predominance of the high-riding vehicles surrounding their sedan. Noting the strong sales for the RAV4, Toyota's newest mid-size SUV, they talked about whether a rough-riding SUV could be cross-fertilized with a luxury sedan. If it were possible, such a car would offer the best of both worlds: the tall ride, high clearance and ample storage of an SUV, with the smooth ride, creature comforts and fuel consumption of an up-market sedan. Suddenly, they realized they were on to something. "We had hit the target in the bull's eye," said Press. "If anybody could pull it off, we knew Lexus could."[14] That crossover vehicle, which became the RX 300, was officially proposed by TMS at a Joint Product Planning Development meeting in Toyota City in 1994. "The engineers in Toyota City responded very enthusiastically," said TMS's Tadashi Arashima.[15] In fact, their enthusiasm should have come as no surprise. The idea of building a sports ute on a car platform had been bandied about among many Toyota Motor engineers in Japan in the early 1990s. "Internally, there was a group that questioned why vehicles with a high driver viewpoint, strong body and rugged image were always based on hard-riding truck platforms,"[16] said Yukihiro Okane, a member of the core engineering team. But it wasn't until TMS had come up with a specific product request for its Lexus Division that those musings became a reality. That's where the wily Wada came in. Aware that Toyota Motor and TMS officials had rejected the idea of "car-ute" in the past, he campaigned quietly to build a consensus among top TMS officials.[17] Once that consensus had been achieved and the product program was given the go-ahead, a preliminary engineering team was assembled to discuss the "packaging" — the size of the engine, the structure of the underbody and the trunk space — in October 1995, led by chief engineer Tsuneo Uchimoto. With a target audience of younger baby boomers in mind, the design team, led by Makoto Oshima, began producing sketches and molding their thoughts into clay. By the end of 1995, they had prepared three scale models of competing designs. "We got together a group of thirty-something designers and wanted to create something almighty for people in their 40s," said Oshima, himself a 40-something boomer. The objective was to come up with styling a touch more glamorous and well-appointed than the RAV4, which Oshima dismissed as "more for people in their 20s".[18] But on seeing one of Oshima's early prototypes, Borst, who had been appointed to oversee Lexus product planning, was aghast. He castigated the "ugly" vehicle he laid eyes on for its "flat and drab, boxy and gimmicky" styling, and asked the designers to start again.[19] After some finessing, the end result was, if not elegant, certainly a head-turner. The vehicle had the long hood of a sedan, the tall seating of an SUV and the back-end bulk of a mini-van. Unkind observers said it looked something like an ES 300 on stilts. But it was born to be the Chariot of the Baby Boomers. "The RX 300 — a splashy new luxury sport-utility vehicle from Lexus — has a front end that says dirt roads and a back end that says carpools," quipped *The Wall Street Journal*.[20]

Instead of building an entirely new platform or using an existing truck platform, Uchimoto's team chose Camry architecture for the chassis, which had been fine-tuned for use in the ES 300 sedan. Further modification of the RX 300 SUV produced a chassis with much higher ground clearance — hence, the reference to "stilts". It also included a new electronically controlled engine mount — later adopted by the ES 300 — with air cushions to cut down on the vibration to the cabin. This was important because a new V6 3.0-liter engine was to be put into the Camry platform to provide extra horsepower. Toyota Motor originally planned to use a standard inline six-cylinder engine, but TMS officials — reflecting the unanimous position of Lexus dealers — held out for a V6 or, better yet, a V8. Uchimoto, a chassis specialist, felt that a V8 was too big for the frame of a mid-sized SUV like the RX 300. Besides, installing an engine of that caliber might eat into sales of the more expensive, V8-powered, LX 470 SUV, which was set to replace the LX 450 in early 1999. "Many car-makers would simply have built a smaller version of the LX 470, or perhaps adapted an existing truck or SUV platform," Uchimoto said. "We were able to throw away the usual constraints and think of this new product not in traditional terms of truck, or SUV, or van, or luxury sedan. Instead, we could incorporate the most desirable attributes of all of those types of vehicles."[21] Although the engineers knew they were entering uncharted territory with this hybrid of a luxury sedan and an SUV, they did keep some competing models in mind as benchmarks. "We had one eye on the Jeep Grand Cherokee and another on the lookout for the Mercedes-Benz ML 320, which was also under development at that time," said Okane.[22] The chief question for the engineering team was how much off-road capability to build into the vehicle. TMS focus groups revealed that many potential customers said they wanted a SUV that could drive off road; but, in fact, surveys found that the overwhelming majority of SUV owners never ventured beyond pot-holed parking lots. So the engineers decided to emphasize the smooth ride over handling characteristics needed in extreme driving conditions. For example, instead of using the Land Cruiser's rugged four-wheel-drive system, they opted to import an all-wheel-drive system from a version of the Toyota Celica sold in Europe. The decision to go "soft" was critical to the vehicle's future success, but for Uchimoto's team it was a big gamble.

While most rivals pieced together SUVs from the architecture of pick-up trucks to bolster off-road handling and hauling credentials, Lexus focused on offering the most comfortable ride available in an SUV. Unlike the body-on-frame structure of most truck-based SUVs, in which the chassis and body rails come together late in the assembly process, the RX 300 was built off a unibody chassis which provided additional rigidity, a lower step-in height and lighter weight. This improved the smoothness of the ride and the dexterity of the vehicle's handling. It was a wise choice, as many SUV drivers would eventually abandon hard-to-maneuver vehicles in search of a softer ride. "The

key issues for people leaving SUVs are ride and price, in that order,"
said Coopers & Lybrand partner William R. Pochiluk.[23] In May and
November 1997, test drives of final RX 300 prototypes were conducted
in Los Angeles, where the crossover seemed very small compared to
the other traffic. In Japan, where a version would be sold as the
Harrier, the vehicle was criticized by dealers for being too wide for
narrow city streets and too tall for many parking garages. But among
American drivers, the RX 300 seemed more akin to a Honda Odyssey
minivan than a hulking Hummer. While 20-something men gave an
unmarked RX 300 prototype unsolicited thumbs down during road-
testing in L.A., TMS officials noticed the SUV turned the heads of
many American women who happened to spot it.[24]

This early anecdotal evidence of a gender divide would prove
prophetic: women made up 44% of RX 300 owners in its first year of
sales. Five years later, women would account for fully 62% of RX 300
buyers. The Lexus Division had inadvertently stumbled upon a
woefully underserved customer demographic, one which it would
come to monopolize: affluent female car-buyers. It found the luxury
SUV's biggest fans came from households with an average annual
income of US$131,000. The RX 300 was, in the words of one newspaper,
"A Sport Utility in Touch with its Feminine Side".[25] In a matter of
years, the RX 300 would become the vehicle of choice for career
women and stay-at-home moms in upper-middle-class neighborhoods
stretching from Orange County, California, to Westchester County,
N.Y. "Soccer moms adore it for its high seating position, as do glitterati
like diminutive choreographer-singer Paula Abdul," said *Fortune*.[26]
One *New York Times* reviewer wrote: "Surveys indicate that many
people — especially women — are ready for such a hybrid of car and
sport utility vehicle. Count me in this group...I concluded that the
RX 300 is about the only sport utility I would consider owning."[27]
An easy-to-drive sports ute like the RX 300 was a valuable asset in
a market where, by 1997, SUVs represented 16% of all new car sales
in the U.S. market, up from just 7% in 1990. And the entry-level SUV
represented a breakthrough in a whole new category of vehicle that
would put Lexus in an enviable leadership position for years to come.
"We pioneered the [luxury crossover SUV] segment," boasted Press.[28]

The US$32,950 3.0-liter V6 RX 300 fell into a comfortable niche between SUVs such as the US$28,730 4.0-liter V6 Ford Explorer twin Mercury Mountaineer and the US$33,950 3.2-liter V6 Mercedes ML 320. Nissan's even more expensive 3.3-liter V6 Infiniti QX4 (US$35,550), essentially a re-badged Pathfinder, priced itself out of contention. What's more, the RX 300 had respectable fuel efficiency, getting 19 mpg (8 kpl) in the city and 24 mpg (10 kpl) on highways. "We think [vehicles like the RX 300] could be the mainstream car of the future," Lexus marketing chief Steve Sturm said with great foresight.[29] Following a preview and test drive for the media in the snowy mountains outside Vancouver, Canada, the RX 300 was unveiled at the Detroit auto show in January 1998 and went on sale in March alongside its bigger brother, the LX 470. Early reaction was generally supportive, though some critics didn't seem to know how to react to the half-breed vehicle. "For better or worse, Lexus has built us a sport ute for people who'd rather be driving a car. If that's you, give it a look," said *Newsday*. "[But] this is not a truck, and it comes up short, literally and in other ways, when you stack it up against the best-seller in this class, the Ford Explorer. Not in strict performance parameters, though. The Lexus offers an inch more ground clearance — 7.7 inches."[30] A writer for the *Detroit Free Press* wrote this of his initial impression of the RX 300:

"I admit to a disdainful snort when I encountered the idea of an 'on-road sport-utility', a term that applies to the new Lexus RX 300. After all, this rugged-looking breed traces its lineage to a single primal progenitor, the World War II Jeep, a small-scale brute that could go just anywhere and do just about anything. So the notion of a sub-species that, by definition, has pretty much the same limits as an ordinary passenger car seemed heretical. But that was before I met the RX 300. And since making its acquaintance, I'm beginning to think that the on-road concept makes sense. For one thing, the percentage of sport-utilities that actually trundle over anything more irregular than a gravel road is tiny...Even though the [Mercedes] ML 320 still ranks as a trend-maker, the RX 300 moves the sports-utility needle just as much. Maybe more."[31]

Not all commentators were so impressed, however. *USA Today* said the "boring" RX 300 had "the pizzaz of a minivan, the handling of a tall car and no sense of beefy truckishness at all".[32] While *Consumer Reports* criticized the RX 300 for "imprecise and numb steering", it wound up calling it "a neat crossbreed of SUV and station wagon". This was positively glowing compared to the magazine's comment on the rival Infiniti QX4, which it castigated as "a wimpy cargo-carrier that's too slow, too thirsty and too cramped".[33] Whatever the experts said, the RX 300 soon began to make its mark among the car-buying public. First-year sales clocked in at healthy 42,191, not far short of the 48,644 ES 300s sold. The buying was stoked by a series of clever Team One ads using Cirque du Soleil performers on ice skates — a loose tie-in to the 1998 Winter Olympic Games. A follow-on ad campaign, also using the circus performers, was darker. This played off the GS's "Something Wicked" theme and depicted the capture of a "wild" (and apparently driverless) RX 300 in a forest glen. The vehicle was shown being impounded in a rogue encampment by freakish, fire-breathing circus types led by a madman in a Napoleonic hat. But the valiant RX 300 manages to escape and roam free once again, leaving the circus madman shrieking after it: "Bring me its head! I want it now!" Car buyers liked the corniness, but some general managers and owners of Lexus showrooms reacted strongly against the campaign. "The dealers accused us of devil worship and complained that their kids burst out crying every time the ads ran on TV," said an exasperated Tom Cordner.[34] Soon after, Team One dished up lighter fare for the RX 300, but TMS was pleased with the reception to it and other product roll outs. "Not to sell short our marketing effort, but it really has been a product story," said Bryan Bergsteinsson, who succeeded Press as Lexus Division chief in April 1998.[35] By then, the RX 300 was a smash hit and the new GS 400 and LX 470 were turning in impressive sales figures as well. Lexus reclaimed its place as the No. 1 luxury import, simultaneously displacing Cadillac as the overall best-selling luxury car in the U.S. Sales of the RX 300 and LX 470 alone accounted for one-third of the brand's total volume. In 1999, *Motor Trend* magazine declared the RX 300 the Sport/Utility Truck of the Year. And the number of RX 300 models sold that year nearly doubled, to 73,498 vehicles, far outpacing the 45,860 total for the ES and positioning the RX 300 as the brand leader and one of the top-selling luxury imports overall.

Today, the RX 300 is as ubiquitous as traffic lights. But back when the vehicle made its debut, it caught on most with car-buyers who liked its uniqueness. "It seems like everyone and his brother has a Jeep," said Peter Giles, who traded in his Jeep for a RX 300 in September 1998. "I wanted to break away from the pack."[36] One survey showed that 56% of RX 300 buyers were first-time Lexus — and Toyota — customers, almost double the industry average and also well above the Mercedes ML 320.[37] What that meant was that car-buyers were abandoning other brands for Lexus-style luxury at a much higher than average rate. By the time that competitors awoke to the explosion of the luxury-crossover market and began producing rival products such as the Acura MDX and BMW X5, Toyota Motor was hard at work on the second — and then third — generations of the popular vehicle line. Americans were in love with the Lexus entry-level luxury SUV.

GROWING PAINS

The RX 300 was the catalyst Lexus needed to catapult itself back to the top of the luxury imports rankings and also to take the crown, in 1998, as the overall best-selling luxury brand. Thanks largely to the RX 300 and to the ES 300 sedan, Lexus sales reached 185,890 vehicles by 1999, almost double the number sold just two years earlier. TMS felt comfortable enough to tinker with the Lexus Division's old standby tagline, changing it to "The Relentless Pursuit of Exhilaration". Indeed, it was a time for celebration. Lexus was 10 years old and stronger than ever. In a fit of exuberance, the TMS unit threw a party for itself at the 1999 Detroit auto show. The "Lexus Lounge" area in Detroit's Cobo Hall convention center was stocked with champagne and chocolate-dipped strawberries. And in front of the world's automotive press, division manager Bergsteinsson rattled off a Top 10 list of accomplishments in a performance worthy of late-night television comedian David Letterman:

TEN: Deep pockets — Let's face it. Toyota has them.

NINE: Pushing the envelope — sure, Toyota was known for great econoboxes, but luxury cars?

EIGHT: No rocks or trees — Lexus's marketing and brand management have been exceptional.

SEVEN: Outstanding public relations — Jim Olson and his group think they deserve credit.

SIX: Great leadership — If Jim's going to take credit, so am I.

FIVE: If we build it, they will come — We took a chance on a car-based SUV, and the RX 300 has been selling like hotcakes.

FOUR: Baby boomers — We all think they're so smart, but the truth is affluent baby boomers are driving the luxury market.

THREE: No plaid jackets — Now, I'm not picking on plaid jackets, but we avoided that stereotype of salespeople and established the best dealer network in the world.

TWO: We're really, really nice to our customers.

...And the top reason Lexus has grown from a question mark to a benchmark...

ONE: It's the product, stupid. Lest we sales and marketing guys think we can do it on our own, the fact remains that it all starts with outstanding products.[38]

Yet, as with any adolescent, signs of growing pains were becoming more apparent for the brand. Lexus tied with GM's no-haggle Saturn brand for first place in J.D. Power and Associates' Sales Satisfaction Index in 1999, but then slipped into second place behind Saturn the following year. Unlike the crisis of the mid 1990s that had gripped the brand when sales dropped, this time the problem revolved around having too many sales. Lexus dealers were having trouble servicing all the cars they sold, especially since the planned expansion of the number of dealerships had been delayed and cut back. By 2000, just 16 showrooms had been added to the dealer network over the previous five years at a time when sales had more than doubled. The upshot was that Lexus had the highest unit sales-per-dealer of any auto franchise in the U.S. The dealers, of course, couldn't have been happier with the money, but long wait times and other inconveniences were beginning to tarnish the brand's image. "It was easy when we just had the ES 250 and LS 400, but we've strained a bit with this growth," said Bergsteinsson. "I'm wary of [of claiming that] every customer is treated the way a Lexus customer should be treated."[39] A toll-free customer-service line, for example, had waiting times so long that many callers simply hung up before reaching an agent. The Lexus Division was being stretched to the limits. Yet the national marketing campaign plowed on, setting up million-dollar "ride and drive" events to woo ever-more new buyers to the brand with the prospect of free rides, fancy canapes and Latin jazz. At one event on a former Marine Corps base in Orange County, Lexus invited 2,500 owners of rival marque luxury vehicles, using lists provided by magazines such as *Gourmet* and *Vogue*. The joy rides came sans sales pitch, but Lexus officials monitored these potential customers' every move with bar-coded guest badges and an advanced computer-scanning system.[40]

Back at the dealership garages, though, tempers were flaring. "Customers were telling me that Lexus was getting arrogant," said Tony Fujita, who became head of service, parts and customer satisfaction in 1997 after a 20-year career at TMS. "[Customers] were second-guessing their [own] purchasing decisions [to buy a Lexus]."[41] To cope, the Lexus Division encouraged dealers to open more satellite branches to service clients and began dispatching more highly trained engineers from Japan to regional field offices in the U.S. for troubleshooting on the front lines. "We'd rather have our existing dealers make the dollar commitment with bricks and mortar, to concentrate more on the processes than [on] having a better cappuccino machine," said Bergsteinsson.[42] At the same time, TMS asked the head of quality control at the factory in Tahara, Kazuo Umemoto, to redouble efforts to clamp down on defects and glitches in production that were affecting sales in the U.S. Here, too, the problem was one of too many customers chasing too few cars. With all six Japanese factories making Lexus vehicles reaching maximum output, it had become difficult to maintain the same high standards everywhere. To counter this, Umemoto set up a cross-checking body called the

Lexus Quality Improvement Committee. The committee was tasked with serving as a liaison between the plants in Japan and customers overseas by inspecting factories and meeting with dealers and clients.[43]

Despite these wrinkles, the brand continued to thrive amid an unprecedented expansion of the luxury-car market. Lexus was selling — and generally selling well — in 35 countries around the globe. "We want Lexus to be synonymous with luxury, whether it's in the U.S., Europe, Australia, Asia or anywhere else," Bergsteinsson said at the 2000 auto show in Detroit.[44] More people than ever before aspired to own a prestigious car, and the longest period of economic growth in the U.S. since World War II meant that more Americans than ever before could actually afford it. Soaring pension funds and real-estate prices in the U.S., coupled with high employment and low inflation, were the ingredients for what economists called a "Goldilocks economy" — not too hot and not too cool. To steer car-buyers newly flush with cash to Lexus showrooms, the division spent US$183.7 million on advertising in 2000, according to a consultancy that tracks ad spending.[45] Having the world's largest economy firing on all cylinders helped fuel growth around the world, and even pulled Southeast Asia and Russia out of financial crisis. It was a golden age for luxury. And it wasn't just the German and Japanese brands that basked in the new affluence. Cadillac, Lincoln and Jaguar also saw sales start to take off, albeit at a slower rate than their overseas rivals. The overall luxury market in the U.S. grew from a low of 1.03 million vehicles in 1995 to 1.66 million in 2000 as baby boomers began to help themselves to a larger slice of the good life. "Baby boomers have always been a relatively self-indulgent generation," GM Cadillac division chief John Smith said in 1999. "Now that they're becoming empty-nesters, the luxury segment is benefiting."[46]

THE LEXUS LS 430

Lexus was doing very well in its entry- and mid-level products, but the flagship LS 400 was becoming a little outmoded. The second-generation car had never been all that well received and U.S. sales dropped steadily in the late 1990s, the luxury boom notwithstanding.

LS 400 sales were 20,790 in 1998 and then 16,357 the following year. By 2000 sales had slipped to 15,871 — the lowest since the LS line was introduced in 1989. A new model was needed and, this time around, TMS and Toyota Motor were determined to get it right. This meant refining what was quite possibly already the world's most refined car — not an easy task. Engineers in Toyota City made a careful study of other realms of the luxury world — from five-star hotels to luxury jets — and replicated the skills of the finest jewelers, watchmakers and even guitar-makers.

The work was carried out under the orders of chief engineer Yasushi Tanaka, the spiritual heir to LS 400 godfather Ichiro Suzuki. Tanaka's team evaluated 16 different full-scale prototype models before settling on a design showcasing a new, more distinctive front grille, taller body profile and larger truck. It was still very conservative, but not numbingly so. Not only did it boast a more handsome face and muscular silhouette, but the new LS came with some impressive aerodynamics as well — a tough feat given the original LS 400's already low coefficient of drag (Cd). The third-generation LS was put to the ultimate test in the same wind tunnel used to evaluate Japan's famed *shinkansen* bullet trains, which can reach maximum speeds of 275 mph (443 kmh). The product was another record in automotive aerodynamics — a Cd of 0.25, the lowest of any sedan in the world. The low Cd ratio further reduced the road and wind noise, making the cabin "as silent as a medieval chapel", in the words of one specialist magazine.[47] Under the hood, the LS 430 contained a new 4.3-liter V8 engine capable of roaring from 0-60 mph (0-97 kph) in just 6.2 seconds. Also new was a "torque-activated", electronically controlled, six-speed transmission for more-seamless gear-shifting. The objective this time was to take on the Germans in the one area where the LS 400 had never dared to venture: raw handling. Tanaka's goal was to "exceed the competition from Europe in terms of handling and stability".[48] Inside, amid swathes of top-grade leather and state-of-the-art instrumentation, a dash-mounted six-disc CD changer was standard, as was the advanced air-purification system. "In addition to the usual luxury-car stuff, it comes with a water-repellent windshield, a power rear-window shade, and enough wood trim to build a canoe," said *Car and Driver*. "And if these aren't enough, there's an Ultra Luxury option package that tosses in a variable air-suspension system, an adjustable rear seat, and enough bells and whistles to start a marching band."[49] That was to say nothing of the mini-refrigerator for keeping drinks chilled, which was no doubt a nod to an innovation pioneered for upscale taxis in Japan.

The reception from the auto press was unanimous: Lexus had a winner. "The car is Lexus' latest offering from the 'Relax, we've thought of everything' school of design," proclaimed *Road & Track*.[50] What's more, in a rematch of a fight first fought 10 years before, the LS 430 also handily beat its erstwhile Japanese competition, a new Nissan Infiniti Q45. That car, which still had an analog clock enshrined in the center of its console, featured a 4.5-liter V8 with a five-speed transmission, which was sufficient to propel it from 0-60 mph (0-97 kph) in just under six seconds, bettering the LS 430's 6.2 seconds. But the race out of the showroom wasn't even close. It no doubt helped that, once again, the LS 430 was the first out of the gate, with sales starting in October 2000, well ahead of the new Q's launch the following April. At the end of 2001, LS 430 sales in the U.S. hit 31,000 — double the previous year's total and well ahead of the 5,726 total for the Q45. By then, Lexus had won not only that battle, but also appeared to have won the war. Toyota Motor's luxury-brand sales in the U.S. reached 223,983 — or 13.6% of the luxury market — in 2000, compared to just 71,365 for Nissan's Infiniti line and Honda Acura's 170,469.

LEXUS'S BMW PROBLEM

As good as this was for Lexus, the brand had a nagging problem — an aging demographic — which was beginning to threaten its image. Baby boomers were great for business, but they certainly weren't cool. What the brand desperately needed were cars with youth appeal to attract a younger, wealthier crowd. "Frankly, these buyers may not have considered purchasing a Lexus in the past, and we're anxious to introduce them into the luxury family," said Bergsteinsson.[51] Toyota Motor's answer was the IS 300, the Lexus Division's challenge to the primacy of the racy BMW 3-Series. It was the second pillar, after the LS 430, of a "Triple Crown" project to make the brand more snazzy and appealing. To develop the car, Toyota Motor appointed Nobuaki Katayama, a veteran of the company's Le Mans sports car and World Rally Championship programs, as chief engineer. The wedge-shaped sports sedan over which he was given charge featured a low-slung air dam up front to improve aerodynamics and standard fog-lights — always a magnet for young, car-loving males. The interior had the hallmark touches of Lexus luxury, but also a snug cockpit with highly stylized controls. These included oversized speedometer and tachometer units bulging out from the dashboard behind the wheel. The car's double-wishbone suspension provided a comfortable but secure ride akin to — but not quite in the same league as — the BMW 3-Series.

In fact, the IS program was something of a band-aid approach to Lexus's "BMW problem" in the U.S. and Japan. The car was actually first introduced in 1999 as the non-luxury Altezza model in Japan, where it was voted Car of the Year. A 2.0-liter-engine version called the IS 200 appeared in Europe months ahead of the July 2000 launch in the U.S. And the very name of the car was shorthand for International Sedan. Yet the main market for the car was always intended to be North America. An entry-level sports sedan on par with the more sedate ES 300, the 3.0-liter inline 6-powered IS 300 was priced at US$30,995. Although this was a couple of thousand dollars cheaper than the BMW 328i, the automotive press wasn't uniformly impressed with the IS 300. What rankled the experts most of all was the lack of a manual gearbox, a depressingly common characteristic of the Lexus brand as a whole and a particularly damning one for a sports sedan like the IS 300, which was hoping to challenge the Bavarians. "Don't bring a knife to a gun fight," admonished *Car and Driver*. "That's the advice offered in the movie *The Untouchables*, and you have to wonder if the guys at Lexus missed that part. The weapon they could have brought to a showdown between their new IS 300 and the quick-draw BMW 328i is a manual transmission."[52] The car did win plaudits for tight cornering in low-speed driving, but critics pointed out un-Lexus characteristics such as a noisy cabin and rear-end drift at the high-speed cruising it was purportedly made to handle with aplomb. Nor, it should be noted, did *Car & Driver* like the gearshift knob, which it described disdainfully as "a chrome ball that could be at home in a [Chrysler] PT Cruiser".[53] What's more, its fuel economy rating of 18 mpg (8 kpl) in the city and 23 mpg (10 kpl) on the highway was less than both the BMW 328i and Mercedes Benz C320 Sport. *Road & Track* was more generous with its praise, calling the IS 300 "the unofficial sedan of Generation X". "The shift knob and climate controls look as though they've been lifted directly from a Ferrari Testarossa — bold and very Italian-looking." But it, too, noted that "one chink in the IS 300's otherwise pristine armor is the [automatic-only] transmission".[54]

Team One sought to overcome those reservations with a slick, post-modern marketing campaign under the tagline: "The New Lexus IS 300. Sufficiently Radical". One television ad had a camera trained on the car's distinctively round tail lamp for almost the entire 30 seconds, as gears were heard shifting briskly on the soundtrack. Captions on the screen flashed by: "Look. A Tail Lamp. No Skidding Across the Desert. No Racing Against Cheetahs. No Jet Plane Metaphors. Just a Tail Lamp. Nice, Isn't It?" Other ads in the series did the same close-ups of the gas pedal, speedometer, the "chrome ball" gear-shift knob and front left wheel. Gearbox imperfections aside, the IS 300 did draw a following, selling 15,540 cars in 2001 and 22,486 in its first full year of release. That was enough for Toyota Motor to declare victory of a sort, even though those numbers fell well short of the Lexus Division's forecast of 25,000 a year.[55] But the car was a smashing success at hitting its target demographic. Buyers of the IS 300 in its debut year had an average age of 39 years and earned US$106,000. The average age fell to 33 in 2001 and then to 31 in 2002. By 2004, the IS 300 could brag of a 29-year-old average buyer, by far the youngest demographic in any luxury segment. This was also below the average age for Scion —Toyota Motor's third and youth-oriented brand, which was introduced to the U.S. market in 2003.

PARLEZ-VOUS DESIRE?

The third component of the "Triple Crown" program was also known as the "Crown Jewel" of the Lexus brand — the 4.3-liter, V8, SC 430 sports coupe — which made its debut at the North American International Auto Show in January 2001. The long-anticipated upgrade of the SC 400 was the brainchild of chief engineer Yasushi Nakagawa. He decided early on that the car would be built as a convertible, not artificially altered from a coupe base by cutting off the top. "To be successful, the car needed to look as good as a coupe as it did as a convertible," said Nakagawa.[56] Notably, the SC 430 was engineered so that people could speak or listen to the car's stereo at normal levels even with the top down. In charge of styling were two men from Toyota Motor's European design center in Brussels: the chief exterior designer, Sotiris Kovos, and the chief interior designer, Satoru Kuno. For styling cues, Kovos led a study tour of the French Riviera for several weeks so that his team could draw upon first-hand knowledge of the finer things in life: from architecture to fashion to food. In particular, his design for the SC 430 was influenced by the luxury yachts moored off the French Cote d'Azur. Short overhangs and 18-inch (46 cm) wheels gave the SC 430 a bold stance, which was paired with a sleek bonnet and prominent grille. But the most notable feature by far was the automatic retractable aluminum-alloy hardtop, which folded down in a mere 25 seconds at the push of a button. With the top down, Nakagawa wanted the SC 430 to speak volumes, with rich appointments such as ample burled walnut and bird's-eye maple trim and a special grade of leather called "Comfort Nappa", made for Toyota Motor by German leather manufacturer Bader. It came with most luxury features as standard, with only a US$2000 navigation system, a US$440 rear spoiler and US$400 run-flat tires offered as optional extras. Despite the car's considerable girth — it weighed in at 3,870 lb (1,755 kg) — it was quick off the mark (0-60 mph [0-97 kph] in 5.9 seconds). But critical opinion was lukewarm. The SC 430 had a lot to live up to after the SC 400 design of the early 1990s. By some measures it passed muster in front of a tough crowd. "Exquisite from some angles and downright weird from others, the SC 430's shape nonetheless is refreshingly bold. Hats off to Lexus here for pushing the envelope," was *Road & Track*'s assessment.[57] Others hated it. Years later, the car was still under attack in some sections of the automotive press. "The bloated SC 430 is an unfortunate interpretation of what some Toyota designers on safari in the south of France thought would appeal to the nouveaux riches in Newport Beach," one columnist wrote later in *Automobile* magazine.[58]

The car's target demographic was a decidedly more wealthy, if not an especially young, group with an average age of 48 and an annual income of US$170,000. Although a left-hand-drive version, known as the Toyota Soarer, had been introduced in Japan six months earlier, the SC 430 went on sale in the U.S. on March 15, 2001. While not exactly cheap at US$58,455, it was priced below both the Jaguar XK8 convertible and the Mercedes Benz SL 500. Team One came up with a well-publicized ad campaign spoken entirely in French (*"Parlez-vous desire?"*). Mixed reviews (of both the ads and the car) aside, demand for a Lexus convertible was so great that dealers pre-sold 7,000 even before they arrived in showrooms. "Ever since I took over as head of Lexus, I've been asked 'When is Lexus coming out with a convertible?' Customers ask me, business associates ask me. Heck, I even get cornered at cocktail parties by anxious friends," Bergsteinsson joked at the New York auto show prior to the SC 430's long-awaited launch. "Now I can breathe a little easier."[59]

In the space of just three years, the Lexus Division had its "Triple Crown" and had gone a long way to rejuvenating the brand to keep it at the head of the pack. Yet Toyota Motor hadn't finished reinventing itself to stay one step ahead of the competition. The brand's Achilles' heel was still an unshakable sense that Lexus lacked passion and a true sense of place in the automotive pantheon. Its brand heritage was amorphous and shallow. In a sign of both the confusion at TMS and the Lexus Division's search for a stronger identity, the tagline changed once again; this time to "The Passionate Pursuit of Perfection".[60]

CHAPTER EIGHT

LEXUS NATION

In the 2002 movie *Minority Report*, set in the year 2054, Tom Cruise plays a police officer who becomes a fugitive after being wrongly accused of a crime. He seeks refuge in a futuristic Lexus plant located outside Washington D.C. After eluding his pursuers in a wild chase through the entirely automated plant, where robots assemble futuristic cars that use electromagnetic superconductivity to hover above the ground, Cruise hides in the cockpit of one of the low-slung and shiny maglev pod cars — just as it glides into the paint shop for its carbon composite body panels to be sprayed by a robot. The episode is fanciful, but not because of the automation. Toyota Motor's newest facilities today boast robotic welding ratios of 95% and wholly computer-operated high-tech paint guns. Rather, the most fictional aspect of the movie — at least at the time of its release — was the location of the Lexus plant. For the first 13 years of its existence, the Lexus line-up had been made exclusively in Japan. Since that Hollywood film was released, however, the company doctrine that Lexus vehicles were to be made in accordance with exacting *mono-zukuri* standards found only in Japan no longer holds. In a bid to show that it can meet its own high quality standards anywhere it produces and sells cars, Toyota Motor started up its first Lexus production line outside Japan on September 26, 2003.

Located an hour's drive west of Toronto on the rural outskirts of Cambridge, Ontario (population 113,000), the plant chosen for this operation had first opened as a Corolla factory in 1988 and added production of the Solara and Matrix in later years. Notably, the Cambridge plant had won seven J.D. Power Awards for Plant Quality, including four gold. "It was a huge decision for Toyota to move Lexus outside Japan," said Réal Tanguay, president of Toyota Motor Manufacturing Canada Inc. and head of the Cambridge plant. "In the 1990s, if you'd asked the Japanese [to do this] they would have said no. But Toyota's North American manufacturing base has grown up along with its suppliers. And so the confidence level at Toyota Motor has increased."[1] To prepare for its new assignment, the company invested some US$450 million in equipment and facility upgrades at the plant. The welding line boasts 256 robots, which apply all but 5% of the welds — fairly standard for a Toyota Motor factory. Among the things that make Cambridge stand out, however, are the five *matahan*, material-handling robots, which stand twice the height of a man and lift cars onto overhead conveyor belts for delivery from the assembly line to the paint shop. Cambridge is one of the first plants outside Japan to get these US$130,000 mechanical monsters, which workers have christened with nicknames such as "Godzilla", "Rodan" and "Mothera." Cambridge also boasts the holy grail of Toyota Motor's new Global Body Line system — a yellow and green spider-like device known as the m-jig (or "master" brace). Suspended from the ceiling and lowered down into the roofless car chassis, this piece of equipment holds the frame together as it is welded by 16 robots. The m-jig not only saves the cost of developing and maintaining a fleet of braces, but also allows greater precision since only the master brace need be recalibrated for any changes that might be required. According to Atsushi Niimi, president of Toyota Motor Manufacturing North America, "the end results are improved quality, shortened welding lines, reduced capital investment, and less time [required] to launch new vehicles".[2]

But the true jewel of the Cambridge plant is its new US$200 million paint shop. The 270,000 square foot (25,000 square meters) shop is broken down into three zones, each a concentric circle designed to cut down on airborne contaminants. In some respects, it looks more like the inner sanctum of a biohazard laboratory than a wing of a car plant. Metal grate floors are installed above running water in its passageways to catch any grit that escapes the specially treated dust-collecting nets that hang from the rafters. Technicians wear anti-static coveralls and bathe themselves in air showers that remove even the smallest particles. The vehicles themselves are subjected to an even more intense regimen to remove dust and dirt. Each body shell is washed for as long as 30 minutes and the runoff is collected and analyzed to measure the amount of solid particles shed. (If it ever exceeds four grams, the assembly shop is called to account about the excess grime.) The vehicles are dipped in a phosphate solution and then given an "electro-deposition" protective coating. The newly cured body shells are then dried in a baking oven and inspected for defects. A sealant is applied and this is followed by a coat of spray-on asphalt. The vehicles are blown dry and wiped down with a soft cloth before another coat of primer is applied. Any remaining blemishes are removed carefully with sandpaper before the body approaches the topcoat line. There, electrostatic robot sprayers, spinning at 25,000 revolutions per minute and using specially designed disposable paint cartridges, apply exactly 60 microns of paint. The single-use cartridges eliminate the need for messy hoses. A second coat is applied to give extra luster before the smoothness and color of the exterior are checked by a machine called a Perceptron. On dark-colored vehicles, black lights are used to reveal any smudges.[3] Like a scene from *Minority Report*, Toyota Motor has made science fiction reality.

Impressive as these technical innovations are, Toyota knows from the lessons learned in Tahara that the world's highest-quality luxury cars are not made by machine alone. Some 700 workers selected to work on the Lexus line received 12 weeks of intensive training and 200 were sent for stints in Japan. Only about 20% of those selected had worked on the Corolla production line; the others were new to the company. Toyota sees this lack of previous experience as a plus because it is then easier to teach workers the Toyota Way of doing things without having to counter any bad habits they may have picked up from other car manufacturers. The company prefers to hire people who have had experience in farm work or even stints at McDonald's, both of which instill discipline. That's a common denominator at Toyota Motor plants, from the workers in the gritty milieu of Tianjin, China, to those who grew up among the flowing bluegrass of Georgetown, Kentucky. To ensure that quality levels in Cambridge don't diverge from those at its sister plant in Kyushu, Toyota Motor introduced "Circle L" stations throughout the Lexus production area, which take the company's commitment to *poka-yoke*, or fool-proofing, to an entirely new level. Areas thus designated — most visibly by large hanging signboards — are subject to double- and triple-check mechanisms for the installation of key parts. Electronic sensors on special jigs, or braces, marked with the Lexus logo detect, for example, whether a part has been properly bolted. If there is a problem, a flashing alert light is set off and the line shuts down if it isn't addressed immediately. Circle L quality control is concentrated on items which customers have identified as problem areas, such as the glove box or suspension system. Perfection is the goal. "What we want to avoid is having customers come into showrooms saying: 'I want the Japan-built version'," Greig Mordue, manager of the Cambridge plant's corporate planning office, explained. "Ideally, we want customers coming in to request the Cambridge-built versions."[4]

"WE MAKE THE DIFFERENCE"

The workers in Cambridge seem unusually dedicated to their jobs. Unlike Toyota Motor's Camry plant in Georgetown, Kentucky, there are no dart boards, basketball nets or table soccer games tucked into nooks along the production line.[5] Nor do Lexus workers receive extra benefits or wages for their regimented work on high-margin luxury cars. While workers at other Toyota Motor plants move through two-hour stints at four different duty stations each day, Lexus workers in Cambridge specialize in just two duties, which they do in four-hour shifts. In Japan, by comparison, workers do only one job continuously throughout the day. At times when the Cambridge production line halts temporarily to address a problem, the factory hands busy themselves by sweeping up or putting tools away. There's little idle chatter. Making a Lexus car is considered to be both an honor and a heavy responsibility. "We know that if we can get this right, we may be able to build other Lexus models," said Jason Birt, a 28-year-old Lexus line worker. "That's our goal — to show we can do what no other factory can do."[6] Birt was one of those sent to Japan to work on a test line in Motomachi, Toyota Motor's biggest plant in Japan. He and others recruited for Lexus proved they were more than a match for Japanese *mono-zukuri* expertise, actually beating Japanese teams in quality assessment on a mock production line. "Our vehicles are at least as good — if not better — than Kyushu," said Wayne Warner, general manager of the factory's press and weld shop, who had previously worked at steel plants for 18 years.[7] Yet the shop floor is spared the relentless morale-building slogans that hang from the walls of many other Toyota plants in the U.S. and Japan. At Cambridge, all that can be seen in this regard is a large Lexus seal with a Canadian red maple leaf painted in one corner of the factory floor with the motto "We Make the Difference". And instead of the typical Toyota Motor factory *andon* cords to stop the line when there's a problem and analog scoreboards tracking the daily production, there are push-button, touch-screen Dell PCs and giant flat-panel screens. If an issue isn't resolved within a few seconds, an automatic alert flashes to the pocket-sized Blackberry personal digital assistants (PDAs) carried by plant managers. Line bosses also carry these PDAs linked to the system in real time to get instant updates on the status of any of the workstations along the assembly line.

Despite all of this preventative medicine, glitches can still happen. That's where the Quality Investigation Reports come in. These detail the problem in electronic files, with a brief description of a problem, often with a digital picture attached, enabling the problem to be traced back along the line to be dealt with at its origin. As in other Toyota Motor plants, Cambridge has a "Catch of the Day" program which rewards employees for finding potential problems — and suggesting possible solutions — on the assembly line. This has the potential to save the company hundreds or thousands of dollars by identifying a problem with, say, faulty parts before they are fed into the assembly line and installed. "You treat every car as if it were your own," explained George Wilson, a team trainer on the trim line who has worked for the company for five years.[8] The line keeps parts and finished-vehicle inventory low, in line with a longstanding company policy which dictates that cars aren't produced until orders are received from dealers. Parts are delivered on a just-in-time basis, keeping inventory down to just a 20-day supply — half that of other Toyota branded vehicles and one-third the inventory of German luxury brands. The downside of having such a thin supply line is that a delay in critical parts — for example, a shipment of seats from a supplier — can shut the whole line down for hours. On the other hand, since the assembly line and paint shop are only separated by about 15 vehicles on the assembly line at any one time, when something goes wrong it is often detected immediately and affects fewer vehicles. "At Chrysler, the buffer between assembly and paint was 200 cars, so hours could go by before a problem was detected," said Phil Rodi, general manager of the Lexus assembly line and a former factory engineer at Chrysler .[9]

Fit and finish are accorded the highest priority. After a final four-man inspection for uneven paint or scratches under high-powered florescent lights, the completed vehicles are polished and the carpets are covered in cardboard as a precaution against smudges from workers' shoes. Toyota models produced at the same plant don't get that kind of pampering. What distinguishes the Lexus approach mostly clearly, however, is the gap factor. The spaces between the doors and body frames of the Lexus are kept to within seven millimeters (0.3 inches) — less than half that on, say, a Corolla. The smoothness of the operations at the plant show the effectiveness of the Toyota Way in any culture and language. Commitment to first-rate quality, continuous improvement and the pursuit of perfection transcends national boundaries. Since the Cambridge plant began production, a new vehicle has rolled off the line every 3.3 minutes. In 2004, annual production will reach 60,000, with their engines being supplied by a Toyota Motor plant in West Virginia.

RIGHT ON THE MONEY

The vehicle which Toyota chose for its first "foreign-made" Lexus was the next-generation entry-level SUV, the RX 330. Its design mimicked that of its successful predecessor, but also incorporated sleeker touches, such as a less pronounced incline in the front and rear windows. "It will set the standard for luxury crossover vehicles. Again," declared Denny Clements at the vehicle's unveiling at the 2003 Detroit auto show. "It's just the right size and has distinctive styling that doesn't scream 'soccer mom.'"[10] About 52% of RX 300 owners were female, with an average age of 48. TMS worried that the SUV might simply be perceived in the public mind as a minivan for mothers with money. Seeking broader appeal, the Lexus Division directed the marketing of the RX 330 at 45-year-old males earning US$125,000–US$150,000, with the aim of achieving a 50-50 gender break. Nevertheless, 60% of initial RX 330 owners turned out to be female and the age of the average buyer rose to 52. Yukihiro Okane, who became chief engineer for the RX 330, did his best to instill a more masculine element, upgrading the vehicle with a newly developed 3.3-liter V6 engine, the same as used in the new ES 300. Based on the same platform as the Toyota Highlander, the RX 330 was slightly longer and wider than the original RX 300. This latest version, sold as the Toyota Harrier in Japan, included auto-dimming rear-view and side mirrors, a digital compass and front headlights that turned with the steering wheel to improve visibility around curves — one of the first vehicles with this feature since the Tuckers of the 1950s. Team One ads showed a 40-something New Age man catching a doe in his rotating headlights as he rounds a bend in the road — just in time to stop his RX 330 and smile with relief. At a base price of US$35,000, the RX 330 was about US$500 cheaper than the late-model RX 300. This was mostly a marketing ploy, however, and average prices for models with all factory-installed options ran closer to US$40,000. Something this new SUV did not have — which surprised some critics — was a third-row seat, which by 2003 had became something of a litmus test for family-friendliness. One reason for this may have been to prevent the RX 330 from eating into sales of the more expensive GX 470, a new eight-seat model introduced in

LEXUS: THE RELENTLESS PURSUIT

late 2002. The RX 330 was like a metallic tortoise in more ways than one. *Car and Driver*'s 0-60 mph (0-97 kph) rating of 7.8 seconds was nearly one second slower than the newly launched Infiniti FX 35 crossover. With these potential drawbacks in mind — and notwithstanding the RX 300's grip on 22% of the entry-level SUV market and cumulative sales of 360,000 vehicles — the Lexus Division could take nothing for granted. So the advertising campaign for the RX 330 took a humorous turn, with Team One having a laugh at its competitors' expense. One ad, dubbed "Clean Room", showed what appeared to be Jaguar technicians poring over a RX 330 in a research lab and marveling at its ingenuity. The youngest of the lab workers is seen peering into the optional rear-mounted camera and saying, "Hello, Mum!" Another ad, called "Auditorium", took a dig at Mercedes-Benz by showing an auditorium filled with German engineers listening to their chief sing the praises of the RX 330. A distressed looking board member in attendance then barks "Enough!", with obvious displeasure. Similarly, magazine ads depicted covers of faux European motoring magazines which raved about the new Lexus SUV. One of these, *Uber Auto*, announced in fake German: "Der Neu Lexus RX 330: Fasstensietbeltz! (p.31)."

Critical response to the RX 330 was largely positive, with many reviewers rating it above rivals such as the Cadillac SRX and BMW X3. "Each time you settle into the soft leather seats, turn a precisely calibrated knob or rush through the cacophonous world in soothing near-silence, you marvel at how Lexus makes sophistication seem so simple," said *The New York Times*. Yet, noting the high cost of options, the paper concluded: "Right on the money — for a considerable bit of money."[11] *Consumer Reports*, while questioning its lofty price, gave the RX 330 a coveted "CR Recommend" tag and called it "the most well-rounded vehicle" out of a group of luxury SUVs that included the BMW X5, the Honda Acura MDX, the Nissan Infiniti FX 35 and the Volvo XC 90.[12] The RX 330 was released in March 2003 and first-year sales reached 92,366. Into the first quarter of 2004, sales hit 23,773 vehicles. Much as the next head of the Lexus division, Denny Clements, had predicted, Lexus had, once again, set the standard for luxury crossover SUVs.

Prior to the launch of the RX 330, the Lexus Division introduced two other key products — the updated ES 330 sedan and the mid-luxury GX 470 SUV. The 2004 model ES 330, released in late 2003, was essentially the third-generation car with a bigger, 3.3-liter V6 engine and the same base price. In 2001, the ES had undergone a change that gave it a taller, more streamlined look and a longer wheelbase. Gone was the traditional sloping ES bonnet in favor of a much more highly chiseled and muscular nose. The headlamps stretched well into the hood — making it look as if the car's skin had been pulled back by a frontal blast of supersonic air. And the taillights wrapped around the side of the car like a pair of "high-fashion sunglasses", said chief engineer Kosaku Yamada.[13] The car's initial base price was US$31,505, but few of the extras — which included a California walnut interior trim and leather seats — came standard. Sales of the ES 300/330 remained fairly steady, despite a downturn in the U.S. economy following the collapse of the Internet stock market bubble in 2000 and the terrorist attacks on New York and Washington in 2001. After falling to a five-year low of 41,320 cars in 2000, sales of the new ES jumped from 44,847 the following year to 71,450 in 2002 and held their ground in 2003 at 65,762 cars. This was impressive because, much like the Toyota Camry model in the mainstream sedan market, the ES 330 competed in the most competitive segment in the luxury market.

The other new offering, the GX 470, with a base price of US$45,500, got off to a slower start after its introduction in November 2002. Sales grew from 2,190 over the last two months of that year to 31,376 in 2003 and an average of 2,500 a month in the first quarter of 2004. This newest member of the Lexus SUV family was essentially a re-badged Land Cruiser Cygnus, a vehicle not sold in the U.S. but based on the same platform as the Toyota 4Runner, which came with either a V6 or V8 engine. Inside, the GX 470 differentiated itself from its Toyota cousin with lots of leather and bird's-eye maple. Beneath its bonnet, it carried the same 4.7-liter V8 engine as the more up-market LX 470. The GX 470, which came with an optional third row of seats to comfortably fit eight people, won critical praise from some corners, winning *Four Wheeler* magazine's "Four Wheeler of the Year" award and *4-Wheel & Off-Road*'s "4X4 of the Year" designation. But some critics felt the GX was overpriced. "The GX is a fancy 4Runner with a price premium of roughly US$9,000 to US$16,000 [depending on the options]," declared *The New York Times*, advising its readers to "Take the 4Runner V6 and the [US]$15,000 [instead]."[14] Many car-buyers followed that advice.

THE PARALLEL UNIVERSE

In the Japanese market, the Lexus ES has long sold under the name Toyota Windom; the Lexus GS as the Toyota Aristo; the GX as the Land Cruiser Cygnus; the LX as the Land Cruiser Prado; the SC as the Soarer; the RX as the Harrier and the top-of-the-line LS as the Celsior. The reason for the development of this odd parallel universe was that Toyota Motor never bothered to bring the Lexus Division to Japan, where a convoluted and overextended network of five dealer channels prevented the company from starting up a new brand. While the Lexus Division had been conceived from the outset as a marketing strategy aimed at the U.S. market, this didn't mean that Japanese dealers were any less anxious to get their hands on Lexus models. Although no authorized Toyota Motor dealer could sell under the Lexus name, Japanese showrooms did offer kits made by third parties containing Lexus badges for the front grille and Lexus model names for the rear deck. These do-it-yourself facelifts proved immensely popular among frustrated Lexus fans in Japan. Although essentially the same vehicles, right-hand-drive Japanese versions of Lexus models sold for far less than the same vehicle in the U.S. The latest IS 300 model, for example, sells for about US$30,500 in the U.S. and British markets; but in Japan, where it's called the Toyota Altezza, it cost little over US$13,500. While American Lexus owners were oblivious to this discrepancy, wholesalers in parts of Asia — where right-hand-drive models are the norm and Lexus models are sold for a premium — have taken advantage of an arbitrage opportunity. They began to ship Celsior and Harrier models — and Lexus makeover kits — from Japan to places like Thailand, at a mark-up that was still less than the price being charged locally by Toyota Motor for "real" Lexus models. By the late 1990s, a thriving "gray market" for these faux-Lexus vehicles had sprung up in Southeast Asia to the tune of about 700 vehicles a year, mostly as rebadged RX 330 and LX 470 models. To counter this, in 2001, Toyota Motor set up Lexus Asia Pacific in Singapore to expand sales of official Lexus models. Its initial sales target in 2003 was 300 vehicles, or about 1.6% of the Thai luxury market. This is expected to rise to 1,000 vehicles by 2005, which would still only put a dent in the unofficial Lexus trade. More worrying to Toyota Motor has been the recent growth of a similar gray market in China, where more and more Lexus sedans have been imported from Japan and the U.S. through unofficial channels.[15]

All that is set to change from August 2005 when the Lexus brand finally debuts in its home market as part of a massive restructuring of Toyota Motor's domestic dealer network. The company will offer just four Lexus cars — the next generation of the IS, GS, SC and LS models — as part of an overhaul of all models by 2007.[16] Toyota Motor plans to sell about 60,000 a year in Japan, a figure which will rise over several years to an annual volume of 100,000, at some 180 Lexus showrooms. This long-rumored move comes in response to surging sales of imported luxury brands — notably Audi, BMW and Mercedes-Benz — in Japan. While Toyota Motor dominated the Japanese luxury-car market with 73.7% as recently as 2001, the company has had increasing difficulty meeting the challenge of European brands in its home market. A particular sore spot is newer models that have been aimed at younger buyers but sold under the Toyota brand, which many rich young professionals consider *Ojisan-kusai*, or cars that "reek of older men". One notable failure in this regard was the much-vaunted, Japan-only Toyota Verossa, a BMW "3-Series Killer", which flopped miserably after its introduction in July 2001. With the advent of the Lexus brand in Japan the Altezza, Harrier, Aritso, Soarer and Celsior nameplates will be retired. That should have the effect of deflating the gray market in Lexus vehicles as pricing differentials disappear along with those hoary Japan-only model names.

In the last quarter of 2004, Toyota Motor also plans to launch Lexus in China, the world's fastest-growing car market.[17] It is expected to initially open six dealerships in four cities: Beijing, Guangzhou, Shanghai and Shenzhen — where the wealthiest Chinese live — and eight more by mid-2005. Global Insight Inc., a London-based market research firm, estimates that China's market for luxury cars will exceed 207,000 by 2008, which is 5,000 more luxury vehicles than it forecasts will sell in Japan that year.[18] Toyota is also gearing up for a renewed push in Southeast Asia, where its sales lag behind those of locally assembled German luxury brands. The company sold just 5,000 Lexus brand cars in the rest of Asia outside Japan in 2001. While this was on par with its sales in other parts of the world, such as the Middle East and Australia, it was way behind the market penetration of its European rivals. Sales in Asia outside of Japan reached just 16,400 in 2003, or about 20% of the combined market. Lexus Asia Pacific aimed to increase this to 30% of the market in those five nations, which it has projected will grow to some 85,000 vehicles by 2008.[19]

SCALING FORTRESS EUROPE

As difficult as it has been for Lexus to gain traction in the developing world, it has been even tougher going in Europe. After 13 years of trying to break into the European luxury-car market, Toyota has little to show for its efforts. Sales in 2002 reached a mere 21,156 vehicles — down 11% from the previous year — and ended 2003 only marginally higher. About half of the European total comes from one country —Britain. In Germany, Europe's largest single market for cars, where luxury sales account for 19% of the total, the Lexus name is recognized by only about 5% of Germans.[20] Since European import quotas were lifted in 1998, sales of cheaper Toyota brand vehicles, such as the French-made Yaris sub-compact, have soared. Toyota's non-Lexus sales rose 10% in 2003 alone, to a record 813,010, giving the company 4.7% of the European market. But Lexus hasn't enjoyed the same gains. While Americans like Lexus vehicles for the comfort and dependability, Europeans tend to place more importance on handling, performance and heritage. These have been widely recognized Lexus weak spots. The derivative styling of early Lexus models was greeted with derision in the European auto press and this image as a copycat brand without a distinctive personality of its own has stuck with many car-buyers.[21] Toyota Motor executives in Europe have acknowledged that this remains something of an uphill battle. "Lexus has to establish its own heritage, not just chase BMW and Mercedes," said Tadashi Arashima, who was sent to spread the Lexus gospel in Europe in 2000 and became chief executive of Toyota Motor Marketing Europe three years later.[22]

Toyota has done itself no favors, however, by refusing to follow the recipe that made Lexus a success in the U.S. Unlike the independent franchise system at its American operations, for example, most Lexus models in Europe sell at Toyota showrooms alongside cheaper, down-market models, which makes it difficult for the luxury brand to establish itself as a serious contender in the minds of status-conscious Europeans. There are signs, however, that Toyota Motor has started to make headway with such innovative marketing moves as offering a six-year warranty that includes three years of free maintenance and roadside assistance. This has become a key selling point, since most European luxury brands only offer a two-year warranty. Indeed, Lexus stunned the German motoring world by taking first place in six of seven categories in a 2002 J.D. Power and Associates survey of quality and reliability. Toyota Motor also plans to replace about a quarter of its dealers with retailers who have more experience with luxury brands. The idea is to move Lexus models from shared Toyota-Lexus showrooms into dealerships which deal exclusively in luxury brands.[23] Most importantly, Toyota Motor has plans to start selling diesel-engine versions of some Lexus models, a key concession to the European taste for vehicles that run on fuels cheaper than gasoline. (Fully 90% of SUVs sold in Germany are diesel-powered.) The diesel-engine option marks "a major sea change in our approach to the European market," according to Lexus Europe director Stuart McCullough.[24] Once these changes are made, the company expects its European Lexus sales to reach 60,000 vehicles a year by 2010; by which time it also finally hopes to turn a profit on its luxury operations.[25] Establishing Lexus in Europe is crucial for maintaining the brand's momentum and for enabling Toyota Motor to reach its goal of a 15% global market share by 2010. That's particularly important at a time when BMW is seeking to expand its sales by 40%, to 1.4 million vehicles, over the next four years and overtake Mercedes-Benz as the world's leading luxury brand. "We won't accept the position of No. 2," BMW chief executive Helmut Panke told

BusinessWeek in 2003.[26] This was more than an idle threat, for BMW has already passed Benz in the U.S. market, to establish itself as No. 2 behind Lexus.

To get to the top, BMW planned to launch a new or upgraded model on average every three months through 2005. This push comes at both ends of the price spectrum: having introduced the US$377,760 Rolls Royce Phantom in 2003, BMW was on track to the launch its US$20,000-range 1-Series in late 2004. Lexus Division executives in the U.S. have duly noted the challenge. "I have to give BMW credit for consistency in their message," said vice-president for marketing Mike Wells. The engine and styling variations offered by BMW are, he said, "clearly an advantage".[27] Lexus also has to keep an eye on Nissan's Infiniti line and GM's Cadillac, both of which have enjoyed a resurgence in popularity. Cadillac, in particular, has made a surprising comeback, especially among younger car buyers. At the height of its popularity, at one time one out of every eight cars sold in the U.S. was a Caddy. But from the late 1970s, the brand's sales began to drop and continued to do so for the next 30 years. Now, with a US$4.5 billion revival program in place, GM has succeeded in repositioning Cadillac in the luxury market. The program has included unburdening the brand of some of its historical baggage by dumping some models and renaming others. This resulted in vastly improved quality and a wave of stylish sedans, SUVs and roadsters. In 2003, Cadillac delivered 216,090 vehicles — an 8% increase on the year and its best showing since 1990. In J.D. Power and Associates' 2003 vehicle-dependability study, Lexus took top honors, with just 163 defects per 100 vehicles. Cadillac ranked seventh with 209 defects, but this was below the industry average of 273 and far better than either BMW (No. 13) or Mercedes-Benz (No. 27). Higher quality and improved consumer perceptions have also helped raise resale values. The SRX crossover SUV, which retains about 51% of its original value after three-years, has moved to within striking distance of the Lexus RX 330's industry-leading 58%.[28] This represents a considerable improvement for the brand particularly at a time when arch rival Ford Motor's Lincoln division was said to have lost US$1 billion in 2001.[29] While Cadillac may not overtake Lexus in the near future,

Toyota Motor knows it cannot ignore the resurgence of this American icon.

Similarly, Carlos Ghosn has effected a remarkable turnaround in the fortunes of Nissan's Infiniti brand, sales of which rose by 35% in 2003 to an all-time high of 118,000 vehicles. The Infiniti GS 35 sedan was named *Motor Trend*'s Car of the Year in 2003, and the company enjoyed similar successes with its FX 35 and FX 45 crossover SUVs. Infiniti ranked second only to Lexus in the 2003 J.D. Power and Associates vehicle-quality ratings and, with the launch of the QX 56 SUV and the M 45 sedan in early 2004, the competition is expected to intensify.[30] What's more, many of Toyota's competitors have begun to adopt the simple brand positioning moves pioneered by the Lexus Division more than a decade ago, such as introducing uniform design, logos and layouts in their showrooms.[31]

Under pressure from newcomers at the low end of luxury such as Hyundai Motor, from the revival of mid-tier luxury brands like Cadillac and Infiniti and from the incessant drive by the German to seize the No. 1 spot in the U.S., the Lexus brand's hegemony is under siege like never before. Amid an escalating war of incentives, in early 2004 some Lexus dealers in the American midwest were direct mailing US$500 "gift certificates" toward the purchase of an ES 330 or RX 330. As early as 2001, the Lexus Division seemed to be at a loss about where to take the brand next. While sales remained strong across most models, a certain sense of malaise had begun to set in once again. The brand's dominance in sales satisfaction ratings slipped in 2000. Recognizing there was a problem was half the solution. In July 2001, Denny Clements replaced Bryan Bergsteinsson as general manager of the Lexus Division. While TMS described the reshuffle as a standard personnel rotation, others interpreted the end of Bergsteinsson's tenure — the shortest since Borst's — as a sign that the company was unhappy with the lack of clear direction at Lexus.[32]

THE SECRETS OF LEXUS
Clements was plucked from a job as chief operating officer for Central Atlantic Toyota Distributors Inc., where he'd served since 1991, to

help the brand redefine itself. He had spent the early years of his career at Ford Motor and its Lincoln-Mercury division before joining TMS in 1983. He honed his skills with successful postings as a regional sales manager in Denver and then general manager for New York State. This was followed by a job as a national logistics manager, a key post in Toyota Motor's "pull-system" of fine-tuned inventory management. Clements immediately set out to "figure out Lexus' DNA", in the words of one of his chief lieutenants.[33]

Lexus had managed to reach the top by doing what its more well-entrenched rivals did — only better. But once on top, the brand needed to start thinking less like an imitator and more like an innovator. It needed to stop refining and start defining its own character. In short, Lexus faced an identity crisis at just the time Toyota Motor wanted to turn it into a global brand. In a November 2000 speech entitled "The Secrets of Lexus", Clements was confident that Lexus was "poised to become the world's leading luxury brand".[34] But before Lexus could truly begin to spread its wings globally, it needed to decide how it would distinguish itself from other luxury brands and stop the deterioration in its U.S. customer satisfaction ratings. In 2001,TMS was rattled when Lexus was displaced by GM's Saturn unit after five years at the top of the J.D. Power and Associates study of customer satisfaction and dealership service. By 2003, it fell to No. 3 in the U.S., behind Saturn and Infiniti. That was a red flag indicating not all was well in the world's foremost Lexus nation. To improve service at showrooms, the Lexus Division put pressure on dealers to invest more money on upgrading their facilities. Not all complaints from customers were to do with poor service, however. Some revolved around the unwillingness of most Lexus dealers to offer sales incentives at a time when potential customers were being bombarded by such incentives from other brands.

To begin the process of redefining itself, the Lexus Division brought in an outside consultantcy, Siegelgale, to organize a 13-city tour of "back to basics" sessions for almost 10,000 corporate and dealership employees. The purpose was to boost morale and to warn against complacency. TMS could no longer assume that everybody shared the goals outlined in the Lexus Covenant because, by 2002, just three members of the 200 staff at headquarters in Torrance had been around when the brand was born in 1989. During the tour, there were tutorials on the Lexus Division's history and what had made it so special, and employees were asked to consider ways of overcoming the brand's perceived weak points. "You have to stop and remind yourself of who you are, or else you lose track," said Lexus Division's marketing expert Mike Wells, adding: "Lexus has quality, value and performance, but it doesn't have the absolute clarity like BMW or Mercedes."[35] By 2002, the median age of Lexus customers had reached 52 — the oldest among the top three luxury brands — and this was beginning to have an effect on younger buyers, who viewed the car as being too old and staid.[36] Of course, Lexus was not alone in seeing its demographics change in line with the aging of the baby boomers and it took comfort from the fact that it sold none of the top five cars preferred by the very oldest buyers, but one of the top five bought by the very youngest buyers — the IS 300. This was important not only for attracting new buyers to the brand, but also because older people like to identify with younger car-buyers. According to Karl Brauer, editor in chief of the car-buying advisory website www.edmunds.com, "There is one general rule that people in the auto industry swear by: you can sell a young person's car to an old man, but you can't sell an old man's car to anyone."[37] To keep its brand image fresh, Toyota began planning to boost the Lexus product range significantly and speed up the development cycle. The move was a timely one, reflecting the increasing importance American society put on hipness and vitality. For Lexus and other luxury brands, *Brandweek* noted that "the focus had shifted to younger owners who seek power and performance as much as leather and walnut, and a ride more in tune with fans of the Autobahn than the back nine."[38]

One product issue bedeviling the Lexus Division stemmed from the brand's earliest days: the engineering side of the business operated in standard Toyota Motor fashion. The two vehicle development centers in Toyota City assigned to work on Lexus and other models did so almost independently of one another. Moreover, the Japanese chief engineers with almost total authority over vehicles in their stable had little incentive to tailor their projects to the needs of the U.S.-centric Lexus Division. They still reported to headquarters in Japan — not Torrance — and were responsible for both the Lexus and its domestic equivalents. These divided loyalties led to endless tension between the engineers and TMS. So, in a move designed to make the parent company more responsive to the needs of the Lexus Division, in December 2001 Toyota Motor decided to integrate its luxury-car development programs into one department. It also created a 15-member Lexus Planning Division in Toyota City, carving it out of Toyota Motor's North American division in Japan and giving it lines of authority reaching up — to senior management — and out — to Torrance. The purpose of this was to better synchronize the activities of the brand, from manufacturing to marketing. It was the first time Lexus had been accorded such status as an entity in its own right at headquarters in Japan and signaled its growing importance to the company's global strategy. From within this structure a sharper identity and a new, more muscular product line-up for the company's luxury line is expected to take shape over the next several years. When measured against the development of the US$357,000 Mercedes-Benz Maybach stretch sedan or the US$234,260 Aston Martin V12 Vanquish sports car, the Lexus Division has found itself wanting, a fact acknowledged by its chief, Shinzo Kobuki: "Lexus needs more sportiness...something that's above and beyond the ordinary." [39]

Quite apart from these astronomically priced vehicles, BMW and Mercedes-Benz also offered several sport and saloon models that were more expensive than the SC 430 sports coupe which, at US$62,875 was the most expensive non-SUV in the Lexus range . The benefit of these upper-echelon models had more to do with brand building than sales. Even if relatively few of these vehicles sell, they add a certain mystique and prestige that counter the dilution of a brand's "luxury" tag from high-volume sales of entry-level luxury vehicles. Some in the industry note Toyota is in danger of being left behind as the competition has moved further up the curve toward super luxury. In response, Toyota Motor and TMS plan to augment the Lexus product line as Clements hinted in 2003: "As our next generation of products evolves, we have an opportunity to make the same statement at the high end as we did in 1989 with the LS 400."[40]

Even as officials in Toyota City prepared to reposition the Lexus brand, Clements and others in the Lexus Division were busy dealing with the business fallout from the September 11, 2001 terrorist attacks in the U.S. Their chief concern in the weeks following the disaster was inventory management. To prevent a stockpile of unsold vehicles, Tahara and other plants cut production levels so as not to flood the market with unsold vehicles. "This adjustment helped our dealers achieve a steady flow of cars and SUVs to continue to offer a wide selection to customers, but not so many as to lose the exclusivity that is so important to our brand," Clements explained.[41] To reassure dealers that Toyota was in control of the situation, three teams of executives visited 15 cities in 10 days for meetings with showroom owners and managers to explain that strategy. Despite these precautions, sales continued to climb across all product lines. In 2001, sales grew 8.7% to 223,983 and then climbed to 234,109 the following year. In 2003, the LS 430 was chosen by *Consumer Reports* as its top pick among five leading luxury sedans, including the BMW 745Li and Mercedes-Benz S430, and the Lexus Division celebrated another year of record-breaking sales. Total sales hit 259,755 vehicles, with the figures for the ES 330 and the RX 330 each increasing by 20,000 cars. That marked an overall increase of 11% over 2002 which enabled Lexus to retain its crown as the best-selling luxury brand in the U.S. for the fourth consecutive year.

By then the luxury brand even had its own poster child, Isabella A. McDevitt, whose parents, after realizing they couldn't make it to the hospital in time for her delivery, pulled into a Lexus dealership in Plano, Texas. Isabella was born on July 1, 2000 in the back seat of a LX 450. In choosing a middle name for their newborn daughter, the McDevitts called her Alexus. A year later, the dealership threw Alexus a birthday party and presented her with her very own miniature Lexus car, complete with vanity plates. Indeed, the brand name had developed such recognition and cachet among the American public that, according to the U.S. Social Security Administration, 353 baby girls were named Lexus by their parents in 2000. It was, in fact, the single most popular name taken from any major luxury brand product.[42] Lexus, ill-defined as it was, had crossed an invisible line and become a staple of American culture.

A bout 155 miles (250 km) southwest of Tokyo, hidden in the heart of Toyota Motor's global headquarters campus stands a domed structure that's more reminiscent of a bunker than an office building. The windowless facility, off-limits to mobile phones and recording devices, is enveloped by trees. Like a scaled-down version of Fort Knox, the dome holds the company's most precious assets: its next generation of vehicles. Used for viewing new prototypes in an environment free of angles and shadow, the facility is an appendage to Toyota Motor's global design center. Here, some 650 stylists and technicians plot fender lines on powerful computers, program machines to whittle giant blocks of clay into the profile of cars and trucks, and use advanced three-dimensional holograms to depict virtual vehicles. The curved hallway of the recently renovated, US$40 million center follows the outer wall of the dome and is lined with shelves showcasing dozens of miniature clay models of the company's best-known vehicles. This spills out into a central foyer where meter-long, jelly-bean shaped sculptures lie about in a riot of colors. These plastic baubles were commissioned by Toyota Motor from a New York-based graphic artist and are meant to inspire the designers who work within. But the sculptures also, unintentionally, highlight the schizophrenic nature of a company which produces some 99 different vehicles. "Our line-up is like a series of vibrant colors that stand out up close but look gray when viewed from a distance," said Hideichi Misono, a veteran designer and head of Toyota Motor's new global design management division.[1] Middle-of-the-road styling has helped the company sell products that appeal to a wide cross-section of the car-buying public. But that plain vanilla design can only take a brand so far, particularly where a luxury marque is concerned. "Lexus has been so successful because there's nothing harsh about the design," said Lexus design chief Kengo Matsumoto. "But the flip side is that there isn't much to grab you visually."[2]

Once upon a time, Lexus was an unknown quantity, an image half mysterious and half mischievous. But these days, with some two million Lexus vehicles having being sold, the brand has lost much of its early mystique. Moreover, servicing existing and new customers from a limited, 207-dealer network in the U.S. has dented the brand's reputation for consistent white-glove treatment. No other automotive brand sells so many cars through so few showrooms. Largely to keep its dealers content, TMS plans to maintain a high customer-to-showroom ratio by limiting its expansion to about four or five new dealerships per year. But to meet the growing service needs of its customers, the Lexus Division has won commitments from dealers to spend US$750 million on expanded and improved facilities over a two-year period from 2003. That appears to be the price that dealership owners must pay to prevent dozens of new showrooms from sprouting up on their turf.[3] Already, the number of service stalls at dealers in the U.S. increased from 3,376 in 2001, to 4,171 by early 2004. And the ranks of Lexus technicians grew from 2,783 to 3,746 in the same period. So far, Lexus buyers seem willing to put up with the hassle. But sluggish service isn't the only issue at Lexus. The persistent strength of the yen, and the resurgence of rivals such as Cadillac and Infiniti also present potential dangers for the Lexus

Division. Once the underdog and low-cost leader, the comfortably established brand now must guard against complacency. "We are no longer the upstart, the newcomer," acknowledged division chief Denny Clements, the man charged with seeing Lexus through the growing pains of its teenage years.[4] Indeed, Lexus officials are aware that more must be done to keep their product line up-to-date in the minds of luxury-car buyers, who are increasingly demanding sportier rides and technological innovations. This has raised the bar significantly for all car-makers, but particularly at Lexus, where sex appeal has never been a strength. To its credit, Toyota Motor has become keenly aware of the potential for stagnation at Lexus. Hence the quest for a clearer brand identity in the marketplace and in the design department. "If there is one area where we and our owners see a major opportunity to take Lexus to a new level in luxury, it is in styling," said Clements.[5]

That task of adding some panache to Toyota Motor's lucrative luxury line falls to the company's Global Design Center. And Misono and his design team have drafted a new styling language for Lexus (and six other product groups at Toyota Motor). The overarching theme plays heavily on something called the "J-Factor" — an attempt to provide more gravitas based on Japanese characteristics as opposed to something more derivative of other makes and models. This involves an infusion of Japanese sensibility as interpreted through the lens of a surprisingly diverse staff. "We're looking back to our roots as a Japanese auto-maker," said Simon Humphries, a British-born designer and a key member of Misono's team.[6] Achieving a unified look will require even more cooperation and coordination among Toyota Motor's far-flung network of studios and its multinational team of designers. The Global Design Center has begun living up to its name, with designers from the U.S., Europe and Japan gathering in Toyota City with greater frequency than ever before to exchange ideas. This design philosophy espoused by the center blends old and the new: Samurai aesthetics mixed in equal parts with *anime* quirkiness and video-game high tech. One expression of that is the bB sub-compact, a car popular among 20-somethings in Japan, and which has been re-launched in the U.S. as the Scion xB. But in a Lexus context, this means incorporating what has recently became known in Global Design Center parlance as "L-Finesse", a somewhat oblique concept conjured up to give designers more styling direction without short-circuiting their creative impulses. At its core, L-finesse breaks down into three themes: meeting customers needs before they ask ("seamless anticipation"), incorporating high-tech but user-friendly gadgetry ("incisive simplicity"), and mixing topicality with timeless beauty ("intriguing elegance").

The first manifestation of this effort in concept form showed up on a remodeled front grille fascia, to be shared among Lexus models to give them a more familial look. In 2003 and 2004, Toyota Motor presented a peek at the new face of Lexus in a trio of concept cars — the LF-C entry sports sedan, the LF-X (or HPX) crossover SUV and the LF-S upscale sports sedan. The LF-C, LF-X and LF-S were, in fact, thinly disguised versions of the next-generation IS, RX and GS models, respectively. Each features a low-slung look accented by slender horizontal grille bars on which rests a large Lexus logo. In a departure from classical luxury-car design, the grille has been positioned well below twin sets of headlamps, which are set in slanted grooves on either side. Other notable styling elements include much shorter overhangs which stretch the wheels to the far corners for a sportier look, prominent crease lines alongside panels that hint at an origami influence, and highly beveled shoulder lines running up the sides of the front hood that represent the "sculpted blade" of a shimmering samurai sword. A slightly muted version of the new look first appeared in a production model with the 2006 model year GS 430, which was slated to go on sale in early 2005, and closely follows the design of the LF-S concept. This latest GS was designed to be a more elegant manifestation of the modern mid-luxury sports sedan than its predecessors, with a graceful yet striking profile: a hammerhead shark of cars. Yet some touches struck observers as a little overdone. The 2006 GS 430's push-button ignition hints at a racing car heritage Lexus never had. And the overall look of the car has its detractors. Jim Hall, an analyst at AutoPacific, found the LF-S concept-cum-GS 430, which was shown at the Tokyo Motor Show in October 2003, still to be too highly derivative of BMW sedans, especially in areas such as the shape of the rear door and windows. "It's showing direction for Lexus, which is pretty damn important," Hall said. "But they've also used the two most notable design cues of BMW."[7] In a similar vein, an *Automobile* magazine columnist wrote disparagingly of the 2006 GS 430's new grille, which evolved directly from that on the LF-S: "This GS 430 front end could just as well be on an economy model as on a luxurious sport sedan, which means that despite the excellent proportions of the car, it still lacks the visual authority that a well-realized car should possess."[8]

But even its harshest critics acknowledge that Toyota Motor has started down the right track with Lexus by attempting to inject more passion into the brand. The very fact that these concepts were so close to being production-ready models was a big step forward for Lexus, which had concentrated in the mid 1990s on dreamy concepts which had no chance of being realized commercially. For example, neither the Lexus Street Rod roadster introduced at the 1997 Los Angeles auto show nor the Lexus FLV minivan unveiled at the 1995 Tokyo auto show got beyond the pipe-dream stage. Now, Toyota Motor has become more interested in testing more plausible vehicles to gauge the reaction in the press and the public.[9] In much the same way that the LF-S served as a precursor to the GS 430, the reception given to the LF-C and LF-X were expected to heavily influence the design of the upcoming IS and RX models. Both were expected to be part of a wave of new products due out in 2006 and 2007 which Toyota Motor and TMS hope will put the buzz back in their Lexus brand.

This new product push will also showcase Toyota Motor's lead in so-called hybrid engine technology, which combines the convenience and power of a typical gasoline engine with the fuel savings and lower emissions of an electric engine. The company's first hybrid vehicle, the Prius, was a compact car that went on sale in 1997 in Japan, and from 2000 in the U.S and other markets. Once the system had been perfected with the launch of a second-generation Prius in 2003, the Lexus Division wanted to use the futuristic technology on its up-market range. The result is the 2005 RX 400h, a hybrid SUV scheduled to make its debut in late 2004. This first "green" Lexus, made in Japan like the Prius, will have 20% more horsepower than the RX 330 because of its dual engine structure and what the company calls a "high-voltage power converter". The key selling point won't be the added power, however, but the tremendous fuel efficiency in an SUV. TMS expects the vehicle to run 600 miles (965 km) on a single tank of gas, which exceeds the 27.5 mpg (11.7 kpl) average fuel economy of a compact car, let alone that of a comparable SUV. Moreover, the low fuel consumption reduces tailpipe emissions on a trip from New York to Los Angeles to no more than the amount produced painting a room with a gallon of house paint. The Lexus Division wants to sell 24,000 RX 400h models in its first year on the market — a high target considering that Toyota Motor exported a grand total of 24,583 Prius models worldwide in 2003. Apart from savings on fuel, the RX 400h will test whether car-buyers are willing to pay a substantial premium over the RX 330 for the same amount of comfort and utility. The RX 400h may also face competition from another hybrid SUV — the 2005 Toyota Highlander, which is to be built on the same platform (including the chassis, engine, transmission and rear suspension). TMS positioned the RX 400h to appeal to a slightly older, wealthier demographic than the RX 330 . But even if the RX 400h meets its ambitious sales targets, this would only amount to a fraction of annual sales of the RX 330. Its real utility lies elsewhere. Lexus Division officials have said the RX 400h's chief value to the brand has less to do with its horsepower, fuel efficiency or even environmental credentials, than its role in "delivering a better total package" for the brand.[10] In other words, it makes Lexus buyers and owners feel better. So even if few of the RX 400h actually sell, the fact that Lexus is identified as a progressive brand will comfort those who choose to drive much less environmentally sensitive models such as the LX 470. Whatever the business case, the strong push into hybrids —even at the high end of the market — demonstrates Toyota Motor's long-term corporate commitment to hybrids at a time when many of its U.S. and Japanese rivals remain skeptical about the technology. This, too, has significant public relations value. But Toyota Motor's senior leadership shows every sign of betting on the mass-market potential of hybrids. As late as early 2004, Toyota Motor president Fuji Cho held fast to his goal of selling 300,000 hybrids worldwide in 2005, even though it had sold fewer than 160,000 cumulatively by the end of 2003.[11]

While the RX 400h burnishes Lexus's qualifications as a technology leader, the next stage in its makeover has more to do with making the blood race than with saving the human race. One of the first products due for a tune-up: the entry-level IS 300, which never quite lived up to its billing as a serious rival to the BMW 3-Series. One main reason for this has been that the two versions of the car (sedan and hatchback) compete against 15 variants of the 3-Series, including those from its M brand performance division. TMS has made no secret of its desire to expand the IS line beyond the current offerings and, in early 2004, provided a glimpse of what's to come in the form of the IS 430 "project car". That concept model included a 4.3-liter V8 engine and Getrag six-speed manual transmission. The IS 430, which was built for Lexus by Rod Millen Special Vehicles, showed what could be done with existing technology and components. But the LF-C was even more visionary, with an undercarriage longer, lower and wider than the current IS 300 and all BMW 3-Series vehicles. The future IS displayed an extreme "sculpted blade" hood design with snowdrift-like patterns up both sides, and complex lines etched into the side panels. "We used a combination of convex and concave surfaces to control the balance of light and shadow on the car, which creates this beautiful contrast of having sharp lines within the sculpted exterior surfaces," said CALTY vice-president Kevin Hunter.[12] The interior mixed F-1 racing car minimalism with Fifth Avenue elegance. A trio of round gauges stood out from the aluminum dash behind a rectangular steering wheel, while a neon blue-hued floor pillar (meant to evoke the fluidity of running water) ran the length of the interior between the bucket seats. But the most compelling feature was the LF-C's retractable hardtop, which slid like a giant paper fan into any of four positions at the push of a button. Under the hood, the car packed V8 engine and six-speed transmission, a first for Lexus. Even the Lexus "L" logo on the trunk lit up — in hot pink. Although the company denied that a production version of either the IS 430 or

LF-C was in the offing, it has openly signaled its interest in offering performance-grade and convertible versions of the next generation IS. An early 2004 edition of the company's own magazine for owners left little doubt of the LF-C's role as a template for future production models of the IS: "This striking if unusual sports coupe could be the automotive equivalent of a crystal ball, showcasing the IS series' potential and possibly influencing an upcoming IS series update. And specific features of the LF-C, such as the four-position folding hardtop, could very well make their way into production."[13] In fact, in addition to the standard sports sedan, Lexus has plans to offer a coupe, convertible, all-wheel drive and at least two different engine sizes for the next generation IS. That would be a significant expansion of the IS line and put it on more equal footing with BMW. A long-unfulfilled goal at Lexus has been to boost sales of IS cars from the current 1,000 each month to 5,500, which would put it on par with the volume of the other entry-level Lexus sedan, the ES 330, and go a long way toward expanding the brand's toehold among rich young professionals. "The key to volume growth is the IS 300," said Jim Press at the Detroit auto show in 2004. "It's in a price category where having volume is OK. [And] it's feeder stock for future Lexus purchases."[14] Expanding this franchise is important because unlike the ES, a product earmarked for North America, the IS will join the GS and LS as so-called global models designed for sale worldwide. And to make them truly global, diesel engine and "L-Sports" performance versions are being planned — a draw for buyers in diesel-friendly Europe.[15] New versions of the IS, GS and RX lines fill out the bottom of the Lexus pyramid, much as mid-level luxury vehicles such as the GS 430 and GX 470 stoke demand in the US$50,000 range. Beyond that range, Toyota Motor has planned something very special to serve as a bright lodestar for the famously nebulous brand.

As recently as 2002, the company itself was unsure of just what the core marketing message for Lexus should be. Internal documents actually had a question mark in flow charts showing how the "L-Finesse" brand personality should be translated to a mass market as part of the brand's communication strategy. The Lexus Division seems to have resolved this issue by stressing perfection and passion in equal measure in its makeover of the fleet. Nowhere will this be clearer than in the next generation flagship vehicles, most likely a standard LS sedan and a sportier, "Super LS" model. The latter could be the first in a series of what Toyota Motor has dubbed "image leader vehicles", which include proposals for a 5.0-liter GS sports sedan, a V12-engine RX SUV and a 6.8-liter top-of-the line sports car.[16] Whether any of these get beyond the drawing board won't be known for several years, but a US$150,000-range Super LS has moved fast toward production. Details remain vague, but speculation was rife in 2004 that the car would run on a V12 engine like that used in the Toyota Century limousine (sold only in Japan), or a powerful new gas-electric hybrid, or some combination of both. What seems clear is that Lexus has a very special vehicle in the works. "It's not an issue of if, but when," said Press. "We just need to work out the business case, development cost and volume estimates."[17] Early indications suggested the car would look more sporty than sedate, yet have ample accouterments to pamper the driver and passengers. One two-door clay prototype sported a long nose which resembled a Corvette, chiseled side panels echoing a Mercedes-Benz SLR McLaren, and a sloping tail end similar to a Ferrari.[18] However it looks, the Lexus Division plans to make quite a splash with a vehicle that rivals the impact of the original LS 400 in 1989. "It's going to be a phenomenal product," crowed Clements. "It's going to change the definition of luxury."[19]

Almost two million luxury cars were forecast to sell in the U.S. in 2004, some 270,000 — an industry-leading 14% — will carry Lexus nameplates. But Toyota Motor, as much as it claims not to care about market share or sales targets, has set its sights much higher. Officially, Lexus Division officials acknowledge they'd like to see sales of 300,000 vehicles by 2008. But internal documents show that, in fact, TMS expects Lexus vehicle sales to reach at least 350,000 by that time, and that's assuming no growth in market share.[20] Some industry analysts warn achieving that goal of growing the brand by another third entails more peril than promise. Even amid a growing market overall, they caution Lexus faces special issues related to its lack of heritage.

Too many similarly badged cars could erode an already tenuous sense of prestige affixed to the luxury marque. Adding to the pressure: its chief competitors also want to cross the 300,000 annual sales threshold in the U.S. "They're risking dilution of the brand," said Eric Noble, a consultant at The Car Lab in Orange County, California. "There is no evidence that a luxury brand can sell more than 250,000 units sustainably. That Lexus, Mercedes Benz and BMW are all flirting with the cliff edge doesn't make it any safer."[21]

Not so long ago, a once-fabled luxury brand name from GM was sullied from pushing too much product onto the market in search of too few buyers. The upshot: prices plummeted and demand evaporated. Lexus officials recognize the danger. "Cadillac did 350,000 [vehicle sales] in the 1980s and they still haven't recovered," said Clements.[22] GM itself was responsible for this decline because, along with a perception that quality had slipped, it failed to maintain control of its inventories. Unlike GM, Toyota's modus operandi centers on maintaining two key pillars: high quality and low inventories. It goes back to the essence of the Toyota Motor "pull system", which holds that only enough vehicles will be produced as justified by demand, which is in large measure a function of perceived quality. With inventory in check, TMS has felt confident Lexus can grow organically with the overall luxury market and eat into rivals' share by making a superior product. Greater volume will be sustainable, according to this thinking, as long as car-buyers are willing to pay premium prices for quality. This means keeping true to Toyota Motor's traditional focus on *mono-zukuri*, or making things well. "Lexus is really the purest expression of the Toyota Way," said Clements, noting that philosophy pervades its business relationships. "It creates advocacy. Suppliers tell us they save the best cuts of leather and most highly trained personnel for their business with us."[23]

TMS and Lexus Division officials shrug off dire predictions of diluting their luxury brand. Their confidence stems from the popularity of Lexus vehicles among baby boomers. Fifteen years after the relentless pursuit began, Toyota Motor has positioned Lexus to take full advantage of even greater demand for luxury cars in the coming years. The 1.9 million-vehicle U.S. luxury market forecast for 2004 accounts for 11.4% of an overall auto market made up of about 16.9 million vehicles. That percentage has risen from just 8% in the mid 1990s and industry officials predict it will continue to grow. The reason for the optimism is that the baby boomers — some 78 million people between the ages of 40 and 58 in the U.S. alone — have entered their peak earning years. Someone in the U.S. celebrates a 50th birthday every eight seconds. While most are not wealthy, the generational bulge is expanding the size of the upper middle class — people who are prime candidates for luxury cars. At the same time, the very rich are getting richer. In 2001, Americans in households earning US$100,000 or more each year made up about 13.8% of the population, up from 10% a decade earlier. What's more, record-low interest rates and greater outsourcing of manufacturing of everyday goods to low-cost labor markets such as China mean consumers in the U.S. and many other industrialized nations pay less than their parents (in inflation-adjusted terms) for basics such as food, clothing and shelter. This, of course, means that more disposable income is available to buy a more expensive type of vehicle. Changes in buying trends, too, have shifted over the past two decades in a way that is sure to benefit Lexus. TMS research into customer preferences in the 1980s found that acquiring a luxury product like a car was all about making a social statement. These days, however, luxury buyers place more emphasis on utility, performance and store of value.[24] In other words, luxury-car buyers increasingly want a brand they can trust, first and foremost. And on that score, Lexus delivers. Not only has it accumulated more J.D. Power and Associates awards than any other brand, it also boasts the highest loyalty rate (53%) of repeat buyers in the U.S. Toyota Motor recognizes that this is a valuable asset at a time when many people have begun to question their faith in other institutions, including vaunted car-makers with far longer pedigrees than Lexus. "We live in an era where far too many of our traditional icons of credibility have proven unworthy of our devotion," Clements told journalists at the 2004 New York auto show.[25] While that could be viewed as a veiled jab at Mercedes-Benz, which has suffered from a recent slide in initial quality and customer service ratings, the comments seemed to evoke a deeper sense of longing on the part of car-buyers. Speaking at a Morgan Stanley-sponsored auto conference, Clements elaborated on the Lexus Division's campaign to leverage the brand's goodwill: "Americans are more skeptical these days than ever before of everything from Martha Stewart to terrorism, corporate scandals to political scandals. Our research confirms consumers are looking for a brand they can trust...And that's what we believe is driving our growth."[26]

The subtext is that what Lexus lacks in heritage it has more than made up for in its efforts to meet or exceed car-buyers' expectations. The Lexus logo, unrecognizable 15 years ago, now adorns more than two millions vehicles on the world's roads. It took more than 10 years for Lexus sales to hit the one million mark, but just a little more than another four years to reach two million. And TMS expects its luxury division's sales to reach the three million mark in another three and a half years. The brand has already begun to transcend its automotive origins. Dealers now offer a 30-page catalogue of Lexus brand merchandise — from US$3.00 golf balls to US$60 polo shirts to US$200 pens. Can a spicy Lexus cologne and line of Lexus floral curtains be far behind?

For all the accolades heaped upon the cars themselves, the brand's success has been primarily a testament to the many men and women in Japan, the U.S. and other parts of the world who have sought to achieve what many industry hands thought impossible. People such as engineering master Suzuki and sales guru Illingworth took the precepts of *mono-zukuri* and the simple wisdom of the Lexus Covenant to build up the brand from scratch. They inspired thousands of others at Toyota Motor and TMS to rally around Eiji Toyoda's drive to create a world class car. Even in the years when Lexus was caught in the doldrums, few inside the company questioned the brand's ability to rebound from its setbacks. Lexus prevailed over more established players by obsessing about quality and service. At every juncture long-term goals trumped expediency.

The pride in being associated with Lexus has become as palpable among workers in the Global Design Center in Toyota City as on the production lines in Tahara and Cambridge, or at the Lexus Division headquarters in Torrance and its 200-plus dealerships. No wonder veteran employees in the U.S. still carry around cards printed with the Lexus Covenant in their wallets. Likewise, the storybook success of Toyota Motor's luxury brand has earned a special place in the annals of business. Few other brands have come so far, so fast, in an already-crowded industry. Lexus has joined the popular lexicon. It seems only a matter of time before it wins a place in the dictionary under the definition of the closest mankind has come to automotive perfection.

January 1989	LS 400 luxury sedan & ES 250 entry-level sedan introduced (sales of both models officially begin in September)
May 1991	SC 300/400 sports coupe debuts (sales start in June)
September 1991	ES 300 entry-level sedan replaces the ES 250
January 1993	GS 300 mid-luxury sports sedan unveiled (sales start in March)
November 1994	Second-generation LS 400 luxury sedan debuts
January 1996	LX 450 luxury sports utility introduced
September 1996	Third-generation entry-level sedan, the ES 300, launched

September 1997	GS 400 mid-luxury sports sedan joins the GS 300 (sales start in October)
December 1997	LX 470 luxury sports utility replaces the LX 450 (sales start in March 1998)
January 1998	RX 300 entry-level sports utility debuts (sales start in March)
January 2000	IS 300 entry-level sports sedan launched (sales start in June)
September 2000	GS 430 sports sedan replaces the GS 400/300
October 2000	LS 430 luxury sedan replaces the second generation LS 400
January 2001	SC 430 sports coupe replaces the SC 400 (sales start in March)
September 2001	ES 330 entry level sedan replaces the ES 300
September 2002	GX 470 mid-luxury sports utility introduced
March 2003	RX 330 entry-level sports utility replaces the RX 300
Autumn 2004	RX 400 entry-level hybrid engine SUV launches
Spring 2005	GS 430 mid-luxury sports sedan debuts

Source: Courtesy of Toyota Motor Sales U.S.A., Inc.

E N D N O T E S

CHAPTER ONE - THE TOYODA WAY

1 *Fujin* and *Raijin* are depicted in all their ferocious glory in a famous folding screen painting by early Edo-era artist Tawaraya Sotatsu. The screen is classified as a National Treasure in Japan and is housed at the Kennin-Ji Temple in the city of Kyoto.

2 "Rethinking the Town That Toyota Built; As Carmaker Moves Plants Overseas, Its Japanese Base Fears for Its Future", Ken Belson, *The New York Times*, October 21, 2003, p.1.

3 Text from speech by Teruyuki Minoura, "Toyota Philosophy: The Foundation for Present & Future", August 7, 2000.

4 The Timken Co. press release announcing quality awards from Toyota Motor for Europe, Japan and North America, May 1, 2003, at www.timken.com

5 "Toyota [Internal] Case Study No. 7: Beikoku ni Okeru Rekusasu Furanchaizu Tenkai [Opening the Lexus Franchise in the U.S.]." Toyota Motor Corp. Global Human Resources Department, 1999; pp. 1, 5.

6 *LS 400: The Lexus Story*, 1989, Toyota Motor Sales USA; p.29.

7 Keller, Maryann, *Collision: GM, Toyota, Volkswagen and the Race to Own the 21st Century*, 1993, New York: Currency/Doubleday, p.62.

8 Speech by Shoichiro Toyoda. Delivered on July 20, 1989 at meeting of U.S. dealers (6th Draft copy).

9 "Here Come Japan's New Luxury Cars", Alex Taylor III, *Fortune*, August 14, 1989.

10 *LS 400: The Lexus Story*,op.cit.

11 *Fortune*, August 14, 1989, op.cit.

12 "Toyota [Internal] Case Study #6: LS 400 no Tenkai [Development of the LS 400.]", Toyota Motor Corp Global Human Resources Department, 1999, p.3.

13 Eiji Toyoda, as quoted in preface of *LS 400: The Lexus Story*; p.3.

14 "Lexus Turns Introspective at Seminars", Mark Rechtin, *Automotive News*, December 9, 2002, p.3.

15 As the company's official history says: "Toyota, not wanting to revise its policy of avoiding direct competition with the American automakers, changed its major export car to the United States from the New Corona to the even smaller Corolla as of April 1968…Although Toyota was initially concerned that the Corolla's engine displacement and other performance features might not gain popularity in the United States, these fears were allayed as sales of the Corolla grew rapidly." *Toyota: A History of the First 50 Years*, 1988, Toyota Motor Corp., p.212.

16 Weston, Mark, *Giants of Japan: The Lives of Japan's Greatest Men and Women*, 1999, Tokyo: Kodansha International, p.64.

17 Eiji Toyoda, as quoted in preface of *LS 400: The Lexus Story*, p.3.

18 Wada, Kazuo and Tsunehiko Yui, *Courage and Change: The Life of Kiichiro Toyoda*, 2002, Toyota City: Toyota Motor Corp., pp.187–189.

19 Ford entered the Japanese market in 1925 and built a plant in Yokohama, outside Tokyo. It was capable of manufacturing 8,000 cars a year from "knock-down kits" shipped from the U.S. Not to be outdone, GM followed suit with a factory near Japan's No.2 city of Osaka in 1927, which produced 10,000 cars a year. *Toyota: A History of the First 50 Years*, 1988, Toyota Motor Corp., p.41.

20 Nagoya Newspaper, April 9, 1930 as cited in Wada and Yui, op.cit., p.233.

21 Kiichiro and a colleague later recalled that, in choosing a model for a prototype, "common sense would tell you it's better to choose a Chevrolet". From Corpus of Kiichiro Toyoda's Documents, as cited in Wada and Yui, op.cit., p247. For the DeSoto Airflow reference see Togo, Yukiyasu and William Wartman, *Against All Odds: The Story of the Toyota Motor Corporation and the Family That Created It*, 1993, New York: St. Martin's Press, p. 52.

22 *Toyota: A History of the First 50 Years*, p.61.

23 In an interesting historical twist, it was Japan's growing trade *deficit* with the U.S. by 1931 that prompted the Japanese Ministry of Commerce to reverse its previously welcoming policy toward foreign automakers' operations selling cars made from knock-down kits in Japan. *Toyota: A History of the First 50 Years*, p.43.

24 The other license to manufacture cars went to Nissan Motor Co. Only two were given out then to prevent "chaos" in the budding industry. *Toyota: A History of the First 50 Year*; p.58.

25 As Toyota's official history says of the name Toyota (as opposed to Toyoda): "It simply sounded better." *Toyota: A History of the First 50 Years*, p.65.

26 The Toyoda family's connections with the Mitsui run deep. In 1899, Mitsui & Co. bought exclusive rights to the first Toyoda power loom, which it hoped to use in China. The regional manager of Mitsui's branch office in Nagoya, Ichizo Kodama, put up part of the capital to build Toyoda Loom Work's first spinning mill in 1914. A year later, Kodama's son Risaburo, an accomplished manager in his own right, married into the clan and adopted the surname Toyoda. He then went on to run the family business, a source of unending friction with Kiichiro and his acolytes. In 1935, the head of Mitsui's office in Seattle and later GM-Japan executive, Shotaro Kamiya, was recruited to oversee Toyota's sales and marketing division. To this day, the Kamiya surname is common in the company's upper echelons. *Toyota: A History of the First 50 Years*, pp.28, 30, 32, 62.

27 Togo, Yukiyasu and William Wartman, *Against All Odds: The Story of the Toyota Motor Corporation and the Family That Created It*, 1993, New York: St. Martin's Press, p.77.

28 Toyota and Nissan took over a role previously played by their American rivals. "Ford and Chevrolet trucks requisitioned from Japan played a very active role in the hostilities in Manchuria, and this prompted the (Japanese) government to make a thorough reassessment of its automobile policies." See Wada and Yui, p.73.

29 See"Japan's Big-Three Service Enterprises in China, 1896–1936", by William D. Wray in Duus, Peter, Ramon H. Myers and Mark R. Peattie (eds.), 1989, *The Informal Japanese Empire in China, 1895–1937*. p. 58; *Toyota: A History of the First 50 Years*; p. 33.

30 *Toyota: A History of the First 50 Years*; pp.69–70.

31 Weston, op.cit., p.60.

32 Ibid, p.61.

33 Ibid, pp.61–62.

34 *Toyota: A History of the First 50 Years*; pp.154–158, 203.

35 Togo and Wartman, pp.127, 129.

36 Quote from *Asahi Shimbun*, ed. *The Pacific Rivals*. 1972. Tokyo: Weatherhill; as citied in Dower, John W., 1999, *Embracing Defeat: Japan in the Wake of World War II*, New York: Norton, pp.543.

37 Toyota was, however, slow to trim its dependence on military orders. Procurement from military sources accounted for more than 10% of its total output as late as 1962. See Samuels, Richard J., 1994, *Rich Nation Strong Army: National Security and the Technological Transformation of Japan*, Ithaca: Cornell University Press, pp.141, 163.

38 Weston, op.cit., pp.63–64.

39 Long, Brian. *Lexus: The Challenge to Create the Finest Automobile*, 2000, Dorchester: Veloce Publishing Plc, p.10.

40 "'We Achieved the Dream' In Just Three Years, Lexus Redefined Luxury", *Automotive News*, September 28, 1992, p.16.

41 Phone interview with Dick Chitty, Senior Vice President of Toyota Motor Asia Pacific, October 4, 2002.

42 Phone interview with Jim Perkins, June 3, 2004 "Lexus ES250 and LS400 — Coming soon: Battle of the Titans", *Car and Driver*, Vol. 34. January 7, 1989, pp.138–140.

43 "New Kid on the Dock", S.C. Gwynne, *Time*, September 17, 1990, p.62.

44 Reitzle was quoted in an interview three months after the launch of Lexus in 1989. See *Automotive News* op.cit., p.18.

45 Speech by Denny Clements, "The Secret of Lexus", delivered before the Iowa Better Business Bureau/Integrity Awards Lunch in Des Moines, Iowa, on November 10, 2000.

46 Data on luxury car sales as a percentage of overall car sales in the U.S. from Ward's Automotive, as cited in "Classy Cars: Why Everyone Wants to Make Luxury Autos", Gail Edmondson, *Businessweek*, March 24, 2003, p.63. "PAI Competitive Sales/Inventory Query System" luxury car unit sales and Lexus market share data from Toyota Motor Sales U.S.A., Lexus division.

47 Speech by Shoichiro Toyoda, delivered on July 20, 1989 at meeting of U.S. dealers (6th Draft copy).

48 "PAI Competitive Sales/Inventory Query System" data from Toyota Motor Sales U.S.A. Lexus division.

49 Phone interview with Dick Chitty, October 4, 2002.

50 Toyota's own research also found that, on average, Lexus owners are less wealthy and have lower levels of education than Benz and BMW buyers. See "Lexus' Big Test", Chester Dawson, *BusinessWeek*, March 24, 2003, p.68.

51 Consumer Reports: "A Question of Balance: Luxury Sedans — Five No-Compromise Models with Premium Prices and Different Characters", November 2003, p.56.

52 "Two Days in Boot Camp — Learning to Love Lexus", Wendy Zellner, *BusinessWeek*, September 4, 1989, p.87.

53 "Channel Management: A Framework for Revolution", *Brandweek*, Nov. 15, 1999, p.28.

54 "This Lemon is Certifiable: What A Used-Car Guarantee Really Means", Michelle Higgins, *Wall Street Journal*, September 17, 2003, p.D1.

55 "The Coming Traffic Jam in the Luxury Lane", Wendy Zellner, *BusinessWeek*, January 30, 1989, p.78

56 "Full Court Press; The Success of Lexus", *Brandweek*, July 27, 1998, p.22.

57 Ibid.

58 Interview at Toyota headquarters in Toyota-City with Shinzo Kobuki, August 23, 2002.

59 "Lexus LS 400", P. Bedard, *Car and Driver*, September 1989, pp.50–53.

60 "Lexus LS 400", Peter Egan, *Road and Track*, September 1989; p.117.

61 *M Magazine*, February 1990.

62 *LS 400: The Lexus Story*, p. 3.

63 "Lexus Takes the RX 330 Sport Wagon to the Next Level", Mark Rechtin, *Automotive News*, January 6, 2003, p.28.

64 "PAI Competitive Sales/Inventory Query System" data from Nissan Motor Co.

65 "'We Achieved the Dream' In just Three Years, Lexus Redefined Luxury", *Automotive News*, September 28, 1992, pp.1,16.

66 "Two Days in Boot Camp — Learning to Love Lexus", op.cit., p.87.

67 Comment to author by Toyota chairman Hiroshi Okuda.

68 "Full Court Press; The Success of Lexus", *Brandweek*, July 27, 1998, p.22.

69 "Here Come Japan's New Luxury Cars", *Fortune*, op.cit.

70 "The coming Traffic Jam in the Luxury Lane", *BusinessWeek*, op.cit., p.78.

71 "Surprisingly Mixed Results for Lexus", Larry Armstrong, *BusinessWeek*, January 15, 1990, p.21.

72 *Toyota: A History of the First 50 Years*, p. 189. Note the Cressida was sold in Japan — and in the U.S. until the early 1970s — under the name (Corona) Mark II.

73 Perkins interview, op. cit., Nakajima, Yasuhi. *Rekusasu/Serushio he no Michinori: Saikou wo Motometa Kuruma-hitotachi* ("The Road to Lexus/Celsior: The Car Guys Who Demanded Perfection"), 1990, Tokyo: Diamond Co., pp.30–31.

74 Ibid.

75 "Toyota (Internal) Case Study #6"; p.2.

76 "Here Come Japan's New Luxury Cars", op.cit., p.62.

77 *Against All Odds*, p.196.

78 Dryden, Steve, *Trade Warriors:USTR and the Crusade for Free Trade*, 1995, New York: Oxford University Press, p.271.

79 Ibid, p.269.

80 Ibid, pp.273–274. Prestowitz, Clyde V. Jr., *Trading Places: How We Are Giving Our Future to Japan and How to Reclaim It*, 1988, New York: Basic Books Inc., pp.421–422. Indeed, on the eve of the accord struck between the U.S. and Japan, the Japanese entertained visiting U.S. diplomats with dinner at one of Tokyo's finest restaurants and a geisha dance performance. Naohiro Amaya, the Ministry of International Trade and Industry's vice minister for international affairs, was forced to step down to take responsibility for the unpopular accord.

81 Nakajima, pp.29–30.

82 *LS 400: The Lexus Story*, p.25.

83 Fairlady Z is the name Nissan used for the car in Japan. It was sold simply as the Z in the U.S. The Fairlady prefix came at the behest of Nissan CEO Katsuji Kawamata, who was a fan of the 1964 Audrey Hepburn film *My Fair Lady*. Yutaka Katayama, who pioneered Datsun brand name in the U.S and is known as the 'Father of the Z', thought the prefix Fairlady made the car seem too feminine, so it was dropped. Legend has it that Katayama personally removed the "Fairlady" tags with a crowbar on the first batch of Z cars sent to the U.S. from Japan.

84 "Toyota (Internal) Case Study #6", p.2.

85 "Here Come Japan's New Luxury Cars", op. cit., p.62.

86 Officially, Toyota's first exports to the U.S. commenced in March 1958, when it signed an agreement with an importer and distributor in Hawaii. *Toyota: A History of the First 50 Years*, pp.166–167.

87 The Crown remains Japan's most popular entry-level luxury car. Several grades are sold, the most ubiquitous of which is a stripped-down version which is the preferred model of taxi cabs nationwide. *Toyota: A History of the First 50 Years*; p.167.

88 Ibid, p.167.

89 Taking a back seat to Nissan in the U.S. was especially hard for Toyota to swallow because it came just five years after Nissan passed Toyota to become Japan's single biggest auto manufacturer. *Toyota: A History of the First 50 Years*; p.168.

90 Eiji Toyoda, as quoted in preface to *LS 400: The Lexus Story*, p.3.

CHAPTER TWO - SEARCHING FOR BOBOS

1 Toyota Case Study #6; pp.2–3.

2 Nakajima, pp.33 and 36.

3 *LS 400: The Lexus Story*, p.30.

4 Toyota Case Study #6; p.3.

5 Nakajima, p.37.

6 *LS 400: The Lexus Story*, p.30.

7 Togo and Wartman, p.229.

8 Ibid, p.231.

9 *LS 400: The Lexus Story*, p.35.

10 Toyota Case Study #6, p.4.

11 This was according to Toyota Motor spokesman Mike Michaels. Interestingly, some members of the focus group also mistakenly identified the Honda Accord as European.

12 Togo and Wartman, p.232.

13 "'We Achieved the Dream: In Just Three Years, Lexus Redefined Luxury", *Automotive News*, September 28, 1992, p.16.

14 Brooks, David, *Bobos In Paradise: The New Upper Class and How They Got There*, 2000, New York: Touchstone/Simon & Schuster, pp.10–11.

15 Interview at Toyota headquarters in Toyota-City with Shinzo Kobuki, August 23, 2002.

16 Togo and Wartman, p.232.

17 Toyota Case Study #6, p.4.

18 Ibid, p.5.

19 Italics inserted by author. Togo and Wartman, p.232.

20 Ibid.

21 "36 Hours: Laguna Beach, Calif", *New York Times*, December 5, 2003, p.F4.

22 Nakajima, p.46.

23 Ibid, p.8.
24 Ibid, pp.61–62.
25 *LS 400: The Lexus Story*, p.30
26 Figures on 777 development program obtained from Boeing spokesperson for the company's Everett, Washington-based wide-body airshop, September 25, 2003.
27 *LS 400: The Lexus Story*, p.36
28 Togo and Wartman, p.236.
29 Nakajima, pp.65–66.
30 *LS 400: The Lexus Story*, p.28
31 Toyota Case Study #6, p.5.
32 *LS 400: The Lexus Story*, p.35.
33 Nakajima, p.66.
34 *LS 400: The Lexus Story*, p.35; Nakajima, p.173.
35 Nakajima, p.18.
36 Ibid, p.74.
37 Ibid, p.87.
38 Togo and Wartman, p.236.
39 Interview with Ichiro Suzuki at Toyota headquarters in Toyota-City, October 15, 2002.
40 Ibid.
41 Ibid.
42 Toyota Case Study #6, p.9.
43 Interview with Ichiro Suzuki op.cit.
44 Nakajima, p.87.
45 Ibid, p.77.
46 *LS 400: The Lexus Story*, p.35
47 Frustrations boiled over to the point that Keiji Sumitani, a 29-year old whiz kid charged with actually conducting the wind tunnel experiments, once threatened to resign if the styling mavens didn't back down and allow a traditional spoiler to improve the aerodynamics of the LS. Nakajima, p.100.
48 *LS 400: The Lexus Story*, p.48; "Here Come Japan's New Luxury Cars", *Fortune*, August 14, 1989.
49 Nakajima, p.101.
50 *LS 400: The Lexus Story*, pp.39 and 40.
51 Ibid, p.40.
52 *Fortune*, op.cit.

53 Togo and Wartman, pp.241–243. This account would also have us believe that Hostetter, in a lame attempt to confuse the motorist, turned to his Japanese counterparts and started speaking to them in German. For Suzuki's awkward first encounter with a vanilla shake, see Nakajima, p.196.

54 *LS 400: The Lexus Story*, p.36

55 Long, pp.24–25.

56 Interview with Ichiro Suzuki, op. cit.

57 *Fortune*, op. cit.

58 Toyota Case Study #6, p.12.

59 Long, p.26.

60 Nakajima; p.165.

61 Nakajima, p.19.

62 Long, p.27.

CHAPTER THREE - DEUS EX MACHINA

1 Phone interview with Ichiro Suzuki, February 10, 2004.

2 Dower; pp.94–95.

3 Suzuki interview, op. cit.

4 Ibid.

5 Ibid.

6 Weston, p.44.

7 Suzuki interview, op. cit.

8 Ibid.

9 *Toyota: A History of the First 50 years*, p.186.

10 Wartman and Togo, pp.141, 154.

11 *Toyota: A History of the First 50 years*; p.187.

12 Wartman and Togo; pp.172–175.

13 Suzuki interview, op. cit.

14 *Toyota Case Study #6*, p.13.

15 Togo and Wartman, p.234.

16 "'We Achieved the Dream' In Just Three Years, Lexus Redefined Luxury", *Automotive News*, September 28, 1992, p.17.

17 Nakajima, p.78.

18 Ibid, pp.138–142.

19 Nakajima, pp.137–138.

20 *Toyota Case Study #6*, p.13.

21 Nakajima, p.34.

22 Interview with executive involved in LS 400 launch, February 19, 2004.

23 As quoted in Samuels, pp.116–118.

24 Toyota Motor pulled the plug on the project without ever trying to sell a single engine. The project was halted in 1998 after the company deemed it too heavy and expensive to commercialize successfully. "Toyota Gets the Urge to Fly", Chester Dawson, *BusinessWeek*, August 5, 2002; p.16.

25 Nakajima, pp.143–145.

26 *Automotive News*, op. cit., p.17.

27 *LS 400: The Lexus Story*, p.65.

28 Long, p.33.

29 "Showdown: What Happens When Lexus and Infinity Meet the World's Best?", Patrick Bedard, *Car & Driver*, December 1989, p.42.

30 *LS 400: The Lexus Story*, pp. 62 and 66.

31 Long, p.21.

32 "Long-term test: Life with Lexus 400", Don Schroeder, *Car & Driver*, November 1991, p.164.

33 *LS 400: The Lexus Story*, p.65.

34 "Long-term test: Life with Lexus 400." See Schroeder, *Car & Driver*, November 1991, p.166.

35 Perkins interview, op. cit., Comparative data are official Toyota internal estimates provided in materials handed out during interview with Ichiro Suzuki at Toyota headquarters in Toyota City, October 15, 2002.

36 "Lexus LS 400: Toyota's Prestige-Car Division Raises the Stakes in the Luxury Wars", Peter Egan, *Road & Track*, September 1989, pp.117–123.

37 Schroeder, op.cit., p.163.

38 Toyota Motor Sales U.S.A. Inc., *The Lexus Story*, New York: Melcher Media, p.77., Brooks, David, *Bobos In Paradise: The New Upper Class and How They Got There*, 2000, New York: Touchstone/Simon & Schuster, pp.10–11.

39 "Infinity Q45 versus Lexus LS 400: Orient Express; luxury transport Japanese style", *Road & Track*, February 1990, pp.46–51.

40 "How to Tighten-up That Suspension", Csaba Csere, *Car & Driver*, November 1991, p.164.

41 Bedard, op.cit., p.41.

42 "Owner Survey, 1990-1992: Infinity Q45, Lexus LS 400", Peter Bohr, *Road & Track*, July 1994, pp.153–157. The magazine found that when it came to timeliness "just 9% of the LS 400 owners and 15% of the Q45 owners had to keep their cars out of service for more than a day while awaiting parts. This compares to 12% of Honda owners and 51% of Jaguar owners." And for repairs other than routine maintenance, it said: "just 27% of the LS 400 owners and 39% of the Q45 owners had to make trips to the dealership for unscheduled repairs in the first 10,000 miles."

43 Bedard, op.cit., pp.53–56.

44 Suzuki interview, February 10, 2004. In his own words, *"yari-sugita"* ("I did too much"), he acknowledged criticism of perhaps having been too obsessed with perfection on the LS 400.

45 The "Disneyland" jibe came in reference to a stop on the test drive itinerary at Neuschwanstein Castle, which was the inspiration for the Disney theme park castles. Peter as quoted in *The Lexus Story*, p.16.

46 Bohr, op.cit., pp.153–157.

CHAPTER FOUR - FROM TAHARA TO THE WORLD!

1 *Tahara Ju-nen no Ayumi (A Walk Through Tahara's [First] Ten Years)*, Toyota Motor Corp. Tahara Plant, February 1989, pp.2 and 7.

2 Ibid, p.3.

3 Tahara was the only plant to receive the platinum designation in 2003, and the next two factories ranked by J.D. Power were also Toyota plants in Japan — Motomachi (with 81 defects per 100 vehicles) and Tsutsumi (86 per 100). GM's Oshawa #1 plant in Ontario, Canada, was ranked No. 4 (with 87 per 100). "J.D Power & Associates 2003 Initial Quality Study", May 6, 2003.

4 "Robot-filled Tahara Sets Standard for Toyota, World", Christine Tierney, *The Detroit News*, February 22, 2004.

5 As quoted in *Niju-nen no Ayumi (A Walk Through [Tahara's First] Twenty Years)*, Toyota Motor Corp. Tahara Plant, December 1999, p.18.

6 *Toyota: A History of the First 50 Years*, p.256.

7 *Niju-nen no Ayumi,* op. cit., p.18.

8 Ibid, p.19.

9 Ibid.

10 *Tahara Ju-nen*, p.4.

11 Plant workers said the saving grace of the rustic Hotel Tahara was its open-air *onsen* (hot spring) baths, which soothed many a bad back and strained shoulder. *Tahara Ju-nen*, p.8.

12 *Niju-nen no Ayumi*, p.25.

13 *Tahara Ju-nen*, p.10.

14 *Toyota: A History of the First 50 Years*, pp.257–258.

15 "Here Come Japan's New Luxury Cars", Alex Taylor III, *Fortune*, August 14, 1989, p.62.

16 *LS 400: The Lexus Story*, pp.51 and 58.

17 In fairness to the oft-maligned consul, he later recounted in a letter to President Franklin Pierce that he had not been asked specifically to remove his shoes before entering the castle's inner keep for his meeting with the shogun. "We crossed this bridge, and at some 150 or 200 yards from the [castle] gate I entered the audience hall. Before entering here, however, I put on new shoes I had worn on my visit to the Minister, and the Japanese did not even ask me to go in my stocking-feet." As quoted in Eva March Tappan, ed., *The World's Story: A History of the World in Story, Song and Art.* (Boston: Houghton Mifflin, 1914), *Vol. I: China, Japan, and the Islands of the Pacific*; pp 438–442 and cited in "The Internet Modern History Sourcebook" (http://www.fordham.edu/halsall/mod/harris-japan1.html)

18 *LS 400: The Lexus Story*, p.42.

19 Ibid, p.90.

20 Long, p.25.

21 *LS 400: The Lexus Story*, p.51.

22 Long, p.25.

23 *LS 400: The Lexus Story*, pp.48 and 58.

24 Phone interview with Ichiro Suzuki, February 10, 2004.

25 "From the Nexus of the Lexus", Chester Dawson, *BusinessWeek*, September 3, 2001, pp.28B and 29D.

26 Ibid.

27 Ibid.

28 Figures cited from interview with plant officials at Tahara, August 1, 2001.

29 The comparisons aren't exact because these figures come from German transplants making entry level luxury vehicles, not the flagship sedan factories in Germany. The two are BMW's Spartansburg, South Carolina factory, which makes the 3-Series and the Tuscaloosa, Alabama. Mercedes-Benz plant which manufacturers M-Class SUVs. See Pries, Ludger, "Emerging New Product Systems in the Transnationalization of German Carmakers: The Case of BMW/Spartanburg and DaimlerChrysler/Tuscaloosa", Center of European and North American Studies (ZENS), University of Gottingen, Germany. (http://www.univ-evry.fr/labos/gerpisa/actes/30/30-2.pdf)

30 *LS 400: The Lexus Story*, p.51.

31 Interview with Yuji Horii in Tahara, August 1, 2001.

32 *LS 400: The Lexus Story*, p.51.

33 Fujimoto, Takahiro, *The Evolution of a Manufacturing System at Toyota*, 1999, Oxford University Press, p.248.

34 Ibid.

35 *The Lexus Story*, pp.78 and 91.

36 Ibid., pp.80–81.

37 *Toyota: A History of the First 50 Years*, p.256.

38 *The Detroit News*, February 22, 2004.

39 Ibid.

40 "An Endurance Test for Japanese Carmakers", Chester Dawson, *BusinessWeek*, April 26, 2004, p.55.

41 Oddly enough, Toyota Motor's workers' union backed the automation scheme because, at the time, they too believed Japan faced a grave labor shortage in the year ahead. See Fujimoto, pp.224–225.

42 Ibid., p.249.

43 Ibid., p.263.

44 "Roaring Into China: If 'Toyota Way' Teamwork Clicks, It Could Mean a Big Jump in Sales", Chester Dawson, *BusinessWeek*, April 7, 2003 (Asian Edition), pp.72–73.

CHAPTER FIVE - THE LEXUS COVENANT

1 All of the above biographical background was gleaned from a telehone interview with J. Davis Illingworth on March 11, 2004.

2 Phone interview with Robert McCurry, March 15, 2004.

3 Illingworth interview, op. cit.

4 McCurry interview, op. cit.

5 "Lexus Case Study #7: [The] Lexus Franchise." Toyota Motor Corp. BR Global Personnel Office. 1999; p. 3.

6 Ibid.

7 *Toyota: A History of the First 50 Years*; pp.344-348.

8 McCurry interview, op. cit.

9 Interview with J. Davis Illingworth in Philadelphia, on September 9, 2003.

10 Phone interview with Yale Giesel on March 12, 2004.

11 Perkins interview, op. cit., Illingworth interview, September 9, 2003.

12 "U.S. Managers' Input Welcomed by Japanese Bosses", *Automotive News*, September 28, 1992, p.16.

13 As cited in "'We Achieved the Dream': In Just Three Years, Lexus Redefined Luxury", *Automotive News*. September 28, 1992, p.18.

14 The Lexus Covenant was disseminated in the form of wallet-sized laminated cards issued to dealers and still carried around today by some TMS true believers. The words are also carved in granite in an eerie display (vaguely reminiscent of the Vietnam Veterans Memorial) at the Lexus headquarters building in Torrance. "Lexus Case Study #7, op. cit., p.5., "Lexus Case Study #7: [The] Lexus Franchise." Toyota Motor Corp. BR Global Personnel Office. 1999; pp. 2-4.

15 Togo & Wartman, p.247

16 Interview with Scott Gilbert on February 19, 2004.

17 McCurry interview, op. cit.

18 Togo & Wartman, pp.244-245.

19 Gilbert interview, op. cit.

20 While use of the Toyota name was largely shunned, some early advertisements introducing the brand noted that Lexus was "the luxury brand from Toyota". Gilbert interview, op. cit.

21 French says he was the first to come up with the exact term. "I created that name!" John French June 7, 2004; Phone interview with George Borst, March 15, 2004; *The Lexus Story*, p.57; Togo and Wartman, pp.238–239.

22 In focus group testing with luxury-car employees and TMS employees, the Lexus "L" ranked first or second with 75% of the respondents among the eight final designs for the logo. In 1989, gold was the primary color for the Lexus logo, unlike the silver which is more prevalent today. The logo's ovular shape is "not a true ellipse, but a mathematically based shape", according to TMS. Interview with Rollin "Molly" Sanders on June 16, 2004; "Lexus Case Study #7, op. cit., pp.5–6; "Lexus Learning the Lexis of Luxury", Chuck Wingis, *Advertising Age*, February 29, 1988; *The Lexus Story*, p.57.

23 "Creating the New Gold Standard (selling Lexus)", David Kiley, *Brandweek*, July 27, 1998.

24 Gilbert interview, op. cit.

25 Ibid; interview with Tom Cordner, March 13, 2004.

26 Gilbert interview, op. cit.

27 Cordner interview, op. cit.

28 One account states Suzuki carried out a "shoebox" with the keys of the other car makes, but Scott Gilbert says that is mistaken and that it was a cigar box. Similarly, Cordner quibbles with the account that he scribbled the famous tagline "on his airline cocktail napkin." Cordner said he jotted it down in the pages of his trip journal on the flight.

29 Togo & Wartman, p.241.

30 Gilbert interview, op. cit.

31 As cited in "U.S. Managers' Input Welcomed by Japanese Bosses", *Automotive News*, September 28, 1992, p.16.

32 "Consider the Urushi Tree — Is It Not Like a Luxury Car?", Larry Armstrong, *BusinessWeek*, September 4, 1989, p.84.

33 "How Do You Build a Luxury Image?", Jerry Flint, *Forbes*, April 3, 1989, p.60.

34 "No Joyride for Japan", Mark Landler, *BusinessWeek*, January 15, 1990, p.20.

35 There is evidence, however, that Team One flirted with the idea of a more artsy, less product-focused ad campaign as late as Jan. 1989. One early newspaper ad at the time showed only a "slice" of the LS 400 and David W. Wager, then president of Team One was quoted as saying that: "We're trying to make the car look like art." See "The Coming Traffic Jam in the Luxury Lane", Wendy Zellner, *BusinessWeek*, January 30, 1989, p.78; Gilbert interview, op. cit.

36 "Dogville", Joe Morgenstern, *The Wall Street Journal*, March 26, 2004, p.w3.

37 Illingworth was quoted at the time as saying: "Our preliminary research indicates that maybe a celebrity spokesman wouldn't work for us, but we're certainly not going to overrule that possibility. We've only begun to work on our creative [publicity] and we're not going to eliminate any approach too early in the game", Wingis, op. cit.

38 Interview with former Team One official.

39 Togo & Wartman, p.249.

40 Illingworth interview, September 9, 2003, op. cit.

41 Wingis, op. cit.; Zellner, op. cit., p.78; Landler, op. cit., p.21.

42 Gilbert interview, op. cit.

43 Cordner interview, op. cit.

44 Ibid.

45 Ibid.

46 "Lexus Case Study #7, op. cit., p.5.

47 Phone interview with Dick Chitty, March 25, 2004.

48 Togo & Wartman, p.248.

49 As a souvenir from that ad campaign, one of the Team One employees stacked the glasses used in the commercial up against the wall in his office and glued them together so they wouldn't fall over. But when Team One executives saw the sculpture they immediately ordered the employee to get rid of it. They feared someone might draw the conclusion the glasses had also been glued together for the ad shoot. Gilbert interview, op. cit.

50 *The Lexus Story*, p.96.

51 Togo & Wartman, pp.248–249.

52 Wingis, op. cit.

53 "Lexus Case Study #7, op. cit. p.8.

54 Togo & Wartman, p.247.

55 *The Lexus Story*, p.58.

56 Illingworth interview, September 9, 2003, op. cit.

57 One account says that McCurry, upon seeing the initial design sketch for Lexus showrooms, said "It looks like a Kentucky Fried Chicken store!" *The Lexus Story*, p.68; Long, p.30.

58 As of early 2004, Lexus dealerships owned by women or minorities totaled 22, or 10.6% of the 207 in the U.S. according to TMS data; "Here Come Japan's New Luxury Cars", Alex Taylor III, *Fortune*, August 14, 1989.

59 Penske, who retired from racing at his peak in 1965 at the age of 28, bought the Longo Toyota dealership in Los Angeles (originally set up by Dominic Longo) in November of 1985. Two years later, it became the biggest single dealership in the U.S., selling 19,000 cars a year. *Toyota: A History of the First 50 Years*, p.348. McCurry interview on March 15, 2004.

60 Armstrong, op. cit., p.85; Flint, op. cit., p.60.

61 As cited in "Lexus Case Study #7, op. cit., p.9.

62 Togo & Wartman, p.251.

63 Kiley, op. cit.

64 Illingworth interview, September 9, 2003, op. cit.

65 Togo & Wartman, pp.249–250.

66 Flint, op. cit., p.60. See also "'We Achieved the Dream': In Just Three Years, Lexus Redefined Luxury", op. cit., p.18.

67 *The Lexus Story*, p.97.

CHAPTER SIX - ZEN AND THE ART OF AUTOMOBILE MAINTENANCE

1 Phone interview with Tadashi Arashima, March 5, 2004.

2 Ibid.

3 It has been noted that MDC's action was not entirely unprecedented. General Motors paid out $500,000 to Italian gun-maker Beretta to settle a dispute about a GM car of the same name. See *The Lexus Story*, p.75.

4 Nakajima, pp.8–9; Perkins interview, op. cit.

5 In fact, TMS drafted a proposal and tapped Jim Perkins to negotiate for an out-of-court settlement with MDC, and at one point, he reached a tentative deal involving joint marketing and free Lexus cars. But the data company would have none of it and sought to fight it out in court. TMS took that to mean the suit was all part of a campaign by MDC to drum up publicity. Perkins says money wasn't the reason he left TMS, but acknowledges that options GM offered made his decisions easier. "Toyota didn't have anything like that." Nakajima, pp.13, 15, 20–21, 209.

6 Perkins interview, op. cit., Long, p.32.

7 Nakajima, pp.208–209.

8 As recalled by Toyoda and quoted in Nakajima, p.207.

9 Perkins interview, op. cit., Nakajima; p.208.

10 Arashima interview, op. cit.

11 Perkins interview, op. cit., Interview with an official involved with TMS who requested anonymity. Several other officials also spoke about Perkins's "surprise" exit on the condition that it was not for attribution.

12 Phone interview with Richard "Dick" Chitty, March 24, 2004. "Lexus Case Study #7: [The] Lexus Franchise", Toyota Motor Corp, BR Global Personnel Office, 1999, p.10.

13 To this day, Chitty still has one of the old switches taken out of the original LS 400. "Lexus Case Study #7", p.10; Togo & Wartman, p.253.

14 "New Kid on the Dock,", S.C. Gwynne, *Time*, September 17, 1990, p.62.

15 *The Lexus Story*, p 99; Togo & Wartman, pp.251–253.

16 Chitty interview, op. cit.

17 In one case, a technician at a Lexus field office for the West Coast area tracked down a LS 400 owner who was hang-gliding in the Mojave Desert. After replacing the parts and filling the gas tank, he left a $20 bill on the windshield with a note apologizing for having been unable to find a car wash. *The Lexus Story*, pp.99–108.

18 GM alone bought at least three of the first-generation LS 400 for dissection as soon as it was released, according to Chitty.

19 "Lexus Case Study #7", p.10; Togo & Wartman, p.254.

20 Gwynne, op. cit.

21 Ibid.

22 TMS did an internal calculation of the cost of the parts-replacement campaign, but has never released the total figure publicly. Whatever the cost, it paid for itself many times over in subsequent months and years in customer loyalty, favorable press coverage and greater prestige among the public at large — Chitty interview, op. cit..

23 Phone interview with Tom Cordner, March 13, 2004.

24 *Hokkaido Shimbun*, "August 31, 1990, p.19 (evening edition.)

25 *Hokkaido Shimbun*, July 9, 1988, p.26 (morning edition); July 9, 1988, p.17 (evening edition); and July 11, 1988, p.8 (evening edition).

26 Gwynne, op. cit.; p. 62. Long, p.42.

27 "Surprisingly Mixed Returns for Lexus", Larry Armstrong, *BusinessWeek*, January 15, 1990, p.21.

28 Phone interview with Yale Gieszl, March 12, 2004.

29 Gwynne, op. cit.

30 "Mercedes Finds Out How Much is Too Much", Mark Landler, *BusinessWeek,* January 20, 1992. p.12.

31 "Lexus SC 400: Toyota Hails Its New Luxury Coupe as an 'Original American Design'", Patrick Bedard, *Car and Driver*, June 1991, p.49.

32 "Miscellaneous Ramblings", Thomas L. Bryant, *Road & Track*, December 1990, p.41.

33 Phone interview with J. Davis Illingworth, March 11, 2004; Arashima interview op. cit.

34 Bedard, op. cit.

35 This car, the Lexus SC 400, was actually the third generation of its type in Japan, where it was sold under the name Soarer and first debuted in 1981. See. "Lexus SC 400: Lexus Creates the Target", *Road & Track,* July 1991, pp.54–59; Long, p.46; *The Lexus Story*, p.132.

36 "Lexus SC 400: Lexus Creates the Target", *Road & Track*, July 1991, p.56.

37 Gieszl interview, op. cit.

38 Arashima interview, op. cit.

39 Gieszl interview, op. cit.

40 "Lexus ES 300: The Camry Clone Gets the Broom", Csaba Csere, *Car and Driver*, November 1991, p.108.

41 "Lexus LS 430: Hey, Hans, Bad News. Here Come Those Guys from Japan Again", Fred M.H. Gregory, *Car and Driver,* October 2000.

42 Long, pp.60–61.

43 Interview with Scott Gilbert, February 19, 2004.

44 "Lexus GS 300: All the luxury. Half the Calories. And a Full Dose of Fun", Andrew Bornhop, *Road & Track,* February 1993, p.64; Long, pp.70–71.

45 "Lexus GS 300", William Jeanes, *Car and Driver*, February 1993, pp.64, 66.

46 *The Lexus Story*, p.139.

47 "Lexus LS 400: Better the Second Time Around?", Ken Zino, *Road & Track,* November 1994, p.100.

48 "Lexus, Sales Skidding 10%, Hopes Campaign Can Retool Its Identity", Fara Warner, *The Wall Street Journal,* November 11, 1994, p.B4.

49 "His Mission: Shift Chrysler Out of Reverse", Joseph B. White and Neal E. Boudette, *The Wall Street Journal*, July 16, 2003, pp.b1 and b4.

50 *The Lexus Story*, pp.139–140.

51 Phone interview with George Borst, March 15, 2004.

52 Ibid.

53 Ibid; *The Lexus Story*, p.137.

54 Long, p.82.

55 Ibid.

56 Zino, op.cit., pp.98–101.

57 "Lexus LS 400: Remodeling the Temple of Tranquility", Barry Winfield, *Car and Driver,* November 1994, p.73.

58 "From the Nexis of the Lexus", Chester Dawson, *BusinessWeek,* September 3, 2001, pp.28B–28D.

59 Warner, op. cit., p. B4.

60 Perkins interview, op. cit., Several other current and former TMS officials either declined to comment when asked about Sakai's three-year tenure or spoke only on the condition of not being named. Attempts to reach Sakai, who had since left Toyota Motor, for comment were unsuccessful.

61 Cordner interview, op. cit.

62 "Lexus: Learning the Lexis of Luxury", Chuck Wingis, *Advertising Age,* February 29, 1988, pp.5–6.

63 *The Lexus Story;* pp. 140-141.

64 Borst interview, op. cit.

65 *The Lexus Story*, pp.144–145.

66 Gieszl interview, op. cit.

67 "Full Court Press: the Success of Lexus", *Brandweek,* July 27, 1998, p. 22.

68 "*Semaru Tai-Nichi Jidousha Seisai (3) Toyota 'Rekusasu' no Shimen-soka* [Impending Auto Sanctions Against Japan (Part 3): Toyota's Lexus Brand Surrounded by Enemies", *Nikkei Sangyou Shinbum,* June 19, 1995, p.1.

69 "Lexus 10th Anniversary Speech: A Decade of Pursuing Perfection", Bryan Bergsteinsson, 1999. Text courtesy of Toyota Motor Corp.

70 "Looks good, But What's Under the Hood?", George J. Church, reported by Irene M. Kunii in Tokyo and Adam Zagorin in Washington, *Time,* July 10, 1995.

71 Armacost, Michael H., *Friends of Rivals?: The Insider's Account of U.S.-Japan Relations,* 1996, Columbia University Press, p.187.

72 Schoppa, Leonard J., *Bargaining with Japan: What American Pressure Can and Cannot Do,* 1997, Columbia University Press, p.15.

73 Lincoln, Edward J., *Troubled Times:U.S.-Japan Trade Relations in the 1990s,* 1999, The Brookings Institution, pp.133–134.

74 "Japanese Cut Back on U.S. Parts", James B. Treece, *Automotive News,* January 19, 2004, p.8.

75 Lincoln, op. cit.

76 Borst interview, op. cit.

77 Gilbert interview, op. cit.

78 *The Lexus Story*, pp.145–146.

CHAPTER SEVEN - SOMETHING WICKED THIS WAY COMES

1 Phone interview with Tadashi Arashima, March 5, 2004.

2 Phone interview with Yale Gieszl, March 12, 2004.

3 As quoted in *The Lexus Story*, p.158.

4 Araco Corp. is a minibus- and SUV-making affiliate of Toyota Motor, which owns 75% of the company's shares (the remainder are closely held by Toyota group companies). Press's comment is as quoted in "Full Court Press: the Success of Lexus", *Brandweek*, July 27, 1998, p.22.

5 Interview with Jim Press at TMS headquarters, September 13, 2002.

6 As quoted in *Brandweek*, op.cit., p.22.

7 "Will Lexus Run Rings Around Caddy's New Baby?", Larry Armstrong, BusinessWeek, April 7, 1997, p.114.

8 Nakagawa succeeded first-generation GS chief engineer Hiroyuki Watanabe, who also served briefly as head of the second-generation GS program. See Long, pp.130–132, 139.

9 "Lexus GS 400: The New GS Goes BMW Hunting", Barry Winfield, *Car and Driver*, October 1997, p.97.

10 Press interview, op. cit.

11 "Karen Smith: On the Road Again with Lexus", Bill Dunlap, *Shoot*, February 13, 1998.

12 "Javelinas Grandes: Deep in the Heart of Texas, We put Five Prime Porkers Through Their Paces", Tony Swan, *Car and Driver*, May 1999, p.72.

13 Toyota Motor did nothing to discourage Tinseltown types from thinking well and speaking well of Lexus. In 1996, Honorary Toyota Motor Chairman Shoichiro Toyoda crossed paths with Harrison Ford, who raved about his SC 400 but noted the lack of headroom. Upon returning to Japan, Toyoda quietly instructed engineers to design a driver's seat for Ford's tall frame and then had the finished product shipped in a wooden crate to the actor's ranch outside Jackson Hole, Wyoming. "After it was installed (Shoichiro) Toyoda said that was fine but asked me if I'd personally gone to inspect it and I replied that I had not. The next day I was on a plane to Wyoming where I met the chief ranch hand, who showed it to me me and thanked us," said Richard "Dick" Chitty, who oversaw the installation of the seat. Phone interview with Richard "Dick" Chitty on March 24, 2004. For the LX 470-Hollywood connection, see "Chariot of the Gods of Celebrity", Alex Taylor III, *Fortune*, May 24, 1999, p.48.

14 Press interview, op. cit.

15 Arashima phone interview, op. cit.

16 Interview with Yukihiro Okane, Toyota-City, October 15, 2002.

17 Many take credit for the idea behind the RX 300. Chris Hostetter is said to have teased a Toyota Motor SUV engineer "for years" that a sports ute should be built off a car, as cited in *The Lexus Story*, p.169. Wada's campaign for a car-based SUV is cited in "Autos: If It Looks Like a Truck but Rides Like a Car, It's Hot", Joseph B. White, *The Wall Street Journal*, January 9, 1998, p.b1.

18 "After a Decade of Growth, Lexus Retooling Its Lineup", Terril Yue Jones, *Los Angeles Times*, September 10, 2000, p.C-1.

19 *The Lexus Story*, p.169.

20 *The Wall Street Journal*, January 9, 1998, op. cit.

21 "Lexus RX 300 Leads Way for Big, Fancy Car-Utes", Mark Rechtin, *Automotive News*, January 12, 1998, p.31.

22 Okane interview, op. cit.

23 *The Wall Street Journal*, January 9, 1998, op. cit.

24 Okane interview, op. cit.

25 "Behind the Wheel: Lexus RX 300: A Sport Utility in Touch with Its Feminine Side", Michelle Krebs, *The New York Times*, April 19, 1998, section 12, p.1.

26 *Fortune*, May 24, 1999, op. cit.

27 The New York Times, April 19, 1998, op. cit.

28 Press interview, op. cit.

29 As quoted in "Lexus RX 300 Sport-Utility: The Truck Stops Here", James R. Healey, *USA Today* March 27, 1998, p.4d.

30 "Week in Wheels: Road Test: Lexus RX 300: The SUV for Lovers of Cars", Tom Incatalupo, *Newsday*, June 19, 1998, p.d3.

31 "On or Off the Road, Lexus RX 300 Pleases", Tony Swan, *Detroit Free Press*, August 20, 1998, p.1c.

32 *USA Today*, March 27, 1998, op.cit..

33 "Sport-Utility Vehicles. Road Test. The Future of SUVs", *Consumer Reports*, September, 1998, p.12+.

34 Phone interview with Tom Cordner, March 13, 2004.

35 "Lexus: Products Fuel Sizzling Sales", Mark Rechtin, *Automotive News*, October 12, 1998, p.3.

36 "Lexus: All Revved Up With Someplace to Go", Larry Armstrong, *BusinessWeek*, December 21, 1998, p.58.

37 *Automotive News*, October 12, 1998, op. cit.

38 Taken from speech by Bryan Bergsteinsson at the North American International Auto Show in Detroit, January 5, 1999; courtesy of Toyota Motor Sales.

39 *Automotive News*, October 12, 1998, op. cit.

40 "Test Drives Never Tasted Like This Before", Greg Johnson, *Los Angeles Times*, July 22, 1999, p.c1.

41 *The Lexus Story*, p.178.

42 *Automotive News*, October 12, 1998, op. cit.

43 *The Lexus Story*, pp.176–180.

44 Bergsteinsson speech, Detroit, op. cit.

45 "Lexus Moves to Topical Ads", Julie Cantwell, *Automotive News*, August 6, 2001, p.3.

46 As quoted in "Redefining Luxury: The Fast-Growing Market for $30,000-and-up Cars is the Industry's Next Big Battleground", Ron Stodghill II, *Time*, January 18, 1999, pp.55–57.

47 "Lexus LS 430: Hey, Hans, Bad News: Here Come Those Guys from Japan Again", Fred M.H. Gregory, *Car and Driver*, October 2000, p.129.

48 Ibid

49 Ibid.

50 "Lexus LS 430: Another High-Caliber Round in the Battle for Perfection", Peter Egan, *Road & Track*, November 2000, p.49.

51 Bergsteinsson speech, January 5, 1999, op. cit.

52 "Lexus IS 300: It Isn't as Much a Clone of the BMW 3-Series as It is a Unique Expression of the Genre", Barry Winfield, *Car and Driver*, October 2000, p.103.

53 Ibid.

54 "2001 Lexus IS 300: Our 3 Series Fighter Has Arrived", Jim Hall, *Road & Track*, October 2000, pp.109, 112; and "2001 Lexus IS 300: The Unofficial Sedan of Generation X", Jim Hall, *Road & Track*, July 2001, p.111.

55 The 25,000 unit annual sales target figure comes from a speech by Bryan Bergsteinsson on April 20, 2000 at the New York auto show; courtesy of Toyota Motor Sales.

56 As quoted in January 9, 2001, press release issued at the Detroit auto show by Toyota Motor Sales.

57 "Lexus SC 430: An Acquired Taste", Douglas Kott, *Road & Track*, March 2001, p.58-62.

58 "Not There Yet But Getting Closer", Robert Cumberford, *Automobile*, May 2004, p.44.

59 Bergsteinsson speech, April 20, 2000, op. cit.; courtesy of Toyota Motor Sales.

60 Speech by Denny Clements at the Detroit auto show, January 9, 2001; courtesy of Toyota Motor Sales.

CHAPTER EIGHT - LEXUS NATION

1 Phone interview with Toyota Motor Manufacturing Canada, president, Réal Tanguay, October 23, 2003.

2 "Can Anything Stop Toyota?", Brian Bremner and Chester Dawson, *BusinessWeek*, November 17, 2003, p.122.

3 Description taken from "Lexus Tour Video Script", courtesy of Toyota Motor Manufacturing Canada Inc.; dated September 16, 2003.

4 Interview, October 22, 2003.

5 In lieu of factory-floor diversions, Toyota Motor built a cutting-edge fitness center for employees across the road from the Cambridge plant. The company also sponsors some 20 intramural hockey teams and rents two ice rinks near the plant for five hours every Sunday afternoon.

6 Bremner and Dawson, op. cit., p.120.

7 Interview at Toyota Motor Manufacturing Canada, October 22, 2003.

8 Interview at Toyota Motor Manufacturing Canada, October 22, 2003

9 Interview at Toyota Motor Manufacturing Canada, October 22, 2003.

10 Speech by Denny Clements at the North American International Auto Show, January 5, 2003; text courtesy of Toyota Motor Sales.

11 "2004 Lexus RX 330: Low-Fat S.U.V. Substitute, Now in Extra Creamy", James G. Cobb, *The New York Times*, November 30, 2003, p.12-1.

12 "Luxury Lineup", *Consumer Reports*, September 2003, p.54.

13 "2002 Lexus ES 300: Social Climber", Douglas Kott, *Road & Track*, September 2001, p.X

14 "Sibling Rivalry: A Utility for the Rugged and One for the Rich," Bob Knoll, *The New York Times*, July 6, 2003, p.12-1.

15 "Lexus in Asia", *Bangkok Post* as reprinted by Automotive Resources Asia, December 4, 2002.

16 "Lexus to Enter Japan with Four Vehicles", *Automotive News*, June 16, 2003, p.18; "Toyota to Introduce Lexus Brand and Revise Sales Network in Japan", Toyota Motor Corp. Public Affairs Division, February 14, 2003.

17 "Toyota Plans to Set Up Lexus Dealers in China, Japan in 2005", Kae Inoue, *Bloomberg News*, January 6, 2004, Toyota Motor Corp. press release June 8, 2004

18 "Chitty to Lead Lexus Into Asia Markets", Urs Muller, *Automotive News*, February 2, 2004, p.72.

19 Ibid.

20 "Selling Lexus is Tough Slog on Mercedes, BMW Home Turf", Neal E. Boudette, *The Wall Street Journal*, December 4, 2003, p.b1.

21 "Lexus: Still Looking for Traction in Europe", Gail Edmondson, *BusinessWeek*, November 17, 2003, p.122.

22 Ibid.

23 "Lexus Will Duel with Rivals in Europe", Dorothee Ostle, *Automotive News*, June 16, 2003, p.8.

24 Boudette, op. cit.

25 "Toyota's Lexus Won't Make Money in Europe Until 2010," Brian Lysaght, *Bloomberg News*, August 12, 2001.

26 "BMW: Will Panke's High-Speed Approach Hurt the Brand?", Gail Edmondson, *BusinessWeek*, June 9, 2003, pp.57–60.

27 Ibid.

28 "At 100, Cadillac Shows Signs of Life", Dave Guilford, *Automotive News*, August 19, 2002, p. 22; "The Second Coming of Cadillac", David Welch, *BusinessWeek*, November 24, 2003, pp.9 and 79–80.

29 "Lincoln Goes Looking for a New Flagship", Jeremy Grant, *Financial Times*, March 18, 2004, p.16.

30 "Infiniti Says Sayonara to Contemplation Areas", Harry Stoffer, *Automotive News*, May 20, 2002, p. 3; "Leaving Zen in the Dust," Christopher Palmeri, *BusinessWeek*, February 23, 2004, pp.86 and 88.

31 "Car Dealerships Face the Great Homogenization," David Wethe, *The New York Times*, January 11, 2004, pp.3–4.

32 "Toyota Shuffles Lexus Management", *Ward's Autoworld*, August 1, 2000.

33 The words of Lexus Division marketing vice president Mike Wells, as quoted in "Desperately Seeking Status", Ken Gross, *Automotive Industries*, November 11, 2001.

34 Speech by Dennis E. Clements to the Iowa Better Business Bureau/Integrity Awards Lunch, November 10, 2000; text courtesy of Toyota Motor Sales.

35 As quoted in "Lexus Turns Introspective at Seminars", Mark Rechtin, *Automotive News*, December 9, 2002, p.3.

36 "Lexus' Big Test", Chester Dawson, *BusinessWeek*, March 24, 2003, pp.68–69.

37 "Appealing to Youth, Selling to the Not-So-Young", Robert Strauss, *The New York Times*, October 23, 2003, p.37.

38 "Luxury Goes Into Overdrive", Karl Greenburg, *Brandweek*, January 14, 2002.

39 Dawson, op. cit.

40 "Lexus' GM: 'You Can Have It All'", Chester Dawson, *BusinessWeek Online*, March 24, 2003.

41 Speech by Dennis E. Clements to the J.D. Powers and Associates International Automotive Roundtable, November 11, 2001; text courtesy of Toyota Motor Sales.

42 "Naming the Baby: Parents Brand Their Tot with What's Hot", Stephanie Kang, *The Wall Street Journal*, December 26, 2003, p.B1.

Epilogue

1 "Wanted: Toyotas That Say 'Toyota'", Chester Dawson, *BusinessWeek*, February 16, 2004, p.48 (Asian Edition); "Lexus' Big Test: Can It Keep Its Cachet and Appeal to the Young?", *BusinessWeek*, March 24, 2003, pp.68-69.

2 *BusinessWeek*, February 16, 2004, op. cit.

3 Speech by Denny Clements at the Morgan Stanley Global Automotive Conference, April 7, 2004; text and technician and dealership stall data courtesy of Toyota Motor Sales.

4 *BusinessWeek*, March 24, 2003, op. cit.

5 Speech by Denny Clements at the New York auto show, April 8, 2004; text courtesy of Toyota Motor Sales.

6 *BusinessWeek*, February 16, 2004, op. cit.

7 "Lexus Finally Gets a Design of Its Own", Mark Rechtin, *Automotive News*, October 27, 2003, pp.1 and 52.

8 "Not there Yet But Getting Closer", Robert Cumberford, *Automobile*, May 2004, p.44. Despite the withering critique, the article goes on to say that: "Toyota eventually will get the design aspects of its cars completely right," adding that the 2006 GS 430 was "a harbinger of that change".

9 While the FLV and Street Rod were never meant to be harbingers of coming vehicles, Toyota Motor did preview some concept cars that were close to being production models, such as the HPS concept sports sedan that was shown at the 1997 Detroit auto show. That car's avant-garde styling was closely emulated in the look of the 1998 GS 300/400. For reference to a shift toward commercial concepts, see "Machine Dreams: Concept Vehicles Like the HPX and the LF-C Are the Automotive Equivalent of a Crystal Ball", Paul A. Eisenstein, *Lexus* magazine, second quarter, 2004, pp.42 and 44.

10 Speech, on April 7, 2004, op. cit.

11 In a bid to create a global standard of sorts for hybrids, Toyota Motor agreed to provide the basic technology to Ford Motor and Nissan Motor, which planned to release hybrids in 2004 and 2006, respectively. But Toyota Motor didn't take kindly to subsequent suggestions from Ford that its hybrid SUV Escape model offered superior performance. TMS personnel were instructed to tell the media that: "We don't agree. After seeing and hearing about the Ford system, and the [Toyota Motor] Hybrid Synergy Drive system, it should be fairly obvious which is more advanced." Toyota Motor Sales internal memo dated April, 2004.

12 "Lexus Unveils Luxury Sports Coupe Concept." Press release courtesy of TMS.

13 *Lexus* op. cit.

14 As quoted in "Boss Puts 'Buzz' on U.S. Luxury Leader's To-Do List", *Automotive News*, January 26, 2004, pp.4 and 17.

15 Internal Lexus Planning Division memo detailing brand strategy through 2010 (undated).

16 These "Image Leader" and "F-Sports" models are codenamed the GS 500 F-Sports, LFX-V12 SHV and 680N F-Sports, respectively, as cited in another internal Lexus Planning Division memo (undated.)

17 *Automotive News,*op. cit.

18 As first reported in *BusinessWeek,* March 24, 2003, op. cit.

19 Phone interview with Denny Clements, April 16, 2004.

20 Figures from Toyota Motor Sales internal memo dated April 2004.

21 *Automotive News*, op. cit.

22 Phone interview with Denny Clements on April 16, 2004.

23 Ibid.

24 Speech, April 7, 2004, op. cit.

25 Speech, April 8, 2004, op. cit.

26 Speech, April 7, 2004, op. cit.